As Nasty As They Wanna Be

As Nasty As They Wanna Be

The Uncensored Story of **LUTHER CAMPBELL** *of the* **2 LIVE CREW**

LUTHER CAMPBELL
& JOHN R. MILLER

BARRICADE BOOKS • *Fort Lee, New Jersey*

Published in cooperation with
KINGSTON PUBLISHERS, LTD. • *Kingston* • *Jamaica*

Published by

Barricade Books Inc.
1530 Palisade Avenue
Fort Lee, NJ 07024

in cooperation with
Kingston Publishers Ltd.
Kingston, Jamaica (W.I.)

Distributed in the U.S. by
Publishers Group West
4065 Hollis
Emeryville, CA 94608

Printed in the United States of America.

Library of Congress Cataloging-in-Publication Data

Campbell, Luther.
    As nasty as they wanna be: the uncensored story of Luther Campbell of the
2 Live Crew / Luther Campbell and John R. Miller.
        p.   cm.
    ISBN 0-942637-43-7 (pbk.): $17.95
    1. Campbell, Luther. 2. 2 Live Crew. 3. Rap musicians—United States—
Biography. I. Miller, John R. (John Ramsey), 1949–   . II. Title.
ML420.C223A3   1992
782.42164—dc20   91-42274
[B]   CIP
                                                                          MN

Designed by Paul Chevannes

Contents

This book is dedicated to My Old Gal, my mother, Yvonne Campbell. Her constant and unconditional love, support and encouragement have given me the freedom to take the risks I have wanted to take and the strength to do what I have needed to do. Thank you, Mamma.

—LUTHER CAMPBELL

Acknowledgments

It took a lot of people working overtime to make this book possible. I can't thank them all but my special thanks to Bruce Rogow, the most brilliant attorney I have ever met. Thanks to Debbie Bennett, who did more than anyone else to hold Luke Records together during the trials and was of invaluable assistance in supplying research for this project. Thanks to all my friends, family and fans who stood beside me in spirit and deed during the trials and to those who bought our records and attended our concerts. Special thanks to Chris Wongwon, my friends and associates.

Also thanks to the staff at Kingston Publishers in Kingston, Jamaica, where the editing was accomplished, and to Kim Robinson-Walcott, the editor, who had never, ever seen anything like this book.

Introduction

People who know me know that I never set out to defend the First Amendment. I wasn't concerned with constitutional legal issues, or with religious zealots and right-wing fanatics for that matter. If I hadn't been forced by those idiots to defend basic American freedoms, I wouldn't appreciate what a precious thing the right to free speech is. The Broward County obscenity trial changed my life and made me understand just how delicate freedom of speech really is. My parents, like all of the people of their generation, fought a nitty-gritty struggle for basic human rights. My generation sort of took all that for granted. I was just a little kid when Martin Luther King was killed. It didn't mean a whole lot to me at the time. Today it does.

When the censorship thing happened, I was just trying to make a living the best way I could and seemingly some people decided to stop me from doing that. As long as I was making records for the people in the ghettos, it was fine and dandy.

You could say that I am a rich man. I know that, within reason, I can buy what I like, when I like. But numbers don't really mean shit. I have discovered some important things about having money. You can only drive one car at a time, wear one suit of clothes at a time, sleep in one bed at a time, and play so many rounds of golf. Money is strange. After a while the toys and trappings mean less and less and the hassles associated with the stuff get more and more.

As I have gained access to higher stratas of society I have seen more and more racism. The more money I make the more shit I catch from lawyers and other authority figures.

I have never been afraid to fight. People see my bodyguard and say, Oh, he's afraid somebody is gonna hit him or whatever. The truth is that I have bodyguards to keep me from hitting somebody upside the head and getting sued, and to keep people from pressing in on me. But fighting these "official" bitches is all done in the dark. I wish I could have settled my differences man-to-man with some of those silly fanatics. We would have gotten the same result but I wouldn't have had to pay my lawyers to do the thing for me. But the bitches don't work like that. They do shit to you long-distance and they don't have to know your name or what you look like to fuck with you. They get some washed-up, semi-sane attorney who is practicing out of his kitchen or whatever, and give the bastard a fax machine and the promise of some publicity and he's off making your life hell from his goddamned dining room table.

Being a defender of the Constitution was not my choice. I was trying to defend my right to produce my music and make a living. Maybe my music is at the far end of what people want to hear but it was never designed to be played in elevators or at teen dance parties or on the radio. In fact before the stuff started about *Nasty,* it had sold over a million copies without being handled by major record store chains or having been played on one radio station. It was designed for a specific audience, people like me, people like those I grew up with. I was just exercising my right to sell my work.

It is my hope that this book will set the record straight about the trial, my music, and the world which spawned that music. It is being written with prejudice because it is my book. People may disagree with some or all of it. Fuck them. Let them do their own book.

1 Luther "The Shorty"

I was born in Mount Sinai Hospital in Miami Beach on December 22, 1960. You won't know it but that is one hell of a place for a black man to be born. I was named after a great-uncle, Luther Whittaker, who was dying from cancer. He spoke eight languages and was an interpreter for one of the embassies in Miami. He never had any children and he was dying when I was born. My parents took me down to him in his hospital bed and when they put me on his chest, he put his hand on my head, smiled and died. Or so the story goes.

My father and mother, Stanley and Yvonne Campbell, had already bought this house in Liberty City in 1958 after my brother Brannard was born. The manager of the apartment they were in before that told them they had too many people in it; the nurse next door who worked at night got pissed because Brannard cried all the time. My father saw an ad in the paper showing these nice houses in Liberty City for a mere five-hundred dollars down. He had saved some money in that direction. The houses that were being advertised in the *Miami Herald* were in a lily-white neighborhood, and when my father showed up and the house salesman saw that he was black, he didn't quite know what to do. However, the white man didn't want to miss selling a unit, especially since he didn't plan to live in the neighborhood himself. So he told my father that if he could come up with a twenty-five hundred dollar down payment, and he could qualify for credit, he could have the house. The salesman figured he was safe either way. If my father didn't get the money, he was just the stereotypical, no-account black man. On the other hand if he did come up with it then the salesman's boss couldn't very well turn down someone who was obviously a worthwhile individual. My father had to borrow a little here and a little there from relatives, but he came up with the money.

My father was surprised to read on that deed, in clear English, that the house was only to be sold to a Caucasian family. His lawyer made them remove that clause from the deed but in those days they did what they did and you had to prove it in court, and the courts in Miami weren't bastions of liberality.

There are still people pulling shit like that around here. If you are white and you answer an ad for an apartment or a house, you can move in; if you are a black man they don't have that vacancy any longer. They will not have a "white only" clause written down but it's there just the same. In some places they have codes for black applicants. I could prove it to you in a few minutes by showing up at most any rich people's condo office and asking to buy a unit. Discrimination at the top levels is often so subtle that if your eyes and ears aren't tuned to it you won't hear or see it at all.

My parents lived in that house until I forced them out and into a new house I bought for them in Miami Lakes. They didn't want to move but one day some drug dealer put a bullet through the sun porch and it could well have hit my father in the head. But I didn't give my mother an opportunity to back out. I simply bought her a large ranch-style house with a pool and I had her shit moved into it. Now they have neighbors that all have nice jobs and kids can ride the streets on their bikes and all that. The Liberty City house is still in a fairly nice neighborhood, compared to some, but it is getting worse every day. My mother still likes to go by there and visit her friends because it brings back good memories. My old friend Chico lives in the house now; I would never sell it because it means a lot to all of us. I can't bear the thought of strangers mixing their memories with ours.

At first my mother didn't like being in the new house and used to cry every day because she missed the old neighborhood and her friends. My father is a proud man who believes a man supports himself. He feels a man isn't supposed to have to support his parents as long as they can work and support themselves. When we were growing up, my parents never took a nickel of the money we earned. My mother said that if you want kids to work and build a solid work ethic, you can't take the financial motivation they are getting for working. My mother and father made us all work unless we were in school. Our spending money had to be earned by each one of us, and our parents stressed that by refusing to give any us an allowance. "In the real world," Daddy said, "money is at the end of a day's work." When us boys were real small he would take us to work with him and pay us a little something to help out. Thus our hanging out on the corner activities were always kept to a minimum. We didn't work, we didn't have money to spend. My mother opened up bank accounts for all of us when we were little and made a big deal about saving money for our future. We were encouraged to save half of everything we earned. This is one of the early habits that separated us from a lot of people that didn't make it out of the neighborhood. But the main thing that separated us from most of the kids our age was that we had two parents who supported us emotionally. Our house was always filled with love and understanding because of my mother.

My father is a janitor. He has been a janitor for the same school, Highland Lakes in North Miami Beach, for twenty-one years. He worked for many years as a forklift operator for Food Fair (that became Pantry Pride) but was fired for insubordination because he wouldn't apologize to a man who felt my father had done something wrong. He took a menial, lower-paying job because there was no way he was going to eat shit for anyone. My father taught us about being a man and being responsible for our actions. His one quirk is that he has never been able to say he is sorry. "If I am sorry I won't do it again. I will show that I am sorry by remedying the situation." But he would never hurt anyone on purpose.

My father demanded that we learn to be men and face up to the responsibility for our actions. He taught us to respect others and gave us a real sense of self-worth, and he set an example by reading constantly and making us think. He always knew what was going on in the world outside South Florida and would sit for hours with us pointing out exotic times and places and talking about them. It was our father Stanley Campbell who instilled in all of us the enjoyment of learning. Where our father was macho and prideful, Mamma was infinitely understanding and trusting and filled with hugs and kisses and laughed constantly.

My father is a Jamaican, but Mamma was born and raised in Miami. My mother had two sons by her first husband, a man named Newbold. Steven and Harry Newbold are a good deal older than Stanley, Brannard and me. Harry and Steven were years older and hung together. When Steven went to Vietnam I was still in diapers. But my father raised Harry and Steven just like he did us. They will tell you that nobody could tell they weren't his own flesh and blood by his words or actions.

We were poor. My parents never made any bones about that fact. But so was everyone else in our neighborhood. But, unlike some of my contemporaries, we never went hungry. My mother always fed us a hot breakfast and had a hot meal on the table in the evenings, and every day there were snacks waiting for us after school. In fact my mother thought that it was her job to keep the bellies of our friends filled as well. If you dared look hungry or skinny near my house, Mamma saw to it you would get fed right on up to full. You can do without a lot of things in life but food is one thing that you miss real fast. I still hate worse than anything to see hungry kids. That's why I and all of my brothers give out turkeys at Thanksgiving. I have a lot of my distributors do the same. Anything you give, in the right spirit, comes back a thousand-fold. That's a fact.

My mother worked as a beautician even though she was always sick. She breathed in that hair spray and those chemicals all those years and she has suffered with cancer and other illnesses. But she kept on working. She has rheumatoid arthritis and her hands became progressively more twisted but she kept right on working till a few years ago. She would have to find new ways to hold the instruments of her trade but she kept on chugging along. She is unflappable and I cannot remember ever hearing her complain about her own problems. She is a truly Christian woman with a golden heart. I call her "My Old Gal."

Our house, located on a large, shady corner lot in Liberty City, was very small for a big family. Cozy, Mamma would say, but it felt cramped to us kids who had to live on top of each other. The entire house was smaller than the master bedroom in the house I live in today but it was always clean and warm. Two bedrooms and one bathroom, a small dining room and kitchen and small living room. One bedroom for my parents and one for the boys. At one time all five of us boys were in the one eight-by-ten bedroom. We got along about as well as five boys can get along sharing one bedroom—we fought all the time. In fact most of my life I would sleep out on the sofa because I just didn't like sharing a bedroom.

I have always had a temper. When I was small and would lose it, there was no way to control it. I remember when I was four or so Brannard traded me a toy for some candy I had. He was the older brother and fairness was an alien concept when he had the ups on me. So naturally when he finished the candy he took the toy back. I asked him for it and he said "kiss my ass" or something along those lines, but in a five year old's vocabulary. I waited a few minutes for him to have a change of heart and when he didn't I went into the kitchen and borrowed a cast iron skillet from the cabinet and I walked up behind him and brought it down on his head. I'll never forget the look on his face. I am pretty sure that it was months before he took unfair advantage of me on a trade again. Another time he got a drum and I got this pair of skates. I liked the drum better, so I waited till he put it aside and I took a knife and slashed the drum head. The next morning when Brannard went to play his new drum he discovered that someone had cut the head into ribbons with a butcher knife. No one had to fingerprint the knife to know I did it and my father gave me a spanking that made quite an impression. You could say I was a problem child.

I had an aunt (Mamma's baby sister, we called her Aunt Baby) who kept us sometimes when we were small because both our parents worked until six o'clock and child care in the sixties was expensive. It seemed to us that she would spank us but never her own children and she always believed anything they said about us. She never would whip her own kids, so naturally, for their own good, we did it for her. One day she was going to spank me with a plastic Hot Wheels truck. I was five or maybe six at the time. I told her, Bitch, if you hit me with that piece of shit I'll kill your ass! She backed down and I walked the twenty blocks home and was sitting on the steps when Mamma got home. Mamma was furious that I had been allowed to walk home and that Aunt Baby had threatened me. When it came to me, Mamma could only see sweetness and light.

My older brothers were angels compared to me. Being the baby, naturally I was Mamma's favorite. The baby is always the favorite especially when they see you as the final addition to the family. The neighbors all said I had a Demon in me but Mamma said I was just full of energy. Yvonne knew that her childbearing was over and that her health was failing. It isn't unusual to find that the baby gets away with a great deal more than his brothers. It's human nature. Even during the periods when little Luther's brothers were excelling in school and winning awards by the truckload, Luther never lost the spotlight for a minute as far as his relationship with his Mamma was concerned. To this day she will readily admit that I am now, and always have been, her favorite child. She was always slow to punish me, although she spanked Steven for being disrespectful while he was in uniform, on leave from his first tour in the jungles of Vietnam.

My neighborhood was a good one back then. But it was full of old people and settled couples without kids. So we would all go over across 12th Avenue. That's where I mostly grew up. There was always action there. And even today if an ambulance drives in there, ninety-five percent of the time it's to pick up a black (body) bag. You can learn more about human nature and life in an afternoon and a night on 12th as you can living a lifetime in Miami Beach. Even at fourteen and twelve, Brannard and I were content to let our older brothers have the studying shit. By then I was already in the process of figuring that it was money and not college degrees and those salaries that were important. You can't make money working for someone else. I figured that to get rich you had to have people working for you, even when you are sleeping.

I was always on the hustle for a quick buck. There wasn't much in the way of loose change in those days around my house. My mother says that I would never smile unless her pocketbook was open. It's true but if you are a kid and you know your Mamma will give you a quarter for a smile it makes you feel like looking stern. She says that she expected me to be a preacher because I never smiled.

I always knew that without money I'd spend my life dodging bullets on 12th Avenue. There in Liberty the odds of making any real money are a thousand to one. Dope is the only way kids can get what they want; get what this society makes them believe they have to have in order to be happy, or in most cases, to put a little something in their bellies. Hunger is a big motivation where I come from. People say, oh these black people think in the here and now, they can't plan for their future because they are this way or that way. The truth is that no man can plan anything on an empty stomach. Any man, white or black, has to fill his belly and have a steady source of food before he can do anything else. People live from hand to mouth because they can't get beyond that first step. Show me a black man with a steady food supply and I'll show you a man moving ahead with his life. Kids can't study when their stomachs are empty. White people seem surprised that there is a lot of crime in black neighborhoods. Hungry people, black or white, have got to fill their bellies and whatever that takes, even crime that will give them relief, will happen. I'm not talking about people wanting dope or money for a car. I am talking about man's number one priority. Pure motherfuckin' survival.

I was lucky. I wasn't hungry for food. I was hungry for a good life where I had freedom of movement, a healthy business, money in my pockets, and a family of my own. That was my goal.

I would do anything for money when I was little. I still will. I had this family full up with overachievers so I had plenty of the right role models. I took the push mower and haunted the streets looking for yards that needed clipping and I worked my ass off cutting grass and doing hedges. I put together a kit and washed windows till the muscles between my shoulders were filled with shooting pain. We sold lemonade, ice cream, frozen cups from the kitchen to the kids that I would get to come over and listen to the music I played out into the yard from the living room. Once I even put a Pac-Man machine in the utility room. I talked the coin-operated machine distributor into renting me a Pac-Man—and Pac-Man was the shit in those days—and split the money down the middle. It was one of the best locations he ever had for a single machine. Since my parents had that big shady lot, kids were always coming over to hang out. Well I knew that all you need for business is bodies with money. I'd open the windows of the house and play music. Sometimes the whole yard would be filled with kids and it looked like a 7-Eleven between the frozen cups and the Pac-Man.

When I was a little shorty about twelve or thirteen, a boy was picking on me, so one day I went in and got my father's .38 and I shot at him. Shot right at the fool. He wasn't the only person I ever shot at but he was the first. I always had a short fuse and it was generally already lit. I used to fight all the time. I was never officially in a gang because there wasn't one that had anything to offer me. When you are blessed with friends like the ones I had, you didn't need a gang emblem to keep people from messing with you. Our faces were our emblems. I never wanted to hang out with people on a corner and take lunch money from other kids and charge people to walk on a certain street. I worked and I didn't have time to sit around waiting for shit to happen. I made shit happen. If I was challenged I fought; it was that simple. Nobody can respect a man, or boy, who won't stand up for himself. I may not have shot anyone, probably because I was less than a great shot. I have practiced since then and I can shoot now that I don't feel I need to.

Liberty City has always been a tough place. Some parts look nice and quiet and stuff; but looks can be deceptive. You could get into a fight to the death at any age, on any corner, anytime. In those days it was more unusual to die for some shitty reason than today. Now it's a combination of cheap drugs, liquor and the fact that everybody packs a piece. These kids don't put any more value on human life than society puts on theirs. These kids have got no hope of getting the fine life they see on TV except for taking it, in pieces, for themselves. It's real sad that they can't see how short-term the flashy cars and jewelry and stuff is. They don't see the things that really matter because they aren't exposed to that side. If they want something you have, they shoot you and take it. When I was a kid, there was less meaningless violence. Drive-by shootings were unheard of. You didn't kill anybody but the one you were after. There was more of a code in those days. Now these shits are shooting like cowboys and people will be falling all over the place, up and down the streets.

I was lucky. My brothers were really smart and their success, coupled with my ability with a football, paved the way for me to learn about life outside the ghetto. The school bused me over to Miami Beach with all those rich white kids, so I could help win their football games for them. Stanley had the highest grades in aerospace engineering in the history of the state school system. All three of my older brothers got formal educations. Steven became a clinical psychologist who was an expert in Post Trauma Syndrome in Vietnam combat veterans. He did two tours in Nam so Harry wouldn't have to go over, because he knew that they couldn't put two brothers in the same combat area. Steven received ninety-five percent disability because of Agent Orange damage to his lungs. He now works for the government doing some secret shit. My brother Harry Newbold got a degree in chemical engineering and is an executive for Monsanto, who manufactured the fucking Agent Orange. Steven returned from his tours in Nam and used the GI Bill to get himself through college. Then he worked to get Harry through and then Harry worked to get Stanley Jr through. Following

Harry's example was as simple as falling off a log for Steven and Stanley Jr.

My brother Stanley went on to become a Navy jet fighter pilot and later a test pilot. He was also one of the men who investigated the military crashes (just like the National Transportation and Safety Board does on the civilian side). Today he is a private pilot and among his steady clients are some of D.C.'s best and brightest. (When I had the "Nasty" legal problems, Stanley's business suffered because D.C.'s best and brightest are also chickenshits.) Brannard was trained to be an executive chef and he works with me running my clubs. He and I hung together more so than our other brothers because of age and interests.

I never truly bonded to my two older brothers because of the age thing. They were old dudes. Stanley was the bridge with all the brothers. The older three went on to academic heights that neither me nor Brannard had any interest in doing. We just simply were not interested in investing the time and energy as our older brothers had done. I'd say we were more closely tied to living from day to day with a reckless abandon that drove my father crazy.

People are always asking why we have been so successful. I have given this a great deal of thought. The reasons are probably complex but the way I see it we had strong, loving, involved parents to care for us. We were taught that we could do whatever we wanted and set out to do. We were taught to work at any job we could find that was honest and to save our money so that when opportunity presented itself we could take advantage of it. Our father always told us to do better than he did. He accepted no excuses. We didn't say we can't do something because we are black or because of anything else. We had to try, and if that didn't work, to try harder. We had two perfect examples of how hard people can work for their families.

Because my older brothers were so smart I was able to go to predominantly white schools. But I was there because I could play football. I always played in the Optimist program at Miami

Beach. I had already gained a citywide reputation for being an aggressive kid with a future in the sport. In those days the Optimists from all over would recruit kids from Liberty City to stack their teams. I quit playing football because the coach couldn't tell me nothing. I knew it all. The last summer before I quit I didn't stay in shape; I partied with my buddies. When I went back to spring training I was seeing stars and shit. The coach told me to do something I thought I was above doing. I refused and he tossed me off the team. He did the right thing. No doubt about it. I thought I was the whole team. That's before I understood that an athlete is only as good as the team as a whole. It's just as well. I could have been one more shade tree athlete in Liberty City reliving those games while the jug or joint goes from one set of lips to another all day. It's easy to find excuses for your failures but it don't do you any good at all. Liberty City is filled with athletes that didn't make the cut in the pros or listened to the guys who gave them bad advice. Everybody tries to give advice but most of the people giving advice don't know shit. How can anybody take advice from people who are in bad circumstances themselves. How can you listen to somebody who doesn't have two quarters to click together? People do and I have seen brilliant athletes listen to fools and lose everything. Then the fools they listened to tell everybody how the athlete fucked his life up. I take advice from people who know what they're doing. When you want advice, go to experts.

I started a Liberty City branch of the Optimist Club International because I wanted the kids in my neighborhood to be able to play organized sports and compete in other Optimist programs. Other Optimist Clubs have always recruited our best athletes for their programs. The kids have to see their neighborhoods as inferior that way. It is hard on our children to be bused out in order to participate in sports. I am helping build physical facilities for that program and putting in dressing rooms and equipment as well as the baseball diamonds and football fields so these kids can have a place to go near home. A place where they can hang out safely. The shorties need to be away from the corners where shit is happening that can hurt them.

I believe in supporting your community, financially. But I buy outside the community those things that I cannot buy within it. I believe that we have to all work together to make this planet livable. I am selective where I spend money and I spend as much as I can on kids. I try to make my money count for something.

If you have self-respect all things are possible. Without it very little is likely. The most important thing we can teach our children is to love themselves and all others, regardless of color or whatever. I was taught to like myself and I do; I won't like you just because you are black or dislike you because you are white. Skin tone is an accident of birth. I have preferences for things of my culture. My Jamaican blood likes spicy food and reggae music. I am comfortable with myself and like my skin dark. I am happy to take money from anyone of any color and I am comfortable in Carroll City or Miami Beach or Miami Lakes, where I live.

A lot of the kids I grew up with are dead or in prison or sitting under some funky tree watching the world pass on by. I always had a fire inside me that dictated that I move ahead. I make a dollar today and I got to make two tomorrow. I have never been satisfied. Even when I was little. It's like I knew my money was out there and someone else had it. I had to get it back. To this day when I see a crowd I know they are holding money with my name on it and I will go crazy until I figure out a way to get them to give it to me. Once it was people in Liberty City that had my money, now it's jitterbugs all over the country that have some of it. I don't ever see myself giving up the quest. I don't hoard money, I use it to build other things.

2 The Ghetto Style Years

Where I come from you can get killed for a quarter or for saying the wrong thing to someone. One time I was at this football game at American High School with a couple of my buddies. This little girl was jumping up and down on the wooden seats we were sitting on and it was bugging the fuck out of us. So we told her to please cut the shit out so we could watch the motherfucking game. And this brainless bitch went and got her brother. Now her brother was in a little piss-ant gang and four or five of these guys, who didn't have two thoughts between them, came up and told us they was going to fuck our shit up. Her brother was all in our faces and these other guys were surrounding us. The bitch was egging them on wanting to see us get beat up. And I said the girl was bugging us and we just asked her nice enough to cut the shit out. He said we was gonna get fucked up, and I told the cat, you do whatever the fuck you have to do. You got the ups on us tonight but we'll have the ups on you sooner or later. I picked out this one cat leaning against the rail at the top of the stands blocking our exit and I was going to push the motherfucker off the shit. I had this picture in my mind of this cat flying in slow motion to the concrete and his brains splashing out and the rest of them freakin' and us gettin' away in the confusion. He would have died falling that far. No doubt about it. I didn't give a shit. We're talking about, I don't know, five stories or better. But the cops saw something was about to happen and they broke it up and we got the fuck out.

Well, a few weeks later we were outside a dance at my school and I saw this same guy in a car with a couple of his buddies and they were blocked in. I said, this time we got the ups on you, and since you were going to kick our asses because your suck-ass sister had bad manners, we're gonna beat the shit out of you bitches. And we did. We beat the fuck out of them. We taught them a lesson. If you have the ups on somebody and you show no mercy, then you should expect none when they got the ups on you. If those bitches had let us be, we would have let them alone.

I never started a fight without reason but in reflection sometimes the reasons were a little short of meaning much. But if you let somebody get up on you and disrespect you, then they will keep on pushing you until you have to act or leave town. I always went the fuck off at the first line someone drew. That kept me out of a lot of shit because people knew to give me some space. Most bitches thought I was crazy. I am lucky I was never shot. I have been into some incidents where people had their shit (guns or knives) and I didn't. I said, "Do what you have to do," and they coulda killed me and didn't for whatever reason.

In high school I didn't work because I played football. In the summers I had jobs for the city of Miami Beach. I worked as a groundskeeper at the Bay Shore golf course on Miami Beach. It never occurred to me that someday I would be out on golf courses hitting at those little balls. I would have found that beyond comprehension. It looked like the biggest waste of time to me. But there was this guy there and he was always fucking with me, and since I was at work I didn't want to do anything to him. Well one day he told me to do something like rake for him, or something like that, and he kept on taunting me and so I had this hoe in my hand and I laid his cheek open with the blade. I could have killed him and it wouldn't have meant shit. I wanted to kill the bitch. Having to do manual labor for minimum wage is bad enough without having to take shit from some major loser.

People usually get shot by people that are scared. The kid that killed my friend Harry was just a punk with an attitude. He was scared of Harry and so he caught him by surprise and shot him. It was just cowardice but more people are shot out of fear than anger. Harry could have taken him in any kind of one-on-one and the guy knew that. He ambushed Harry because it was the only way he could take him.

In my world, dying was easy, living was hard. I think the good get out early, and the worst live the longest.

The couple awakened from their sleep by the shot were peering out from the windows of their pink house. They were probably the ones who had called the police. The cops knew as soon as they saw him, lying there with his eyes rolled open and his lungs rattling, that he would go before the ambulance arrived. The rose bubbles at the corners of his mouth were testimony to the fact that the young man's heart was pumping blood directly into his lungs. He was drowning on the very fluid that had always kept him alive and as he lay there on that cool sidewalk, there was not one thing that could be done about it. Even had there been a trauma team in the patrol car, the results would have been the same. The cops had removed the automatic pistol which had been clenched in his hand and the pathologist's report would show that there was one small, cleanly punched hole in his side.

Mercifully he remained unconscious from the time he collapsed until he expired a few minutes later. Two blocks away from the shooting scene, at the PacJam II teen club, his friends had heard the fatal shot. But shots fired on a Friday night are as common as horseflies and no one had paid much attention. Anyway none of us knew our friend had even left the building.

The dead man's name was Daryl Williams, but we called him

"Handsome Harry." Although his death didn't rate but a few "another black man dies a violent death in the ghetto" lines on one of the rear pages of the *Herald,* it caused deep anguish to us, the Ghetto Style DJs, because Handsome Harry was an integral member of our organization. He was also one of my oldest and closest friends.

I gave Daryl the name Handsome Harry, because though he was not attractive, women loved him. His front teeth were rotten. Even when there were far more attractive men to be had, women would gravitate to Harry because Harry was nice to them and made them feel appreciated. Handsome Harry was found lying on a sidewalk at 57th Street and 12th Avenue because he had said something that had offended someone. Someone to whom a flippant remark uttered in passing was worth the price of a human life. A nothing remark that, at worst, would have created a minor shoving match at most anywhere else, in almost any other world. The boy that had shot him was a little bad dude about fourteen years old. One of the soulless cowards that hung on 61st Street and had had their brains fried under a lifelong barrage of violence, drugs and God only knows what else.

Harry was no stranger to violence, having been ambushed before when he and his cousin were set upon, by a gang they had done battle with at a Ghetto Style concert. Harry was caught almost alone at a Martin Luther King concert by some kids with handguns. In those days gangs would often try to get into concerts without paying and a fight would break among the thirty or so members of the Ghetto Style DJs and whoever was pushing at the gate. Harry was shot in the fingers and the arm and his cousin in the leg.

But Harry's luck, so pronounced on so many occasions over his twenty-four years of life on the streets, had run out. Harry was a lifeless statistic lying on the corner of 12th and 57th Street because of an accidental scratch on a pair of cheap shoes. Earlier that evening in the PacJam Teen Club, Harry had stepped on this kid's shoe. No big deal. It was a minor accident. The kid said something like, "Hey watch it! You scratched my shoe!" Harry, who took offense at the kid's attitude, said, "Well if you don't want 'em scratched, take 'em off and put 'em in your pocket." And Harry carried the kid to the door and tossed him out like he had done a hundred times before. And that was it. Harry was standing there smiling down at this kid. But at that moment, through all the music, the dancing, and the laughter, this young thug flipped an invisible coin somewhere deep inside his head. In those dull bowels that pass for a brain, he decided that Handsome Harry was a temporarily upright, but very dead man. This kid who Harry insulted was one of a bunch of young mini-thugs who had been terrorizing our neighborhood for years. He thought less of killing a man than what his breath might smell like to his kid sister's girlfriend. The boy went straight home and pulled his .22 caliber Uzi replica from under his bed, or wherever he kept it, and came back to the shadows to watch for Harry's departure.

Around eleven o'clock, the club closed. Harry slipped out of the door unnoticed by the other members of the group and was walking a girl home. It isn't real clear how these kids knew Harry was going to be walking the girl home down that particular street, because normally he would be with one or more of the DJs and they usually carried guns. Suddenly these two kids sprang out from behind some bushes and the one Harry had had the falling out with walked up and said, "Why don't you put your shoes in your pocket," and pushed a gun into Harry's side and squeezed the trigger. Harry tried to run but didn't get far. He had a Tech 9 with him, and he managed to draw it, but was unable to fire. By the time he got it out he was too far gone to pull back the receiver to direct a shell into the empty chamber. Trying to get a shot off at the kid who had fired at him was probably the last thing he ever thought about. Harry lay there looking up into the dark sky as his life drained from him, across the short walkway, and into the gutter.

When I was a kid we played with marbles and spinning tops and shit like that. Now the kids play at getting themselves guns. The only recreation is centered around guns and the games in Liberty City all seem to revolve around death.

I took losing Harry real hard because I loved him like a brother. Even now, almost six years later, I cannot talk about

Harry's death. If he was still alive he'd be sitting right here beside me. Our friendship was magic and we communicated like brothers.

I gave Harry a send-off unlike anything Liberty City had ever seen. No expense was spared. Harry was dressed in the colors of Skyywalker: lime green and white. The casket was bright green too. But the focal point was a massive floral piece that was made from a solid wall of dyed green carnations set up behind the coffin with "SKYYWALKER RECORDS" spelled out in white carnations. They still talk about that funeral in Liberty City like it was a coronation ceremony.

The boy who shot Harry got picked up by the cops, but the girl who was there and saw it happen froze up like granite. I can't blame her really. Those kids were guaranteed crazy and talking to the cops could well have introduced her to the same fate as Harry. Besides, the witness protection program wasn't designed for a poor black chick who is testifying against minors. The cops, unable to get her to testify, had to cut the murder-tykes loose.

While Harry lay in state at the funeral home, the older brother of the boy who had shot him came to see me so he could ride down the street in his car without worrying that some of the Ghetto Style DJs might retaliate by sending shots into it. The Ghetto Style DJs were certainly not more than a few deadly inches away from shooting up the son of a bitch that killed Harry. This was all very serious, life and retaliation shit. In the light of day death looks more terrible than it does under the street lights with alcohol, drugs or adrenaline running through your blood stream.

I was inside the club working at my desk. With Harry lying in a coffin a few blocks away, I was not in a forgiving mood. The older brother parked his car right outside the front doors of the PacJam II for a quick getaway. When I was told the boy was outside with a friend, I walked out, locking the office door behind me. I told them to leave. The two guys got hot and soon the verbal shit was flying. These guys were backing for the door with me screaming right behind them. They were saying that the DJs weren't the only ones who knew how to use a gun. In fact, they had guns in their waistbands, and I was unarmed and alone. As fate would have it, most of the DJs were at my house in Coconut Grove cleaning the pool and kicking back.

"Baby Ced" (Cederick Walker), who cleaned up the club, wandered past at that moment. Sometimes Ced's mind seems to wind up a little slowly under some circumstances, but he can read street danger like a traffic sign and when he saw what was happening he went around to my office. He stood at my locked office door and tried to decide whether I needed a gun badly enough to justify replacing the door. After standing there for a few long seconds, he broke into the office and retrieved my Colt AR-15 which he tossed across the club floor to me. The guys took one look at the weapon with its thirty-round clip and ran for their lives.

They got into the car but by the time they started fumbling with the keys I had the barrel aimed at the car windshield. I was not intending to open them up. But they made the decision to leave the car anyway and take off for higher ground on foot. I just stood where I was and walked those high-powered military steel jackets into that car just like I would water my lawn on a Sunday morning. The bullets punched through paint, sheet steel, and layed waste to the window glass. When the first barrage ended, blue water cascaded from the radiator and streamed out of the grill. The car sank slowly to the ground. Just then, a patrol car was driving down 12th, two blocks away. The cop heard the rifle shots and he freaked. He dropped to the seat, slamming the brake pedal so that the car came to a screeching stop in the middle of 12th. Then he opened the microphone and started screaming into it. In his panic the cop had tuned his radio county-wide and he broke into every open receiver with something very close to "Oh Lord, They're killing me! It's an ambush! Oh God, I don't want to die!" It took a while for the man to calm down enough to say where he was. Every cop who heard the "officer in distress" broadcast became like one of the hornets looking for the kid that fired the slingshot at their nest. They converged on the scene in a near riot of smoking tires, screaming blue strobe ribbons and vapor trails. When the first officer got to the scene all they found was a patrol car that was blocking traffic. All around the car it looked like another normal afternoon in Liberty City. The merchants and residents who had initially come out at the sound of shots, had long since gone back to their normal business.

Naturally the cop in the car was humiliated to find out that the shots were fired from two blocks away. By the time the back-up cops arrived, some concerned—or nosy—citizens had phoned in the fact that a lunatic was shooting up a car several blocks from where the "alert" patrolman was stuck to the floorboard with his pistol drawn.

The cops, who rolled to the PacJam II, surveyed the smoking wreck and told me that since I was on my own property protecting myself, it was cool. While they were concerned about where the ricochets may have landed, there didn't seem to be much damage done beyond the target. The gun was legal and properly registered and there was a crowd gathering. As any cop who works Liberty City will attest, it doesn't take murder for a crowd to become a stone-, rock- and bottle-throwing mob that doesn't think twice about leveling every Cuban and white-owned building within five square miles. So the cops warned me to think carefully about firing that weapon in the city limits again and they wandered off to write their reports. The crowd, confident though maybe a tad disappointed that nothing had happened worth tearing shit up over, went back to their jobs—drug-dealing or sitting on the corner watching traffic.

After all the other cops were gone, the one who had humiliated himself dropped by and asked me if I would come with him to look at mug shots. Naturally, I said I hadn't recognized the guys who had threatened me and then left their car there. I drove my Jeep downtown behind the patrol car. When I was in the station house the cop cuffed me in front of his buddies, trying, the only way he knew how, to get some of his flattened pride back. Nothing came of it and the charges were dropped.

I used to shoot dice all over town. I was good at it and I made money at it. You can use loaded dice but you had better be a master at switching them or you'll get killed. I was on the tour. I never got caught with loaded dice and I played with people that had been rolling dice for years. I smoked some reefer but in those days marijuana was no big deal. Now I know that drugs ain't bad in moderation. But it's destroying our communities, our families, and killing off our people.

My brothers and I can all cook. Back then, we wouldn't think twice about preparing the family meal to make it easier on Mamma. Knowing how to cook made us more independent. When I got out of high school I got a job cooking at Mount Sinai hospital where I was born. My brother Brannard was already there. I was installed in the kitchen cooking for the employees' dining room. It was a bitch but it was money. The kitchen, that's where I met Terry Brimberry. She and I had a thing and she got pregnant with Shenetris, my first daughter.

Getting into the Ghetto Style DJs was an accident. First off, when I was still in high school, my Mamma hit the Jai Alai combination numbers (using numbers that came to her in a dream) and spent some of the money on this stereo system. It was a component system with a turntable, cassette deck and speakers. Every afternoon after school we would get it out into the yard and kids would come over and I'd play music. Kids would dance or whatever and just hang out. That was when I put in the Pac-Man in the utility shed. I also made cassette copies of my father's reggae records and sold them to Jamaicans around the neighborhood for reefer or cash. Then I'd trade that for something else and so forth. I put together tapes with good shit all in a row.

A lot of my friends got into drugs and shit but it was a short trip for them. I don't like not being in control of my life even for a few minutes. Dealing drugs has no future, never did. So I would play this music until about the time my mother would be getting ready to leave the beauty shop. Then we'd put the thing back where it was and put the photos back on it like the way she had arranged it. We really rattled the walls all over the neighborhood. But nobody ever told her.

And I hung out at the radio stations, especially WEDR, and I learned about DJ'ing and production and how valuable advertising was. I still use radio for advertising.

When I was seventeen, DJ groups were hot. I knew them all and they fascinated me. Plus, women love DJs and think DJ'ing's glamorous. But it isn't. Almost nothing is. Most everything is hard work if you do it right. But I always wanted to be a DJ. Nat Moore, this football player, had his group called the International DJs. The South Miami DJs, SS Express, and the Jammers were hot shots. Those guys were my idols. They were on the radio and DJ'ing at the parks and I wanted in. This was before rap. It was when rap was being created. We DJ'd different down here.

The Ghetto Style DJs were founded before I came along. They had like three speakers and no way to get the equipment to the parks and all that. I only got in because I had a van and that was more valuable than experience. They could get the shit around to the parks and parties because of me. I started DJ'ing. The other guys were happy to play for free at the parks but I couldn't see where this was a valid plan because it was expensive driving the shit from place to place. So I started going around to all the schools to get some dances. I had a great sales pitch but the other groups had all the shit tied up. We got some little shit. So I dropped the price. But I still ran into a stone wall. The school activity directors were all getting kickbacks. They had relationships with other DJs and they were ripping the schools off, and the student councils had to vote on the groups and it was hard to slide in. It was all politics, serious politics. I went straight to the coaches and pitched them direct and gave them the kickbacks. Because they could change the game by going over the kids' heads, soon I had all the schools. I took over and knocked them all out and they never knew what happened. I went to the top. The coaches. Then I had to get hooked up with the radio stations. All the other groups had radio connections and had the stations behind them. I was an outcast. I wasn't in with them at all.

When I started making money with the DJ'ing and the record sales of "Throw the D," the cops saw me in a new car and wearing jewelry and they assumed I was selling drugs and they started harassing me. So Jerry Rushin, the manager of WEDR radio, called for a sit-down with Chief Dickson and we showed like a million dollars worth of receipts from record sales. That helped some, but see, some of the Ghetto Style DJs and their buddies sold drugs. They had left the group because the money was better in the drug business. They would hang out at the club but they weren't in the group. Some of them got really screwed up on drugs. But it's five or six years later and they are all penniless now. Drug money don't stick to nothing but a good time. But hey, that's all some people want. And for people who ain't never had shit, that's a trade they are willing to make. There's a lot of the guys from then who say I owe them because they was there in them old days. Well, if they had been my friends and had been willing to work, they'd have something. But they think everybody should carry their asses around in wheelbarrows because they was "back in the days" with me.

Well, life ain't that kind of fantasy. In this life you get what you can hold on to. I joined the Ghetto Style DJs as a kid. I had the dream and the direction. They was playing free gigs in African Square with these shitty little speakers. I was responsible for building the gigs into a profitable enterprise. I bought the equipment and I registered the name. Some of those guys went to jail for dope. Some started to hit the pipes and, hey, they go around saying that they made me in the old neighborhood. But they are dreaming. I took each little thing and I built it into something. Some of them helped me here and there but I am the one who kept it all in one piece and made sure that piece got bigger and stronger. So where are they today? They've got to understand this is now and that was then and the two don't necessarily fold into each other. The only thing constant between then and now is Luther Campbell. That's not a brag, that is a fact. I did it all without outside help. I never got one thing from radio stations and they even tried to block my action most of the time. I never got handed one break that I can remember. I paid retail for every ad I ran. I paid for all the equipment. The only break I ever got was from this U-Haul place. We built up enough equipment that we had two full groups and we'd split up on weekends. The U-Haul guy would let us keep the trucks that we rented on weekends all week unless he needed one of them for a customer and we'd drop it off. That was great. A lot of people talk about how much they did for me. Nobody did shit. I fought for everything we got.

One day I got this idea that we could be playing our own gigs and we could cut out the middlemen. I knew there was this skating rink called the Sunshine Skating Center in Homestead, Florida, but I named it PacJam at night when I did my thing in there. That was just one place. There was a deal for dead nights through the week. They charged seven dollars a pop. I even did the advertising. I called that place the PacJam I when we were renting it at night. We had Soul Night on Wednesday and Reggae Night on Thursday. One owner didn't tell the other and he was having the place packed on nights and this partner didn't know it. The cops hated us because we were bringing blacks into the area to party. They didn't like that.

I figured that we were leaving a lot of money on the table. So I rented the PacJam II. It was located at 1205 NW 54th Street at 12th Avenue. Today it's just another boarded up, poorly-painted, concrete block building in a sad, neglected area. But in those days, in the mid-eighties, the PacJam was a great teen club and it was Liberty City's only one. I made it a teen club because that was money on the street that nobody was claiming. I wanted those quarters and dollars. We didn't serve anything harder than soft drinks. It was a place to test music on the jitterbugs and to create a safe environment for kids. It also gave Liberty City DJs a place to appear regularly and provided a venue to bring in other rap acts. I was interested in promoting for fun and profit. The club operated for several years. Parents liked to have the kids in a safe place as an alternative to the corners. We rocked PacJam II with great sounds. Kids loved it. Our customers from those days have followed me to two other clubs, Strawberries and now Luke's Miami Beach.

I opened the club because I knew that kids didn't have a safe place to go to let off steam and dance. So the idea was solid and as far as such things are possible in that neighborhood, it was a safe place. And the jitterbugs spent money just like adults. That whole area of Miami is violent and there were a few fistfights in the club and even killings nearby, but if something happened three blocks away, the cops and the *Miami Herald* attributed it to us. I have always had off-duty cops in the lot to make sure that the kids were safe and weren't taking dope or alcohol on the property. It was as safe an environment as we could possibly make it.

The Ghetto Style DJs had security guys in the group and the PacJam was our headquarters. There were sometimes a dozen of us. I was never a great rapper but I got into talking to the crowd and they'd talk back. We started doing a dance called the "Ghetto Jump" that I did during parties and concerts using a heavy bass dance beat. It was the origin of the Miami Bass sound. So a record producer gets this guy to do the song and I was credited on the record as the originator of the song. But I never got a fucking penny from the producer. I decided that I'd forgo the royalties if the guy (I can't even remember the shit's name) would play the PacJam for free. I figured I'd get a few bills out of the record one way or the other. But the mother-fucker wouldn't do it. So I said that if that motherfucker could do a record of my shit and make money, then so could I.

I had started doing concerts, promoting Run DMC, The Fat Boys, and everybody who was working the clubs. Rap was still a new form and the kids were just getting into it. The PacJam was a hot spot. I decided that I wanted to do a record. I had found this record by a group called 2 Live Crew. These guys were from California. It was started by David Hobbs and Chris Wongwon. Mark Ross came later after the other original guy wanted to get out of rap. Their record crashed everywhere except in Miami where I was playing it, promoting them, you know. Well, I got them in to play here and I decided I wanted them to back me up. So we cut "Throw the D" which is short for "Throw the Dick." It did okay. It got certified "gold" which was unbelievable for a rap record in those days. I don't know, maybe we sold 250,000 before it was over, then we put it on an album and sold half a million of that.

So the guys moved to Miami and we started the group as it is today. We did great. Luke Skyywalker, as I was known before the punk George Lucas double-crossed me, had my Skyywalker

Record company's offices there. When I started making records, there was one small office that held five people and their stuff, and the other larger office was mine. As the company grew, the rooms got filled up with boxes of tee-shirts, crates of twelve-inch vinyl disks, then later albums and the assorted paperwork involved. I had to add a large metal shack behind Mamma's house complete with a ten-foot-tall fence with razor wire to keep punks from the neighborhood from stealing my shit and selling records on street corners. The PacJam grew from a club to an operation center. And the business shit grew faster than anyone could deal with. When my brother Stanley called up a top accounting firm and told them the numbers I was generating, they seemed excited. When they drove up in front of the PacJam and took one look at the building and the guys shooting baskets in the parking lot, they put their Lincoln in reverse and fled back to their high-rise. They're still kicking themselves for judging this book by its cover.

I sold records to "mom and pop" stores all over and I furnished our music to the guys that were doing parties and concerts in other cities. And it grew into an organized thing that is still operating and growing.

We did two things that made us successful. One, we used everyday ghetto language with subject matter that everybody hears all the time, and we had a bass beat that you could dance to. It's that simple.

Pretty soon we had gold records. Then platinum. It was hard work but we did what we had to do.

The thing about the Ghetto Style years that is most amazing is that although I was a man with a violent temper who would fight at the drop of a hat, a man who regularly pissed off really dangerous people, and a man who everybody thought carried a lot of money, I still managed to survive. A lot of my friends didn't. People like Handsome Harry. But I walked out of the ghetto with a pocket full of cash and a dream that was just getting underway.

When I left Liberty City I drove my Jeep Cherokee to a house at 3897 Kumquat Avenue in Coconut Grove complete with a large swimming pool, a security wall and neighbors with real jobs. I moved my fledgling company from the shitbox headquarters at the PacJam into a suite of swank offices in a glass high-rise on Biscayne Boulevard. I was on a roller coaster and the tracks were greased with money from a new type of music that I was helping to refine into a form that could generate millions and millions of dollars well before the major labels had any real idea that there was any potential to be exploited. I was on my way to becoming a multimillionaire. When I moved again I abandoned the house in the Grove and moved into a mansion on a golf course and traded the offices on Biscayne for a building in a location that I liked—a large building right in the very heart of Liberty City. When I returned to my neighborhood it was as a king, the King of Dirty Rap.

3 Life on the Road Is Triple-X Rated
by John R. Miller

Diversions are a major part of life on the road. There is a constant search for any little thing that might break the monotony of weeks of traveling the highways in buses, night after night in antiseptic hotel rooms with the tiny soap and plastic one-jigger shampoo bottles, of Shoneys and Burger King rubber breakfasts, lunches and dinners, the super highs of performing and crashing lows around both edges of doin' the gig. With ninety percent of all rock and roll, rap, country, blues, polka, gospel, jazz, big band, swing, and possibly even classical musicians, sex is the old standby. Sex is a game that gives the towns some significance beyond having a venue or club swap cash for a couple hours of hard sweating, words cast out in an endless string and a driving, soul stirring, heart-thumping Miami bass beat.

The 2 Live road-bound men play hard out there and so do the women that wait for them to come through. For some of these women it is a quick grab at a brass ring. They get touching close to fame and fortune for a few minutes or a few hours. It's commerce. The women can exchange sex (or whatever they have to do during that time) for this little memory they can keep. And they don't realize that except for those moments of glory on stage or the first three hours behind the wheel of that new Ferrari, the stars' lives are pretty much mundane, shitsucko too. Generally, the lives of stars are even emptier and hollower than their own.

It takes two to party but as often as not these guys can have as many girls as they can reach out and touch. The higher up you are in the group the easier the pussy falls. Sometimes girls have to screw their way up through the crew to get to the performers. Sometimes they play sex in a scramble, moving from tumble room to tumble room until the sun comes up.

Near Phoenix, Arizona
1990

In Phoenix, Luke has hired one of the top live record produ-cers in the business, a short elf-like man with a little ponytail who drops big names, to create the first studio-quality live rap album. Thick black cables stretch from the ass end of the eighteen-wheeler, across an expanse of desert floor and into the great hall. Microphones have been placed above the stage and above the seats so that every scream and "fuck me" response is sucked through the cables and slammed into the mixing board in a way that is understood only by the man with the ponytail.

At a press conference Luke says that Arizona sucks, that they have disrespected Martin Luther King, and that he won't come back until there is a Martin Luther King holiday. He also asks how the Indians are treated. "Are they just another kind of nigger here?" "Do you think all women are whores?" the white lady reporter throws back at him. "I say if the shoe fits, wear it." Those were Luke's last words before waving goodbye with a peace sign and a smile.

In the 2 Live dressing room with Chris, Marquis, Hobbs and the Move Somethin' girls, he begins preparing for the concert by drinking a large glass of Hennessy. He has a major toothache. Within minutes all of the other group members are right beside him sucking the thick, dark liquid from large plastic glasses. They drink the cognac like spring water.

Luke humors a group of female fans who have gathered in the hallway just outside the backstage dressing room. One, a tall beautiful young lady, puts out steadily louder protestations of "Oh No, Please I'm a Church Lady!" Luke dances with her to a reggae tune that he carries in his head, with a glass of cognac in one hand and a long unlit cigar (a King Kong from Mike's Cigars in Miami Beach) in the other. As they grind, cheers go through the ranks. People around Luke cheer a lot.

Luke leads the group through the hallways and toward the darkened stage to a deadly thundering Miami bass beat, and the ocean of screaming faces. The group follows security into the darkened hall and through the hand held microphones Luke signals the fans that he is in the house. "BEFORE WE GET THIS MOTHERFUCKIN' THING MOVING, I WANT TO GET ONE GODDAMNED THING PERFECTLY MOTHER-FUCKIN' STRAIGHT. WE ARE THE 2 MOTHERFUCKIN' LIVE CREW!" The hall fills with a chant, "2 Live Crew, 2 Live Crew, 2 Live 2 Live Crew, Boys boys boys," once, then repeats, and then a bass beat that might well be removing paint from jets passing overhead stuns the crowd. Luke starts calling, "Head, booty and cock—what you like, fellows?!" The church lady is on the front row jumping up and down in a frenzy and screaming at the top of her lungs like she has been filled with the spirit. Tomorrow she may well sit in the choir and Amen up a storm as the preacher condemns the concert. Luke smiles and points at her.

For the next hour the group drives this crowd into a voco-pornographic frenzy. The Move Somethin' girls and women from the audience who scale the stage and do the Big Nasty add to the excitement. "2 Live Crew will be hosting a party for women only at the Hilton hotel," booms the P.A. announcement near show's end.

When Luke exits the stage, everyone in the theater is still revved and over-amping, and the pudgy, clam-like man with the ponytail in the truck is clapping furiously. "It's in the can!" he shouts. Being used to working with the biggest acts in the business, he will not, Luther is told later, even let Luther hear the tape over the telephone, until he has been paid in full. You learn fast in the music business that the bigger the star the more likely you are to get stiffed.

"This motherfuckin' show was in the house," says Luther's road manager, Michael Hopkins. "In the house!"

The band is in limos and out on to the dark highway toward their hotels to await the evening's entertainment. Since you never know when the local district attorney in need of some anti-porn P.R. might call for an arrest to be made, encores aren't advisable. Luther has chosen a resort in Scottsdale where he can play golf before leaving for Houston. He and I are driven there while the band settles into their hotel for the night's entertainment. Luther's bodyguard and the driver leave to go to the party. Luther settles in and turns on a college football game.

After an hour or so and a few stiff drinks, Luther's bodyguard sticks his head into the doorway from the adjoining suite and says "I brought you something." He enters and a woman follows like a shadow. Her makeup has been applied in thick layers with deep accents circling her brown eyes and has been smeared as though she has had her face rubbed across the sheets of a bed. She has a nice face but her hair is teased into a standing mushrooming puff. Ebony rivulets of wet dark hair arch across her face, completely obscuring her left eye. When she smiles, a chunk of red lipstick seems to have been thumb-pressed into her front teeth. She wears dusty black heels. Small mirroring appliqués cover her outfit; each echoing incandescent light, like the mirrored ball in a road house. She carries a small matching clutch bag. She has met her heroes tonight—heroes who are as susceptible to her fantasies as she is to theirs. And tonight they are as accessible to her as her next door neighbor.

She sits in a chair and looks nervously at Luther, thrilled that she is in the presence of a real celebrity. He smiles at her and then turns to yell at the television screen.

"What the fuck was that, you dip-shit motherfucker?" he screams at the athletes sweating somewhere in the Midwest.

"Oh, I've seen you on TV so many times and I have all the records, even the first one! You're my favorite," she says.

She knows why she is here, but to make sure, the bodyguard says, "Tell the man what you been doing tonight, honey."

"Sucking cocks . . . and getting fucked!" she says in an excited, singsong voice shot through with nervous giggles.

"You like to suck dick?" asks the man who is stretched across the bed, still with half of his mind somewhere in the Midwest.

"Yes! I really love to suck dick. I just sucked his in the limousine!" she says, pointing to the bodyguard.

"She is one hell of a dick sucker! What did you think about my dick, honey?" he asks.

"It was big, black and really delicious!" She runs her tongue around the circle that her lips have made as she rolls her eyes and giggles from deep in her throat.

"You going to suck their cocks?" the bodyguard asks.

"Please!!!" she says. "Oh, please let me!"

"No problem," the man on the bed says absently. "No problem." Bored with the college game in Nebraska, Luther now switches his undivided attention to the girl.

"Let's have a look at your pussy. You want to show us your pussy?" he asks as he crosses the room toward the bathroom. He stops at his golf bag with "Hurricanes" printed on it and unzips the hood, pulling a club from his bag. "A three-iron, I believe," he says as he approaches the woman who is shifting herself in the chair.

"Show us the pussy," the big man says. She puts her feet up on the chair seat to show herself to the men. No panties. Her vagina glistens as she peels the covering petals of flesh back with her long crimson fingernails.

Holding the club by the blade, Luther gently aims the black muzzle directly at the wet orifice. "You a freak?" he asks. She nods her head quickly up and down. He walks slowly forward until the ebony tip is resting against the damp pinkness. She coos and moves her legs further apart.

"You want this? It's a Ping!" he says. "Ping, Pong Pussy."

"Oh, yes! Please! Give me the Ping!" She arches herself toward the club handle.

He moves the wand gently back and forth until the handle is moistened enough to submerge a few inches. He moves the club in and out slowly, gently. She is making deep noises of satisfaction and she is building the volume. She closes her eyes and smiles. He removes the dripping golf club and puts it to her lips. She tongues it into her opened mouth and sucks it loudly. She cries for more.

"Uh-Oh, a sic-ko!" the big man says. "This bitch is crazy."

"Watch this!" she says as she inserts into herself a small squared scotch bottle that the writer has just emptied. Tiring of this, Luther goes to the bed, leaving her in the chair. He lifts the receiver and makes a call. She seems confused by his sudden disinterest. The vagina is exposed to about a 75-degree angle of view to the writer, her heels planted into the vinyl seat cushion and her knees as wide apart as the arms of the chair will allow.

"Ain't this a trip! You trippin', Casper! The white man wants to eat the pussy! Let the man eat the pussy," Luke says, laughing. "White men like to eat pussy. Ain't that so?"

She looks at the writer. "It's real clean," she says earnestly, a wide smile growing across her dark face. "I washed it a bunch of times before the concert. I'll wash it again if you want to eat it."

She seems genuinely afraid that she may fall short in pleasing the men in the room. But she isn't sure that she is wanted where she is being aimed by the famous man on the bed.

"Maybe I'll pass," I say, unsure of the protocol since this is my first road trip with the group.

"I said LET him eat the pussy!" Luther says again.

"I'll wash it," she adds. "If you want to eat it I'll go wash it. There's nothing wrong with it. It's clean."

"Nothing personal but I'll pass," I say. "But thanks anyway. Really."

"Well suck his dick then!" Luke suggests from the bed. He is engaging in a conversation in Miami as well as monitoring the action and trying to direct his reluctant guest into some sort of perverse initiation ritual.

"You don't have to eat it. Can I suck your dick?" she asks softly. She does not want to displease Luther but neither does she want to force anything. She is unceasingly polite and seems suddenly unsure of herself. It is as though being turned down is a new experience and she is becoming crestfallen; as though the clock is ticking and she is in danger of losing curtain number two if the bell catches her with her task left uncompleted.

"I don't mind. I like white boys. I've sucked a lot of white boys." She seems to be on the verge of wondering out loud if it's because she's black that the writer isn't responding to her willingness. "I screw white guys where I work."

"Where do you work?" I ask.

"At a hospital."

"No shit?" says Luther. "We got ourselves a nurse."

"No, data processing," she corrects him, smiling.

"Really. Thanks anyway. I'm fine," I say again, feeling uncomfortable. I take another one-ounce pull at my glass of scotch, the ice collapsing to the bottom.

"You don't like me? Please let me." She eyes the man on the bed. "Where are the ice cubes? Get some ice cubes!" she says. "If I use the ice cubes? Two cubes, one in each jaw while I suck . . ."

"Well," I say, "I really don't think my wife would like it."

"Where's your wife?" she asks suspiciously, turning from side to side suddenly; as though the other woman might be hiding in the closet.

"At home. Asleep. She'd better be asleep."

"How you know?" she asks.

"Because it is five-thirty in the morning back there," I say.

"Where?"

"Miami."

"Enough talk! Let the man eat the pussy!" says Luke from the bed. "Or suck his dick! Or get out and let me watch the ballgame!" says Luther. The larger man is looking between her legs as though he is trying to make out some words written there.

Under weakening protest from the writer, but under growing peer pressure she will rub his back, in some attempt at foreplay, fidget with his zipper, remove his penis and begin the descent toward the purple head. The tongue darts across the head before he can react. The scotch has slowed his will to resist involvement in this tableau.

"Gee, I haven't been involved in anything like this since high school," I say while wrestling my dick back from her grip and trying to see if the tape is rolling at the same time. It is. This awkward scene evokes howls of laughter from the other two men in the room. All the writer on the couch can think is "God, I just know you can catch AIDS from a wet tongue?"

Tomorrow, I think, I can say I was drunk, but I know what it was. It was an initiation. Now that my penis has been coaxed beyond the folds of denim, seen the florescent lights and been moistened by the velvet tongue, the white man is officially "Down" with the group. After weeks of sullen attitudes, silence and lies, I am finally accepted. The price of admittance was participation in the ritual, no matter how benignly or awkwardly I stumbled through the test. They had thought the writer was a cop but no cop would do that and hope to make a case. How many cops would pose as writers and travel across the country for a ten dollar prostitution bust six states away?

The "stank ho" will stand up by the bed and talk on the telephone with someone in Miami, while Luke lays across the bed and places his hand inside her vagina. A long-fingered mummy of a hand, tightly wrapped in a brown and white plastic shopping bag.

Later, while Luther holds the writer's tape recorder, she will push her tongue deep into the big man's anus while he roars with laughter and shouts instructions. "Deeper. Oh shit! This is freaky!" Then her mouth will move to the penis. And back and forth on command from one to the other. "Ass, dick, ass, dick," loud puppy-like sucking, dove-like cooing and Deep-South slobbering. And, of course, hysterical sheets of male laughter in the background. The big man tries to use the seven-iron on her like Luke did, but he does not have the touch and she squeals with obvious displeasure, "Goddamnit!" He stops.

"She's eatin' the ass!" the man beside the bed holding the recorder says flatly. "Yes, fans. She is definitely eating the ass!

She's not drunk. She in her right mind. Now suck the man dick. Yeah baby. You twisted."

"Yes, I'm a freak!" she yells when she frees her lips for a second and lets her hand take up so not a beat is missed.

After the rimming is completed to the man's satisfaction she takes his penis, puts it in her mouth and she begs him to urinate. Then she drinks at him like a baby calf, until his bladder is dry.

She has managed to execute this maneuver without spilling one drop of yellow liquid on the astroturf that covers the balcony where she kneels for the feat. He calls it a Golden Shower but one of the men says he thinks that a Golden Shower is something that occurs when someone urinates on to your skin and not down a throat.

"You see," the big man says proudly, "the women Luke writes songs about do exist! He didn't make them up. This gal is a flat backed, stank ho. Would you kiss her on the lips? If you kissed her on the lips you'd be sucking my dick."

When this is over she is beaming like she has passed an audition for a starring role in a feature film. She says that she has never had a better evening. Before she leaves, she is given a large red tee-shirt which she pulls down covering the miniskirt. The message on the shirt reads: WE WANT SOME PUSSY.

"I need some money for a cab," she says.

"Oh no, that'd be prostitution," Luther says. "No way. I'll have the limo driver take you home. My treat!" he says.

"I'd hate to have to smell her breath in the morning," Luke says, waving goodbye from the door to the other suite. The big man leads her to the door. Outside under the wide sky the limousine is waiting. The big man later swears that the limo driver jerked himself off on the trip back while the girl was giving head in the recesses of the long Cadillac.

The white man, the writer who once thought he had seen everything on earth at least twice, is probably in shock. He leaves the room to try to shower off the experience. Remembering an old wives' tale he urinates, hoping to push the memory and the pangs of guilt into the recesses of his mind and any venereal disease germs down the drain. He tells himself it was the scotch, fatigue and the strangeness of the event which caused him to participate, killing any objectivity that he might have had. Guilt or no guilt, when he lies down on the rollaway with the unfamiliar lumps he crashes into unconsciousness. Maybe he prays that the woman, the nurse, has had all her shots before he nods out. Maybe he doesn't.

The next day, the bodyguard tells us that after the limo delivered the pair to the hotel in Phoenix where the other band members and roadies were staying, she ended up doing sex tricks throughout the rooms there until well after the sun came up. "I had sooo much fun! I hope I can make it to work!" she said as she was leaving.

"She sucked more dicks in one night and got dicks jabbed in more holes than your average ho gets in a year of Sundays. And she didn't get nearly enough to suit her," a band member says. The writer, totally disgusted with himself, stares out the window at the desert flying past.

The tee-shirt she now wears over her mirrored blouse, he thinks as the cacti streak by, is physical evidence of what may well be the most important memory of her young life. She has weathered twenty-four years of normal, mundane, wind-swept life in the desert. A life of working at a six-dollar-an-hour job in the bowels of a concrete hospital at that big green computer screen, giving occasional fast sex to men that have no respect for her, drinking and eating, dancing and sleeping within spitting distance of cactus and coyotes. Now she can remember living a real fantasy while she taps away at the keyboard searching out the cost of a shot of morphine to tack onto some cancer patient's bill or adds an aspirin to the tab of some accountant who had his gallbladder removed.

"Drink the man's hot piss. Sure, great! Why not!" This was, after all is said and done, her dream and the rigid phalluses, warm urine and the brown elastic spokes of the puckered asshole were merely props, like hollow fiberglass models and single sided sets in that fantasy. She will be free to relive these fantasies day after day. A one-shot deal in some hotel rooms in the desert will weather a lifetime of remembering.

"Want to diddle me with the golf club handle. Go ahead. I'll never forget it." In her mind the fantasy will live forever, a dream to hold dear while she stares at that screen of flashing numbers and billing information. You can't feel that you are missing life when you have such a unique memory to fall back on.

Now she has something wicked to cling to during those long, lonely, desert nights. The writer predicts that someday she will forget the useless facts and her memory will build a white picket fence around itself. The night will become one that she spent in the arms of a famous man who held her, kissed her gently and made love to her in a hotel room outside Phoenix. She will gradually forget about the other pushing and pulling puds, the golf club handles, the little liquor bottle, the way her tongue pushed into the man's tight asshole, and the salty urine.

"She never removed her blouse. In fact, besides lifting her skirt up she didn't expose anything," the writer observes later in the limousine as the tape of the evening blares from the large speakers in the ceiling. "All of the sex was accomplished around her clothing. Opened pant zippers, partially pulled away underpants and that." The limousine driver is in convulsions and the long car weaves, rolling like a sailboat running from the wind.

To the men drained once more in yet another hotel room she was simply another faceless road whore to use as a handy lust receptacle.

"This may well be a song, Golden Shower," Luther Campbell says as he replaces the old number three Ping in the golf bag.

The writer wonders if it's adultery, even if you don't come.

Seven months later Keith Sweat, formerly of New Edition, is playing in Miami. There is a gathering backstage of the road crew and the performers. One of the members of the band asks Luther if he remembers the last time the 2 Live played Phoenix. Luther says he remembers. "I stayed at a golf resort on that trip with this writer pal. We played golf."

"Well," the man says, "there was this girl that was partying with us after our Phoenix show. She told us that you fucked her with one of your golf clubs. Is that true?"

Luther, sitting in the dressing room surrounded by his contemporaries, picks up his pocket telephone to tell the writer that his prediction was indeed correct. She told everyone about that evening as though it had been the high point of her life. "Can you believe that shit!" Luther says.

A Music Convention
Downtown Houston, Texas
1990

There are two of them and they look like sisters. Cute, bubbly. They are standing together in the glass elevator with their shoulders touching. Young, fair-skinned, with cascading golden hair. Behind them, through the clean glass, the Hyatt floor, teeming with tiny, skittering figures, falls away.

They are fixtures on the road. These eighteen-year olds have been pursuing the group across the country and sleeping with them every chance they get. They are on vacation. The taller one says that her father is a bigot. "The idea of us being on the road doing these concert dates with a black group drives him nuts." The shorter one, Ziggy, has no father because he died. Her mom isn't crazy about this either, but the taller, Star, says that her mother is just great.

The girls live in the Valley a block away from each other. They are not groupies. They say so. They are, well, different. Serious. They are interested and involved fans who have followed the band across the Western United States at no small expense. They were at both L.A. shows, the Phoenix show, to Austin where the show was cancelled because Mark Ross's mother had suffered a stroke, and now to Houston for the Beaumont performance. They sit at the table, looking at each other as they talk.

"Well, outside Phoenix, Eddie [one of the roadies] got out of the bus and into our car," says Ziggy.

"This side of Phoenix," corrects Star.

"Was that Eddie or JT?" Ziggy will ask.

"JT." Star answers.

Star is in love, more or less, with a member of 2 Live Crew and Ziggy has a thing for a member of Poison Clan. Poison Clan opened for 2 Live and call themselves "Baby 2 Live Crew."

"Like, I know JT has been in jail a lot but I love him. I know he doesn't like me but I can't help it. He is so deep. And cute. He asked me if I thought that cities and buildings that you didn't go into actually exist."

"The guys are funny," Ziggy says. "They are all just out to get laid, naturally. Well we don't play that stuff because we ain't hos. But they want pussy. All of them. They think all bitches are hos but not us. We told them that we demand respect. So I told one of them that we weren't like that. But I made the mistake of fucking J.T. right off the bat while everybody else was in the room and then "Dep" got offended because I didn't wanna fuck him and everyone else 'cause I'm really not like that. I have to love someone to fuck them. They are still really pissed off. And JT is even pissed because I won't fuck all the guys. Maybe I should have."

"They agree that blonde pussy is something they all seem to want," says Star.

"Any pussy," Ziggy says with a giggle.

"They all use exactly the same lines. It's like some sort of training school for pickup artists," adds Star. "They say, well we are all adults. Right? And if you say yes then they say and we can do adult things. Right? And then we say go ahead but count us out. And they get all pissed but don't push very hard to change your mind. Like they could care."

"But they give you no respect. They expect every girl out here to fuck 'em and they can't deal with a woman on any other level. You want a relationship? Forget it! These guys don't look for lasting relationships. Just sex. They're children in adult bodies. All of them. Almost," says Ziggy.

"Of course intellectual relationships are out. These guys generally don't waste much time thinking deep about love stuff."

"Except," Star says wistfully, "Marquis."

"Marquis is the same," says Ziggy. "Exactly. He just wants to fuck you!"

"Well, so I fucked him. I did. Maybe I shouldn't have. But he talks to me sometimes. He's sweet. The others don't talk and they aren't sweet. It's almost like he cares," she says softly. "I think he might like me but he doesn't want to admit it."

"He only likes himself," Ziggy says.

"They all only like themselves," Star adds.

"We've never met Luke. I don't guess we will. He ignores us. I don't think he likes white girls."

Marquis is in the Luke Records Entertainment Center months later posing for a photographer. When he is reminded of the girls that followed them across the country he smiles and says, "Yeah, that was some shit. That little gal was a'right. I wonder what happened to her?"

Los Angeles
Universal City Hilton
The Day After the Big Studio Fire

There is a concert at Club Vertigo in L.A. Vertigo is one of those snotty "only the hip survive" clubs where the doormen have a burr up their asses and have let their little bit of power go completely to their bone-heads. The venue is basically a raw concrete echo chamber with a stage and colored lights that spin. There is the obligatory private room where celebrities are fawned over.

The show is a sellout and the crowd is white and hip and young. Luke does a press conference with the same used-up questions, dusted off and tossed at him in a new wrapper. Nobody seems to understand that Luke's music is about people who really exist. They can't get it through their white heads that a "stank ho" does not require any respect because she has none for herself, that there are women who will stick their tongues so far up your ass that they can feel your heartbeat or drink piss because they want to, or that the music is simply funny to

Luther and that is enough. Luther is a comedian but that seems lost on the crowd of journalists. It is all he can do not to yawn into the floodlights. To them he is an animal singlehandedly attempting to destroy womanhood.

The concert is a boomer. The crowd is with the group and it seems that everybody in the crowd knows the lyrics. Several girls climb up on the stage to dance with the group and the participation is excellent. A-plus. In fact several of the girls end up shaking their breasts at the crowd. The management freaks and does their best to clear the stage of these women. One of the girls brings down the house when she shoots the bouncing moon at the balcony.

A couple of the girls, it turns out, are professional strippers who want to break into films. They have shown their bodies in the hope of being discovered by someone in the audience. One, a blonde who will find her way to Luther's room, gives several of the Vertigo doormen blow jobs to get inside the club. She is a model and has posed in *Hustler*, she tells the group. "I've done some films," she adds. "Shorts."

"So, would those short films be the five minute loops in stag shops?" Luther asks her.

"Could be," she giggles. But she is looking for a shot at a feature.

She is a blonde and she has a beautiful body. Her breasts are barely confined at all. She is wearing a spandex miniskirt and when she changes position on the couch it is obvious that she has left her panties at home. There between the long muscular legs is a wide patch of blonde pubic hair.

When she disappears into the bedroom with a band member the room grows quiet. Another girl, who has followed the group back, is a tall thin beauty who wants to be an actress or a dancer but in the meantime, she tells the men, she hangs with the Crips. "The Crips treat me with respect," she says meekly.

"Aw honey, ain't no future in hanging with a screet gang." The bodyguard tends to change t's to c's sometimes. He also calls strippers scrippers.

"So baby," says the bodyguard. "Why you hang with the Crips? They ain't no future in that."

"Yeah, I can see the future you have in mind," she says to him.

When the blonde comes back into the room she offers blow jobs all around, and having no takers she makes conversation with the girl on the couch. The bodyguard, being too loaded to resist, begins turning everything that is said into a crude sexual barb.

"Girl, I want to go back to dancing naked," she says.

"I'd like to see you dancing on yo back naked. Wif me on top," he counters.

"You got big muscles," she says after a few of these barbs. "I had me a muscle man once. He had a little-bitty dick!" she says, laughing.

The other girl agrees eagerly. "Yeah, big muscle, tiny dick! That's true!"

"You sayin' my dick is little?" he says, bristling. Everyone in the room laughs loudly. The bodyguard has been attacked where he lives. "Aw baby. I can't believe you said that," he says.

He responds by trying to get her in bed for a personal inspection of his member. He ends up all but pulling her into the bedroom. A few minutes later she comes back and admits that she had been hasty in saying that her experience with muscle men was that they had small penises.

"He has a giant dick!" she says loudly, winking at the blonde.

He smiles, his self-esteem restored.

The next morning, when asked how long the girls stayed, the bodyguard says, "We threw them out when we were ready to go to sleep. No ho is gonna sleep in our room."

One has only to remember what happened to Leon Spinks to understand what they are saying. Everyone knows that Leon had his wallet, clothes, mink coat, and even his false teeth stolen by a ho one night some years ago. Hos can't be trusted with all the money and gold jewelry that the guys travel with.

Luther and the gang spend the morning at a radio station owned by Stevie Wonder doing an interview. When they return, the blonde, still wearing the same spandex outfit, is getting into a Jeep with a tall man. She smiles at Luther but doesn't wave. It would be disrespectful for her to make a big deal out of the fact that she knows him. Especially since he tossed her out into the hallway along with the skinny Crips chick at four o'clock in the morning. She's been around long enough to know the deal and that it was nothing personal.

Los Angeles
On the Rebound

These two girls don't plan to put out for anyone. It isn't really an issue. They are glamorous bimbos, not merely bedrollers tonight. They are pretty and they are wearing imitation designer gowns and they like riding around in the long white limo and drinking free and walking into exclusive clubs where people standing in line for hours are upset when Luther's small party is led up through the kitchen and into the club. There are celebrities here. People you have seen before on television and in the movies. They smile too broadly, look a little too relaxed, and laugh with their arms extended. "The people here in L.A. are sooo superficial," the one woman says to the other.

Later the crew decides to go to Vertigo, the scene of the performance the night before. Luther and the girls are shown to a holding area until room can be made for them inside. The bodyguard, an extremely large man who is very drunk, decides that the time for waiting is past. There is a scene with the Oriental doorman. "Where is the manager. Can you get somebody who can get us in?" the bodyguard demands. "This is Luther Campbell!"

"He'll be coming in a few minutes."

"I bet if I threw you through that fucking wall he'd come in less than a minute," the bodyguard says, putting his swaying bulk inches from the small Oriental. Standing a few feet away, Luther chews at his cigar and watches the bodyguard in action.

Within seconds, from nowhere several bulky bouncers have appeared and the Campbell party is being shown the door. Luther tries to salvage the evening at another club but his bodyguard has forgotten his ID so they are turned away at the door. Besides, the mood is broken. "Time to go home!" Luther announces. "Sometimes things happen for a reason." L.A. closes down at two a.m. anyway and it is one-thirty. "What's wrong with these fucking people?" says the bodyguard. "L.A. should be a twenty-four hour town like Miami."

Somewhere High Over America
A Day Later

Luther is traveling on a red eye back to Miami. He sits in first class reading a movie script. People are relaxing and the cabin is dark. A stewardess comes along and strikes up a conversation with a man a few seats up from where Luther is reading. She is a beautiful woman with dark hair and almond eyes. She laughs in a superficial manner at the fat man's jokes and cuts her eyes at Luther while she talks. He doesn't respond in any obvious manner, but his eyes are talking to her. When she passes toward the rear of the cabin he sits for a few seconds reading. Then he stretches, yawns, and heads for the back of the cabin. He is gone for ten to twenty minutes.

Strawberrys Too
Some Nights Later

At Strawberrys Too, Luther is in the small private office with a beautiful college girl for several long minutes. His bodyguard stands in front of the door with his arms crossed and his face a mask of cold stone.

Luther arrives at the club after midnight a few nights a week when he is in town. It's a club for anyone over eighteen with a few dollars and the desire to join the scene. Luther's clubs are dens of concentrated activity. Usually eight to ten bartenders are making drinks as fast as they can from ten until five a.m. seven nights a week. Being searched for weapons and drugs is mandatory and it slows entrance to a crawl. Most nights there is a long line that stretches down the street.

There have been fights in the club and even a murder. Luther has a roving security team that moves like lightning to a trouble spot and shoves anyone involved (on either side of an altercation) out the front doors with a speed that would impress the secret service.

Later, two men who have a lot of money and are wearing some very expensive silks start a champagne war using bottles of Dom at two hundred and fifty dollars a pop. They run through ten bottles, stopping only long enough to peel bills from the thick wads that they carry in their pockets. "I'm no drug dealer!" he says over and over again. When he pulls up one night at the club in a very expensive automobile he says, "It's borrowed! I can't afford shit like this!"

The Club

He is a drug boy. He hangs out at the club and spends money like a drunken sailor. He spends a thousand dollars or better every night he's in, a waitress confirms. "He's in a lot. Sometimes he gets out of hand. The other night he was in the dancer's dressing room after the place had closed. Brannard and I opened the door and here's this guy butt-assed naked on the floor with two lesbians. The girls were sucking at each other's wet whoppie spots and this guy is naked from the waist down drinking champagne from the bottle. Maybe his socks were still on. Then he starts eating them and they're sucking and nibbling at his dick and it ends up with him fucking one of them. Luke and Brannard are standing there laughing their asses off. This guy has done this shit in his club but he is so out of it that he doesn't even know they are standing there laughing at him. The girls don't care one way or the other 'cause they are gone over the hill as well. Luke was pissed after he thought about it but hell, the club was locked up tight. It was seven o'clock in the morning. They didn't even know the guy was still there."

New Orleans

Rossi, Luke's friendly golf pro pal, enters the hotel room drunk. Luke is auditioning strippers. There are three of them and Luke gets the strippers to hold Rossi down and sit on his face.

"It wasn't too bad!" Rossi says later.

Luke Records

Chackler is behind the desk telling Luther stories. He calls the PA system the "Luke Box" and he is saying that somebody should publish a book containing Luke's public messages. "Once Luke comes on and says, 'Y'all, watch your fuckin' language, we have guests in the building.' Another time he said, 'There is a tornado headed toward Liberty City. It's true 'cause some white people said it on the TV.' "

"Ask Luke to tell you about the hookers who used to come up here and do blow jobs all around," he says. "Oh, better still. Get Luke to tell you about the trip to Europe."

"You tell me."

"Well, first we get to Munich and Luke takes one look at the place and says he wants to retire there. Then he goes to the hotel and shuts his door and sleeps for two days. We had to get the hotel people to open the door because we thought he might have died." Chackler's mind is running across the landscape of the trip.

"He loved Germany because he could say motherfucker or whatever and they didn't beep it out. In fact they showed the lyrics translated into German while he talked. Same with radio. They translated as he spoke exactly what he said. They loved him. He said, 'So this is why black people move to Europe when they get fed up with the United States' bullshit.'

"When we went to Amsterdam we ended up in the Yum Yum, or whatever, which is the nicest bordello in Amsterdam. There is a disco in there and chrome, mirrors and glass and leather furniture. Luke pulled out his American Express and bought all the guys all the pussy they could handle. He had a great time that night. I think I saw him with half a dozen women over the course of a few hours. The man's stamina is amazing. The next day after fucking his brains loose he was up and rearing to go. They loved him in Europe. Especially the women. I bet they're still talking about that night. Luke was definitely in his element.''

Luke's Miami Beach

She is sour-faced, slightly drunk, leaning against the grill of a small Japanese car. She is holding a plastic cup of whiskey. ''Those Campbell men are real freaks,'' the lady says. ''They go out and get their little blow jobs, and freak with they hookers and strippers and . . . they tricks around somewhat. But they're good, decent men. And they always come home to their women. What you gonna do?''

4 Ups and Downs

In 1986, Mark Ross, Chris Wongwon, David Hobbs and I did "Throw the D." That record was the birth of Skyywalker Records and the first product of the Miami 2 Live Crew. I pressed three thousand copies of that record in a twelve-inch single for the record stores, clubs and record DJs. That was all I could afford and I wasn't sure I could sell all those copies. I would load up my Honda Accord and deliver them to the record stores in South Florida, myself. I would introduce myself and play the record for them and I built up my distribution network one store at a time. It was a slow process. And we would haul stacks of records to UPS. I had a beeper and suddenly I was returning calls from Europe at pay phones. I carried a sack of quarters for those long long-distance calls. Those were good days; I thought, 'Oh man! This shit here is a great way to make money!' I sold two hundred thousand copies of "Throw the D." I figured that was a good enough test market. At six bucks a copy that looks an awful lot like my first million dollars. I was twenty-five years old and fresh out of cooking in a kitchen.

Then in 1987 we cut *2 Live Is What We Are* and we had "Throw the D" on that as a single. We sold a half-million copies of that album, making it certified gold. Some record stores refused to stock it. But we weren't depending on the chains at that point. We were selling these albums by word of mouth in the black community. That word spread through the normal, urban grapevine. At that point we were running this company out of our back pockets. We had no experience at all. Especially no experience with this kind of success. It was wild shit.

In 1988 we cut *Move Somethin'*, which is slang for getting pussy. That was when I decided to put a sticker on the records and to make clean versions for kids starting to listen to the music, as kids will do. That's the forbidden fruit thing. We had heard some complaints and I felt they were valid. I don't want my daughter at nine years old to hear this stuff. Kids need to grow up protected as much as possible. When people would say, Oh, my daughter heard this and that, I would say, and does she read *Hustler* magazine too? It is the parents' job to regulate what the kids see and hear. But nobody can watch kids all the time. And the parents would say, How do we know what the kids are listening to? So I said, Well I can put stickers on these albums and that will at least help in most cases. So I was the first person to sticker an adult album with the words "THIS ALBUM CONTAINS EXPLICIT LYRICS. PARENTAL GUIDANCE SUGGESTED." Other entertainers and the record companies were fighting the sticker issue and there were Senate hearings about it. But I said this here shit is for adults. So I stickered the album. And I put PG labels on the clean versions. An added benefit of the clean versions was that the cuts could be played on the radio and it opened a whole new market with the jitterbug set. The kids.

In the early days my music didn't stir anyone up because my audience was almost completely black and urbanized. They heard my music for what it is. Humor. My music came directly from conversations from the streets. Each song we write comes from something we did or something we heard someone say. Sometimes we take a real incident and pull it all out of shape. Our use of street language is what the flap really centered on.

Nobody removed from the streets can deal with those words. The main two things that a black man lies about (and is expected to lie about) is how much money he has and how much pussy he is getting. In a piss-poor world, sex makes all men equals.

"Me So Horny" came from one night when we were watching the film *Full Metal Jacket* in a hotel room on the road. We were so knocked out by what this Vietnamese chick, this prostitute said. This soldier asked her: "What can we get for ten dollars?" She went, "Everything! Ah, me so horny, me love you long time." She wouldn't fuck the black guys because she said their dicks were too big. So we sampled the tape 'cause it was hilarious. Just the few words. And Stanley Kubrick and the studio sued us for a billion dollars or some crazy-ass number. The ridiculous thing is that one movie freak out of one hundred thousand would have figured where those lyrics came from. In fact we told people in interviews and that's how Kubrick's people got onto it. We could have avoided the suit if we had had another chick redo the lines but we didn't have any idea that anyone would care or that that was illegal. We liked it the way we heard it—pure and from the action. Our talking about where we got those lyrics also made the movie rentals soar. But they had us by the balls and they had us by the white man's rules, which is the same thing, and we finally had to cut a deal to do a sound track for a film for them and give them the profits. It was more complicated than that but that's basically how it ended up.

I have never sued any rappers for sampling one of my songs. But if I ever catch Stanley Kubrick or George Lucas ripping off the lyrics to one of my songs, or anything I can claim, I'm going to twist their balls off and push them up their noses.

We released *As Nasty As They Wanna Be* in 1989. The advance orders were half a million which is un-fuckin' believable. We also issued the clean version which sold very well too.

When I started making money, the shit hit the fan, because if you are selling ten thousand units in ghettos, nobody cares. But when we crossed into big sales and high-profile shit we became targets. Rap music is created from cuts on records you find or buy. Now we pay royalties to every note we sample and there are formulas for figuring royalties. When we started there weren't and these people came after millions of dollars. It was scary because we didn't understand the system.

You learn the rules as you play the game. Nobody offered to teach me the music business. I learned it by fuckin' up. And all the big boys did everything they could to keep us on the bottom so we had to fight our way through for everything we got.

There's this lawsuit that we had. We were in a bus touring in California and the bus driver had a fuckin' breakdown. He was driving and yelling and screaming at cars and weaving in traffic. He had a gun and he was waving it around. When he stopped, we called the cops and they took him off, but we missed the concert and had to fly everybody to the next venue. We had twenty thousand dollars' worth of tee-shirts, Iron-Man jackets at over a grand a pop, all the tapes and records and CDs and a whole bunch of stuff that we sell. And we had to leave it with the bus.

And then, right, the bus company wanted us to pay them and I said you fuckin' gotta be shining my ass. And they wouldn't give us our shit back to sell so we were screwed. The company is in Alabama and they sued us in Alabama. Ain't that some shit! We are filing a countersuit because the thing was dismissed. The shit they took was Skyywalker Records stuff that we can't sell now, 'cause it is dead stock since the Lucas suit. Plus I think they sold it anyway.

Luke Skyywalker was my nickname from the DJ days. Since my name was Luther, my family and friends called me Luke. Since I had the touch with the people they said I had the force or whatever. So Luke Skyywalker fit. I spelled it differently because I didn't want to rip the name off from *Star Wars*. I wanted to have the benefit of that name and I wanted it to be my version of it. Well, when my name started getting around, George Lucas heard about it and he thought it was cute or whatever. We wrote him asking if it was alright and his people said sure. See, we were just an obscure rap group and he was this big powerful guy and he said, what the fuck, it's just a bunch of black kids and they'll give us a plug and go away. So his attorney sent a legal document for us to sign saying that we were free to use Skyywalker in conjunction with our acts but couldn't merchandise the name by itself. We never signed it and sent it back because this attorney I had, who didn't know shit, had some problem with it and he said it's cool, Lucas said so, and we went along with that. I'm no fuckin' attorney.

Well, when *Nasty* drew fire from the right wing, the Lucas people freaked out. How can people be so chickenshit that they will run from a handful of extortionists? What is wrong is that the world has lost its balls. I don't let these crazy motherfuckers tell me what I can do. This is America! But Lucas, with all his millions and millions of dollars, folded. Oh no! his people yelled. They found out that we had not returned the agreement they had sent us and so they said we had to drop the use of the name. By then we had a million dollars' worth of product out there under the Skyywalker name and we said that if we called it all in, we'd be ruined. Think Lucas gave a shit if he ruined a bunch of black kids who he had allowed to function under his character's name? He sued us for some crazy sum like three hundred gazillion dollars or whatever. And the lame-ass motherfucker won only because we had never sent back that paper. That means, as far as I can see, his word ain't worth dog shit. And as far as I am concerned he's a fuckin' coward. He's all for children's imaginations, but when these fundamentalist bastards get their way, those minds are deprived of ideas and images these people don't like. He's a mighty powerful man. As far as I am concerned he's also a punk asshole. He almost ruined us and everything we had built. But we survived. We had to pay him several hundreds of thousands of dollars in cash and we are still destroying the old product as it comes back in. We have destroyed nearly a half-million dollars' worth of product that we had paid for. So George Lucas showed me his Dark Side. He had heard our music and knew what it was about, or should have because we sent him records. He just ran scared. Movie people say they can't afford to have those guys come after their films. Well, films should be created in an atmosphere of freedom of expression. He bent over to these moral faggots and buckled under and it was us who got the ass-fuckin'.

Luckily, *Nasty* was selling like crazy and the sheer volume saved us.

Most of the lawsuits we get served with are groundless and we win them. Like the Acuff/Rose suit over "Pretty Woman." They said, oh you have degraded this lofty song by Roy Orbison. Well, they let the movie people put their lofty song in a movie about a ho. But since it was a parody we won and they had said "you do not have permission to do a parody of 'Pretty Woman' " in a letter. Well, admitting it was a parody hung their asses. Parodies are protected by the Constitution. People are so damned greedy.

Sometimes suits are groundless and we lose them anyway. We were sued for not playing a concert in Houston when in fact the promoter's lack of funds was responsible for us not playing. No pay, no play. He won that suit and it cost us a fortune. Right now a cat in Beaumont is trying to sue saying that we didn't play a concert. I was on the stage saying, "I'm here to play. Pay me!" My tour manager, Mike Hopkins, was standing with these guys in the press booth looking down at me standing there. But they didn't have the money so we left and there was trouble. Now they claim we didn't show up. When we walked out of that hall, our tee-shirt stand got looted. Too Short opened for us and as far as I know he didn't get his money either. But these concert promoters pull that shit one time and they have a hard problem getting any acts to play for them in the future. It's a small world, especially in rap. M. C. Hammer slept on my couch and opened for us. I hired the Fat Boys when they started and Run DMC. As a promoter I hired them, or worked with them and still see them at conventions and concerts and shit. So the promoters are just fuckin' themselves.

The law is funny in that justice is as likely not to be served as it is for it to be served. See, if my attorney is incompetent, I may lose, and even though I am innocent, I can be found guilty. If you think all attorneys are competent because they passed the bar, you're wrong. If you think they are good because they have good clients, you are wrong. And if they say they are entertainment attorneys because they have done some entertainment deals, they may still be incompetent as entertainment attorneys. Sometimes, entertainers trust the wrong people. Sometimes lawyers are merely crooks in fancy clothes who are trying to suck clients clean.

In my life, it has gotten to the point where I have had to hire an in-house attorney, Joe Weinberger, just to deal with the attorneys handling my business to make sure they are doing a good job and not just stacking bills for work they aren't doing. Don't get me wrong, I have had the benefit of some talented attorneys. And certainly not all of them have taken advantage of me. But enough have so that I don't feel free to trust any of them any further than I can see them.

There are at least four sets of laws in America. One for the wealthy and another for the poor. One for the whites and one for the blacks and other minorities. As a wealthy black man, I am governed by a whole different set of laws and rules. Most laws are designed to benefit some few at the cost of many. Just laws are designed to benefit all. Unjust laws to benefit a few. What the government says a law means is usually far from what it ends up meaning in practice.

I am lucky enough to be able to afford good attorneys. Also I am high enough profile that when something happens and I am arrested or sued, a lot of people take a close look through the media. But when poor blacks are arrested they are treated like shit.

One of my rap acts was driving a Jeep Cherokee that belonged to his buddy. His buddy was in the car. The police began following the vehicle and all they saw was two black kids in a new Jeep. So when it pulled into my parking lot, about six cop cars pulled in behind them. All of the cops had their guns out. They forced the two kids to lie on the hot asphalt with their hands behind their heads. The cops had their guns out pointed at their heads. Then they threw the kids into the back of two of the cop cars. They thought the Jeep had to be hot, but it wasn't. So they hauled the driver off saying that his license was suspended. It wasn't, and they'll drop the charges, but it graphically illustrates the way blacks are approached by the police. They took him to jail because they had to, since they had made a scene in front of a couple of dozen witnesses. Some of the witnesses, including my attorney, were white. The cops would not give Weinberger any information at all. So why do blacks distrust the police?

The cops are a double-edged sword. I opened a club called Strawberrys Too in 1989 in this Hialeah shopping center. It had operated as a Latin club called Strawberrys for years. We attracted blacks from all over Miami and the Cubans couldn't deal with it. It's no secret that the Cubans don't particularly enjoy the company of American blacks.

When I first leased the club, the Cuban who had owned and run the club for those years agreed to stay for a period. The shakedown cruise, you might call it. About two days after we added a "Too" on the sign outside the building—and that was the only change—a whole gang of these city-code health and fire guys came in and spread out like fire ants. They were everywhere. All at once. The Latin guy came in and said, "What's going on?" The officials said, "Oh! Are you still runnin' this place?" He said he was still there and they said, no problem! Then they all left. Everything was back-slapping cool. The very day the Latin guy left all hell broke loose. Suddenly there were more violations to be fixed than a leopard has spots. And then the occupational license that the club had always run under was wrong. It was a restaurant license, the same one this club had operated under for years with not a squeak from the Hialeah inspectors. They tried to pull the liquor license. They tried to pull the operating licenses. My attorneys went to court and council meetings and everything to clear it. So this attorney who was in with these city officials suggested that if we wanted smooth sailing we should consider "pleasing the powers that be." So I asked what would it take to please them? Easy, a payment. Not too much. A token of respect is all. And I said, Fuck 'em. This is America!

It ain't America. Hialeah ain't near America. Well they wouldn't let me hire off-duty cops like the Latin clubs were allowed to do. "Oh no. Our policemen can't work bars!" they said, while the off-duty Hialeah cops were at every restaurant and bar that could afford them. In fact they wouldn't let us hire off-duty cops from anywhere else, either.

Now they knew just as well as we did that without cops there is gonna be trouble. We had this gigantic parking lot and we couldn't patrol it. We checked everybody at the door for weapons and drugs and alcoholic beverages but the parking lot was the Wild West. The cops said, Well, give us X dollars and we'll put up a sign saying that the lot is patrolled. We did and the sign went up but they wouldn't come unless they got a call. If they came at all.

They were called one hundred and twenty-eight times in one year. And we called them almost every single time. They wanted violence to happen there. It was nuts. There were drive-by incidents. One night we called them and they said, "Fuck you." I'm not kidding about this. So we called 911 and they said, we're not dispatching a car. So we called 911 in Miami and asked if they would send a car. They said that was in Hialeah's jurisdiction. We said, they won't come. The lady said, "I never heard such a thing!" We said it was a fact so she called them up. The whole thing is on tape. They told her that no cops would respond to that location and she said, "Are you crazy?" And they hung up on her.

The fact is that the club was closed by the police after it was destroyed by the same fuckin' police.

I say that historically corrupt city officials set out to close Strawberrys and they did. After Raul Martinez, the mayor of Hialeah, was convicted in Federal Court of extortion and other shit, the people still wanted a kickback. If we had paid them their "pleasing amount of money" they'd be giving me plaques telling the world what a great friend of Hialeah I am. I have Cuban friends and I am not prejudiced against Cubans who are friendly to me. I opened in Hialeah and I always welcomed Latin customers. I have no anger toward the Latin community. But a vast number of their elected officials are scumbags.

I closed the club for good after my off-duty bodyguard pistol-whipped this guy in the flower bed after he was hit in the head by the guy's mobile telephone. The pistol went off when he was slapping the man with the shit. The shot missed the man's head and ended up in the dirt beside his ear. But the shot caused a chain reaction. Some young drug boys standing against the wall think somebody is shootin' at them so they draw their nines and start blasting. Another group standing beside their cars return the fire with Uzis, nines and a twelve-gauge pump. The crowd, caught outside, broke through the fuckin' plate glass window to get inside and off the sidewalk. In the shit this young kid is hit by a wild bullet and falls dead just inside the club. He was a good kid and was an innocent bystander who had just come by to talk to this cat.

I was at home asleep when that shit happened. The cops picked up hundreds of empty shells but the cat that shot that kid has still never been caught. I could have stayed open and sued the city but I was tired of the constant shit, and to remain open without the police protection I needed was crazy.

Any people that were hurt and even died in the parking lot there were killed by the Hialeah police department as surely as if they had shot them personally. I could have made a big deal over it but it wasn't worth losing one human life. In the end I just said fuck Hialeah and fuck their corrupt politicians and government officials.

So now I am paying rent on an empty space that isn't generating thousands and thousands of tax dollars like it was. Two off-duty cops in that lot, which I wanted to pay for, and there would not have been any trouble. I know it and they know it. I offered to pay for six officers every night we were open.

I opened an adult club before Strawberrys Too—Miami's in Pensacola. My brother Harry lived in Pensacola and I wanted to take advantage of a booming economy and a lack of good black dance clubs. There is a bunch of military bases up there. I finally closed Miami's because running a club that far away is taxing and because the economy went to shit there. In fact the only police trouble I had in Pensacola was when I was arrested there one night because a cop I had hired was letting some people fuck up my Jeep. I said stop 'em and he wouldn't so I sneaked the bitch's gun out of his holster and started firing it over their heads. The charges were dismissed. That cop was running around inside the club trying to find his nine and I had it. Well fuck, if he was too chickenshit to do what I hired him to do, I figured I'd do it. His superiors made him press the charges. He was embarrassed by losing his shit.

Luke's Miami Beach is a great club. I hope to put up a chain
of Luke's clubs in other cities. Luke's tries to incorporate the
best features of clubs from New York through Atlanta and L.A.
without any of the shit I hate. There is a doorman, but as long
as you are dressed decently you can get in. Celebrities and
members are admitted ahead of people off the street, but once
inside everyone mixes on the dance floor. I have a private
balcony overlooking the dance floor and two private champagne
rooms. I spent hundreds of thousands of dollars on the sound
and lights and the DJ booth is state-of-the-art. Sometimes,
usually Sunday nights, I DJ myself to test new music.

On any given night you might see Robert DeNiro or some
other actors who are in town, along with directors, producers
and other Hollywood types, entertainers and athletes from
everywhere. I'm at the club four or five nights a week from
midnight to dawn. It's a great place to hang out. It's what I like
about clubs. The crowd is a blend of ethnic groups whether
they're whites, Cubans, blacks or whatever. I like bringing
people of all races together and they all spend money. When I
say Peace, I mean it. It's easier to make money when people are
smiling.

Outside there are cops in the lot. There has not been one
incident in the months the club has been open on South Miami
Beach. For the first month, the new police chief, Huber, would
not let me hire off-duty policemen because of Strawberry Too's
reputation. After the chief watched Luke's for a month, he let
them come on but the Miami Beach police still take every
opportunity to follow me around and pull my black ass over.
The parking lot is strictly under control. The element that makes
trouble can find other places to start its shit where there are no
policemen with radios and their own guns.

Recently I let some people use the Luke Records complex
Entertainment Center for teen dances. In July there was this
drive-by shooting down the street from the complex and a
fourteen-year-old boy was killed. So I can't open that up for the
kids. It's crazy today. Kids are beyond help. I am going to
concentrate on the little kids at the street level. By the time kids
are fourteen or so they are set in their ways and have no idea

what human life is worth. That's a crime. Who do you blame? That's easy, their parents.

Due to pressure from the kids who have no other place to go on weekends, I decided that the teen center can be opened again in the Entertainment Center. I told the kids that if there is one more incident I will close the bitch up, forever.

5 Five Sing-Along Favorites

"THROW THE D"

Listen up y'all, 'cause this is it
forget the old dance and throw the D
let's dance.

It's a brand-new dance and it's coming your way
it was started in Miami by the Ghetto DJs
say some call it nasty but that's not true
it's the only dance that you can do
'cause you need a sexy body, make your partner come alive
if you can't do that, don't even try
so get yourself together and learn it quick
just get on the floor and throw the D.

When I went to Miami, I couldn't believe my eyes
this female was throwin', wanted me to try
if you don't know how to do it
here's what you must do
just listen up close, I'll explain it to you

just jump in the air
and when you land you whine like you just don't care
it's all in the hips so go berserk
and let that (pause) do the work
so while it's workin', you just start strokin'
to show your partner that you ain't jokin'
'cause this ain't a dance from Mother Goose
better freak your body and turn it loose
when you're on the floor you don't give a shhhheee
all you wanna do is throw the D.

DICK ALMIGHTY

Dick Almighty's of no surprise
it'll fuck all the bitches all shapes and size
she'll climb a mountain even run the block
just to kiss the head of this big black cock
it'll tear the pussy open 'cause it's satisfaction
the bitch won't leave, it's fatal attraction
dick so powerful she'll kneel and pray
awaitin' her time, hoping soon to slay.

That dick will make a bitch cry
when fuckin' a bitch that's tight inside
that dick has got a spell on you
once it gets inside you will act a fool
that dick will make a bitch act cute
suck my dick, bitch, it make you puke
jump up on it, grab it like you want it
if you could wear a dick, bitch, you would flaunt it.

Bitches are the one thinkin' dicks gets sore
they fuck one time and then got off
thinking it's slick just to ride the dick
till make 'em think they come and then he'll quit
but not the long one, I won't play that shit
put her ass in the buck and kill the clit
it's fifteen inches long, eight inches thick
last name Almighty, first name is Dick.

That dick is a motherfucker
I can't be pussy whipped by a dick sucker
that dick would drive a bitch crazy
bitches want to fuck when you're tired and lazy
that dick sometimes costs you money
don't be blamed for a child that's not yours, dummy
that dick is a greedy bitch's dinner
I let a bitch feed before I go up in her.

That Dick Almighty!

Bitches go crazy at a all night fuck
startin' from the back and then in the buck
since a good dick is hard to find
I kill that pussy then fuck your mind
bitches like the dick, just claim defeat

forget the salads, just eat my meat
they save big dollars 'cause it comes free
to spend time with the Dick, the Almighty.

That dick will make you cheat on your man
make you so freaky and hot in the ass
that dick will make you hurt yourself
when you don't have dick you're free to fuck yourself
that dick is an awful thing
but you bull-dyker bitches are fuckin' up the game
rubbin' belly to belly and skin to skin
fuckin' like hell but ain't no dick goin' in.

That Dick Almighty!

"HEY WE WANT SOME PUSSY"

Chorus:
Somebody say, hey we want some pussy
hey we want some pussy
let me hear you say, hey we want some pussy
hey we want some pussy!
somebody say, hey we want some pussy
hey we want some pussy
everybody say, hey we want some pussy

hey we want some pussy.

You see me and my homeys like to play this game
we call it Amtrak but some call it the train
we all would line up in a single file line
and take our turns at waxing girls' behinds
but every time it came to me I was shit out of luck
because I would stick my dick in and it would get stuck
the girls would say stop, I say I'm not
that's enough, I quit, because y'all are bustin' me out
I say girls don't hide it
jes divide it and please
don't knock it, until you've tried it
so to all you bitches and all you hos
lets have group sex and do the Rambo.

(*Chorus*)

I'm the Peter Piper of the nineteen eighties
got a long hard dick for all of the ladies
I don't care if you got three babies
you can work the stick in my Mercedes
if you want to blow jus' let me know
we can go backstage at the end of the show
I'll look at you and you will look at me
with my dick in my hands as you fall to your knees
you know what to do 'cause I won't say please
just nibble on my dick like a rat do cheese.

(*Chorus*)

"DROP THE BOMB"

Now, before we get this motherfuckin' thing started we are 2
motherfuckin' Live—in your ass—and my man, Mr. Mixx, is
fixin' to tell you what we came out here to do.

All the people on the left let's participate
and everybody on the right we won't make you wait
and all the people in between just shout and scream
and have a funky good time if you know what I mean
because when we rhyme we move people by the masses

when they say they'll pay we'll play when they ask us.

They say they don't know of us but that is a lie
so they try and play the game so dis and die
and don't you try and take my hand or be my friend
just like a hook made out of rubber I will not bend.

To all you silly suckers who try and abuse us
when we get ignited you can't diffuse us
it'll be on radio and even TV
that we achieved a level you want to be
now step off the pedestal and give us the mike
so we can rock the people the way you would like
just do us a favor, don't be a jerk
'cause all we want to see is your body work.

There's lesson to be taught
that's the one you should learn
you can't buy respect, it's what you earn
'cause when you dis 2 Live
you get yours in the end
it's not a threat, it's a promise, my friend.

So suckers step aside and let the women do their thing
come on y'all and shake that thing.

MOVE SOMETHIN'

I been wanting to tell you this for a while
I like your fake blue eyes and your hoey style
so let's go for a walk through the park
and you can suck my dick in the dark
and do what I ask, bitch, bend over
let me ride your backside like dogs do each other
I know that you're with it so don't start frettin'
I don't want to be your man, I wanta move somethin'.

Listen up, baby, you look real pretty
let me pull up your shirt and suck your titty
yes, pretty lady, I love you so
since the time we met my dick has grown
you've had other men now it's my chance

give me some time to take off my pants
the time has come, don't be frettin'
jus' drop them drawers and move somethin'.

Let's rent a room at a fuck motel
and play this game called ring the sleigh bells
put the do not disturb sign on the door
and ride this dick till it gets sore
then open your legs, put 'em in the buck
'cause that's the way I like to fuck
it's really simple, it's not really nothin'
all you have to do is move somethin'.

Look, baby doll, don't lie or fret
you know what I need and I know what you want
let's go to the beach, we'll lay in the sand
and I'll prove to you that I'm a real man
the way that it felt it was real tight
it chilled my body and the feelin' was right
it's all for love that you have been wantin'
just roll those hips and let's move somethin'.

6 The Jackals Move In for the Kill

The train that I was riding gathered speed with a momentum that was hard to fathom. My "dirty" records sold in numbers that shocked everyone, except me. Each weekly sales report just made my belief stronger that we could do better. If I got gold sales, I wanted platinum sales and when we got that I wanted double platinum sales. But in 1987, '88, '89 and early '90, the money was coming in so fast that I couldn't invest it fast enough. Everything I touched turned to gold. I bought a jet, a large building which I had renovated for the company headquarters, a forty-eight-track recording studio, a house for me, a house for my parents and a new car for my mother. All the financing came straight out of the cash flow. I paid child support. I staffed my company with seasoned professionals and signed promising groups to my label. It is a-one-in-a-million shot to escape the ghetto and make a place in the world of comfort. But I had done it. For the first time in my life the tracks were unobstructed and I had a clear field of vision from the depths of Liberty City to the farthest corners of the world. But at what seemed to be the brightest moment in my life up to that point, something was closing in on me that I did not see coming, something I had no idea even existed.

I had always liked to see the money come in. And I found plenty of enemies between me and the green. But it wasn't any of the people from the neighborhood that would come close to derailing me. The worst problems in my life came from a bunch of strangers. The Moral Majority. They discovered something about Luke Skyywalker that really pissed them off. These people were about to drop a barricade across the tracks and move heaven and earth in an effort to stop this new money train.

The Alabama Case
The Cracker Trial

Alexander City, Alabama, with its population hovering around fifteen thousand souls, is a sleepy little backwater town in the shadow of Mount Talladega on Highway 280, forty-five miles north of Auburn. The chief of police, Ben Royal, is a religious man and he does not hold with the sale of pornography in his hamlet. When he received a complaint from a parent (undoubtedly a parent on some fundamentalist mailing list) that 2 Live Crew's vulgar rap music was in local record stores, he sent a young policeman to one of them called "Take Home the Hits," located less than a city block down main street from the courthouse. Tommy Hammond, the fortyish co-owner, was behind the counter when the policeman entered and began browsing about in the tiny store. It is so small, twenty by thirty feet, that Tommy and his partner, Joe Campbell, chose to keep the rap tapes behind the counter, out of sight. Tommy knew the policeman, and when the man asked if they carried 2 Live Crew, Tommy sold him a copy of *Move Somethin'*. Tommy immediately went back to his business until some time later when the policeman who had purchased the tape returned with a detective and a uniformed officer. The detective showed Tommy a search warrant and told him that he had sold "pornography." Tommy told him that the tape was sold to adults only, even though by law he could sell the product to anyone he wanted.

The detective told him that in Alabama no one could buy it, and seized every 2 Live tape, every other rap tape with a parental advisory, and any tape he simply didn't like the name of. He told Tommy that he should come the half-block to the courthouse and be arrested. The detective issued a stern warning to Tommy that if they had to, they would come get him, shackle him, and drag him down there.

When the churchgoing Chief Royal listened to the cut "S&M," he couldn't believe his ears. This is what he heard:

Female Voice:
Listen all you motherfuckers, calling all freaks, bull daggers, pussy riders, shit eaters, dick beaters, fags, sissies, asshole fuckers . . . or just plain fuckers . . .

Marquis' Voice:
I'm a part of this just like you
I'm a disciple of Satan with work to do
I'll ride you till your death
and squeeze blood from your breasts
and work you like a sex slave, you get no rest
I can see it in your eyes the Devil's deep inside
you're a masochistic freak in disguise
your love is your pain and pain is your game
you'll force the fit just to feel the strain
you worship the bed with your light
holding sessions of confession every moonlit night
you do it so good tasting every ounce
until the last drop, leaving nothing out.

chorus:
S&M—bring yo dick suckin' friends
S&M—let the beatings begin
S&M—bring yo mamma and her friend
S&M—bring all yo horny friends.

I wore my lover in the summer to all the shows
with my whip around my neck I controlled the hos
my sexual fantasies must be fulfilled

or my tensions will increase and then I will
so I pulled a little girlie, this is what I did
jumped into the ride, took her to the crib
rushed her in the room, sat her in the bed
grabbed her by the ears, as she gave me head
then turned her over, got it from the back
the pussy was sorry, so the bitch got slapped
then I took my dick out, laid it on her chest
she put it in the middle and she squeezed her breasts
as I got some feeling this is what I said
baby, baby, baby, just a little more head.

chorus:
Listen here—bring yo dick suckin' friends
S&M—let the beatings begin
S&M—bring yo mamma and her friend
S&M—bring all yo horny friends
S&M—let the orgy begin!

An ashen-faced Chief Ben Royal turned off the cassette player
and dropped the tape into an evidence envelope. I imagine had
the chief been free to do as he pleased, he would have set the
store on fire and shot Tommy and Joe as they ran into the street.
Royal was aware that the same tapes were available in the local
black record stores, but the owner of one of those stores, who
dared the chief to tell his "black ass" what he could sell, was
never spoken to by him. It appears that as long as the "jungle"
music stayed where it belonged, the chief was not interested in
the least. Tommy and Joe and the majority of their clients just
happened to be white as snow owls.

Tommy Hammond was convicted in city court in a hearing
that lasted but a few minutes. Hammond's female attorney met
with the judge in chambers, before the trial. According to
Tommy, she told him well before the trial started that the judge
was going to find him guilty. She also told Tommy that the judge
had said that Tommy should appeal it at once, that a trial of this
magnitude could be drawn out for over a year. "The lady wanted
to make money, pure and simple." She told Tommy not to speak
to the press but to route all calls to her. When Tommy, who

would have been happy as a hound dog to talk to members of the media, got the bill his attorney was sending to me (I had agreed to pay the attorney's fees) there were numerous calls listed to and from the world media billed at fifty dollars an hour.

Tommy Hammond said, "The only difference between most attorneys and contagious lepers is that the skin of attorneys is too slimy to fall off."

The conviction was appealed and a date set for a jury trial in circuit court. Tommy's new defense attorney, Elizabeth Johnson, an ACLU lawyer and now a member of the Southern Poverty Law Center based in Montgomery, Alabama, brought in witnesses to explain, to the twelve Alabamians tried and true, the cultural and historical basis for the dirty music. After the defense witnesses, including music critic John Leland and black cultural expert Carlton Long, testified, the jury acquitted the store clerk. A free Tommy Hammond roared off to the "Donahue" show and all that glittery sort of mess that made him a local hero in Alexander City. Overnight the store became so successful that the partners had to move to a larger space. Now the 2 Live Crew tapes and CDs are right out in plain view and they sell very well, thanks to the publicity. "People drive in from all over the state to buy those 'pornographic' records, tapes and CDs. Chief Royal doesn't even turn his head when he passes. Just think, every time a white child listens to that music it is probably because Chief Royal told them where to get it," said an amused Tommy Hammond to the television camera.

This Alexander City trial was just the start. The major confrontation was brewing in South Florida. Fundamentalist groups had been angered by the defeat in rural Alabama (part of their home territory). So they marshaled their forces and they watched and waited, and when they struck, it was with their most god-awful weapon. The weapon often referred to as the "superiority" weapon or the "Dumb Bomb," equipped with the self-destructing Jack Thompson warhead.

"Morality policmen" demand the right to direct what the rest of us should be allowed to see and hear. They are generally people with tiny, frightened minds who look out at the world through a combination of religious fervor, self-delusion, hypocrisy, suspicion, paranoia and sheer ignorance. Unable to moralize their own lives, they only have time to moralize ours. They feel spiritually superior and as such are only tolerant of their own weakness. This makes them dangerous, and it has always made them dangerous.

The group that brought the dirty 2 Live lyrics to the public's attention was a right-wing "Christian" fundamentalist organization called "Focus on the Family," run by psychologist James Dotson (no known relation to the famous Illinois rapist). Other similar institutions include Tipper Gore's Parents Resource Center and Reverend Donald Wildmon's American Family Association. Philosophically, they all stand within spitting range of the American Nazi Party.

Jesse Helms stands on the steps of Congress holding up stolen copies of Mapplethorpe photographs of big black dicks. Helms, like Jack Thompson, sees a massive homosexual conspiracy undermining America's staunch moral and ethical structure. But the ethical and moral structure they describe is a fantasy which has never existed except in Norman Rockwell's cornball paintings and the twisted imaginations of some elder fundamentalists.

Once they discovered the music of 2 Live Crew, the lyrics were immediately faxed to their South Florida commander, Jack Thompson, on New Year's Day, 1989. Jack Thompson, then just another faceless ex-golf-pro loser with a new law degree, would soon find his personal mission and become one of the very most famous of the Morality Policemen.

Jack sent faxes of 2 Live lyrics from *Move Somethin'* and later *As Nasty As They Wanna Be* to every sheriff's office, prosecutor, media outlet and police chief in Florida. A couple of the state's sixty-five sheriffs did make some noise and some even contacted record stores to tell them that the records were obviously adult material and to keep them from kids. One of the peace officers was the state's prosecuting attorney from Lee County, a well-known, press-hungry, anti-porn crusader. In Lee

County, the sheriff's deputies successfully petitioned a judge who found that there was indeed probable cause that the 2 Live recording was legally obscene under Florida statutes. This incident didn't get much response from the 2 Live Crew attorneys because Lee County is a hick area where there were no sales going on anyway. However, Jack struck gold with the Governor, Bob Martinez. The fax to Martinez elicited this response:

(letterhead)
State Of Florida
Office of the Governor
Bob Martinez

February 22, 1990

Mr. Peter Antonacci/ Statewide Prosecutor
2540 Executive Center Circle West
Douglas Building
Suite 100
Tallahassee, Florida 32301

Dear Mr. Antonacci,

I have recently become familiar with the content of a recording by the rap music group the 2 Live Crew. The group and its record company, Skyywalker Records, are based in Miami. Two weeks ago the album *As Nasty As They Wanna Be* was removed from store shelves in Lee County after sheriff's deputies successfully petitioned a judge to find probable cause to conclude the recording is obscene. Eleventh Circuit State Attorney Janet Reno has informed my office that law enforcement agencies are examining the recording and its sale to minors.

It is appalling to think that recordings that a judge has already determined may be obscene are readily available to minors throughout Florida. Even more horrifying are reports that some of these lyrics are routinely recited by children as young as seventh graders. It's bad enough to think that vulgar, disgusting lyrics would be circulated among adults, but to make them available to minors violates all conceivable standards of decency.

I do not believe that the state of Florida should go about seeking to censor the kind of legitimate public expression protected by the First Amendment. However it would appear the recording in question does not meet that standard. As a society, we have the obligation to ensure a healthy, nurturing environment for our youngsters to grow up and thrive in. Songs like those in question promote the worst in society, and they have no business being available to minors.

Section 847.012, Florida statutes, provides that anyone who knowingly distributes to a minor a sound recording containing matters which are obscene (as defined in section 847.001, Florida Statutes) is guilty of a third class felony. The statute empowers the State Attorney to petition a judge to adjoin further sale of those materials.

Under Section 1656, Florida Statutes, the Statewide Prosecutor has jurisdiction to prosecute any violation of Florida's RICO Act. Under that act, a violation of Section 847.012 is specifically listed as a crime chargeable by RICO. Further the record publisher, Skyywalker Records, could be considered an enterprise within the scope of RICO. Since the sale of recordings of the 2 Live Crew apparently has numbered in tens of thousands, the pattern of racketeering activity is arguably present.

Therefore I ask that your office conduct a full investigation into the possibility that Florida's RICO and obscenity laws have been violated by the widespread distribution of the recordings of the 2 Live Crew and other groups. In submitting this request, I have just two regrets: that this offensive material has already been so readily available to minors, and that I must further disseminate it in order to provide you with the enclosed supporting documentation.

Sincerely
Bob Martinez

Peter Antonacci responded to the governor's letter by saying basically that each county's state prosecuting attorney should proceed with this matter as he or she saw fit. Most of them dropped the correspondence in the garbage can. The end result was that each went on about prosecuting cases they knew they could win. Janet Reno, Dade County's chief prosecuting attorney, infuriated Jack by saying that she had real crimes to worry about.

Had Martinez understood people better, he would surely have ignored the "lyrics" letter. But as it turned out, he hadn't a clue as to how the majority of Florida's adults felt about the subject. He would have been well-served to have made a cursory inquiry into the reputation of Jack Thompson and how the voters felt about having government officials and religious fanatics deciding what information and entertainment forms they can be exposed to.

Jack Thompson, especially when he is on the other end of the telephone and one cannot see his eyes, can initially hold a fairly coherent conversation. But when he talks about me he begins unraveling. He will start ranting and giggling about me being the Antichrist and a pornographic racketeer and about how the government is going to sweep in and take everything I own thanks to the RICO statute.

Prior to setting his sights on 2 Live Crew, Jack Thompson already had a history with the media. He harassed Neil Rogers, a self-admitted homosexual and South Florida's highest rated on-air personality, by staking out Mr. Rogers's house and taking down license numbers of the cars in his driveway. Then Jack was caught trying to get the owners' names through the state motor vehicle registration office in Tallahassee. He put pressure on Mr. Rogers's sponsors and other station advertisers to drop their ads on WIOD, Mr. Rogers's station. Once when Mr. Rogers was announcing a Cubs baseball game from Chicago, Thompson called Chicago area hotels until he found the one where Neil had registered. Then, according to the newspaper story, he told hotel personnel that they had a pervert, a child molester, registered. Because of his sleazy methods and outrageous excesses, a judge ruled that Jack can neither mention Neil Rogers's name nor come within a thousand yards of him. He also cannot call, or cause others to call, the advertisers of Mr. Rogers's radio station. Rogers, who had retaliated by giving out Jack's telephone number over the air, agreed to lay off, even in self-defense. (This is why, on the Phil Donahue Show, I goaded Jack Thompson by saying, "Say Neil Rogers, Jack!")

Jack Thompson, having either been sacked (say some), or come to a parting of ways because of the ethics of his contemporaries in his law firm (says guess who?), announced that he would run for the position of Dade County state prosecutor against Janet Reno who then held the job. Reno, who had so far refused to prosecute the crimes that Jack was digging up by the bushel, had angered Jack. During the election, Jack announced that she was obviously a lesbian because he had accused her of it and she hadn't denied it to his satisfaction. (After the election Janet Reno said that her interest was in real men and that Jack did not measure up in any degree to that description.) By coincidence, "Skyywalker Records" had donated a rap tune, which aired on black radio stations, supporting Janet Reno for her effectiveness in making fathers responsible for the welfare of their children. At that time, I didn't know Jack Thompson from Felix the cat.

Jack Thompson lost the election by a lot. And he was more than a little upset that he had been beaten by Janet Reno, after he had told everyone that she was a dyke.

Thirty-minutes from downtown Miami on the interstate highway, Fort Lauderdale was made internationally famous as the "spring break" haven for students from all over America in the '50s, '60s, '70s and through the mid-'80s. Broward County Sheriff Nick Navarro then put an end to the frolicking hoards of drunken teens and the problems they brought with them. Also the millions and millions of dollars of daddy's money that was a shot in the arm to the local economy. But Navarro's cronies wanted a Fort Lauderdale that wasn't turned over to the thundering crowds for one week every year. Fort Lauderdale was ready, they felt, for a new, cleaner image. Navarro decided that the voters wanted a nice, quiet, clean place to raise their kids.

Navarro read the infamous "Thompson" fax and passed it down his chain of command. Somehow it ended up in the clutches of William Kelly. Now old William Kelly knew smut when he read it and these particular lyrics sent the blood coursing through his rusty old veins. Kelly is a long-retired, honest-to-God, J-Friggin'-Edgar-Hoover-saluting FBI agent. An old-guard, bulldoggin'-devoted investigator of pornography. He had been hired by Navarro as a "Special Porn Consultant" with ties to certain "conservative, family-oriented" fundamentalist organizations just like our Jackie Boy. And though Jack Thompson had no credibility in Dade County, he certainly did with William Kelly. And just like Thompson, Kelly is not widely known for his sterling sense of humor where sin is involved.

So William Kelly gives Detective Mark Wichner a ten-dollar bill and sends him out to find him an actual copy of this record. Wichner runs right out to a record store and returns with a cassette tape that he paid eight dollars and ninety-nine cents for. Soon Wichner is sitting at his desk with his earphones smoking, and his eyes rolling, trying to pencil the lyrics, which is no small feat for a white cop whose contacts with blacks usually involved being heavily armed and ready to use deadly force. Next he grabs the cassette, the transcript and his description of the purchase and beats a path to the Broward County circuit court for a "probable cause" determination. Mel Grossman is the judge on duty and he takes the cassette, the affidavit, and the transcript from the worried-looking detective. This is how it's done. A detective buys a magazine or a tape and then gets a judge to say whether it is legally obscene. Then they are required to have an adversary hearing, or trial of the questionable material, to get an obscenity ruling. If they can get the ruling against the material, they can go out, make a buy, and bust the person standing at the cash register.

Judge Grossman, in his official capacity, said the following:

ORDER FOR DETERMINATION OF PROBABLE CAUSE OF OBSCENITY

Upon application of Detective Mark Wichner of the Broward County Sheriff's Office, and prior to the filing of any criminal charges with the office of Broward State Attorney, the court, in its Magistrate capacity, on March 2, 1990, did review in its entirety the following material, to-wit, a recording: "AS NASTY AS THEY WANNA BE", by the 2 Live Crew as released by Skyy Walker [sic] Records, 3050 Biscayne Boulevard, Miami, Florida.

THE COURT being fully aware of the contents of the aforesaid material and in conformity with this court's duty to satisfy the requirements for a speedy judicial determination as to the issue of obscenity, finds probable cause to believe that the aforesaid material is obscene within the purview of Florida Statute section 847.001 and the applicable case law.

THE COURT also notes that the application of contemporary community standards is shared by as avid a First Amendment proponent as the Miami Herald. That newspaper stated in an article appearing in its edition of February 28, 1990 that "Many of 2 Live Crew's lyrics are so filled with hard-core sexual, sadistic and masochistic material that they could not be printed here, even in censored form."

DONE AND ORDERED in Chambers at Fort Lauderdale, Broward County, Florida, this 9th day of March, 1990.

[s] _____

CIRCUIT COURT JUDGE MEL GROSSMAN

With the judge using an article from the *Miami Herald* to indict the dirty record, Kelly and Wichner took this piece of paper to Nick Navarro. Navarro was as excited as they were. They were sure that this would cinch the next election for sure. They would be the first to silence a bunch of dirty-mouthed Nigrahs that the white people felt threatened by anyway. It looked like a win/win deal. The sheriff would be a popular hero fighting pornography, whether in print, film or cassette record-ing. Win or lose, he wins!

The deputies were hitting the record store owners and clerks, saying that if the record was obscene, and if they sold it after it was so declared, they could end up in jail. They released their threats to the media. Missionary zeal took over; these men were engaging in prior restraint. They were saying the record was obscene before that determination had been made in the courts. In other words, clearing the tapes which they felt were obscene off the shelves, they were breaking the law. Meanwhile, they were not making further moves to take the record to court. So the sheriff violated 2 Live Crew's right to free speech and the deputies' statements had a "chilling effect" on sales of the records in Broward and even Dade Counties. And a lot of money was lost since few record store owners wanted to risk arrest for one nine-dollar tape even though there was no way they could be arrested until a judge formally ruled the tape obscene.

Up to this point over one million records had sold, mostly through word of mouth since the record had never been played on the radio in this country, featured on TV or spotlighted in widely circulated magazines. After the trial, another million copies would sell. But Navarro's men effectively ended sales in Broward County and Broward County is a big market for 2 Live Crew's music.

Since the sheriff did not seem to be moving toward the required adversary hearing to resolve the probable cause into a conviction of the record, or an acquittal, my attorneys decided to press the issue. They believed that Navarro thought he could score a victory without having to take the chance of being beaten in court. So Skyywalker Records' entertainment attorney, Allen Jacobi, suggested that we hire Bruce Rogow, a law professor at NOVA University in Fort Lauderdale and one of the country's leading First Amendment attorneys. Rogow sued Navarro, on behalf of Skyywalker Records, for damages arising from the sheriff's obvious prior restraint of trade.

Rogow's strategy was simple. He would sue in federal court in Fort Lauderdale because he felt certain that a federal judge would be friendly to the First Amendment issue. On our side was the fact that a rural jury in Alabama had already ruled against the obscenity motion in the *Move Somethin'* trial. All we had to do was win, and then I could continue to sell the tape.

Bruce Rogow's thinking was that we would go before a federal judge, slap the sheriff for the prior restraint, and have the record declared not obscene, and that would end this oppression once and for all. It should have been a breeze. Never in the history of recorded sound had a record been declared obscene. Never. In history. Oh, what the fuck. First time for everything.

7 The Trouble with Obscenity

Congress shall make no law respecting an establishment of religion, or prohibiting the free exercise thereof; or abridging the freedom of speech, or of the press; or of the right of the people to peaceably assemble, and to petition the Government for a redress of grievances.
> —The First Amendment of the U.S. Constitution

The First Amendment was designed to act as a restraint on governmental abuse of the awesome political power it holds. Never, it stated, should anyone be jailed for his thoughts, spoken words or writings. These were the only forms of expression available to the framers. Later the First Amendment was upheld to cover all communication channels. It is intended to counteract the tendency of political entities to react to criticism with lengthy jail terms, or other punishments, to dissuade criticism. It was specifically designed to protect the free exchange of ideas, most especially unpopular ideas, and information on which we base our beliefs. This, more than the threat of our combined armed forces, serves to maintain our free state.

In Bruce Rogow's words: "Nothing inhibits government misconduct more than criticism from a free press." A free press may in fact be the only thing that keeps this country free. The press, for all its many failings, keeps information flowing and acts as a watchdog, alerting the population to abuses of basic freedoms. Obscenity is not protected as free speech, and judges are faced with a real problem in deciding whether or not material is in fact obscene. There are specific criteria set forth in Supreme Court decisions which govern what may be declared obscene, thus losing the protections guaranteed by the Constitution. The Constitution assumes that something is protected under the right to free speech unless it is proven to lie outside that protection. Free speech does not entitle someone to yell "fire" in a crowded theater, or "Nine in the house!" at a club—meaning someone has pulled a gun (nine-millimeter) and is going to start blasting.

The courts have recognized that sex is such a big part of human life that sexual materials are to be accorded the same degree of protection as political speech. Nasty isn't necessarily obscene. 2 Live Crew's music is nasty. But is it obscene because the language is dirty and the message can be alarming to a majority of men and women? I push the boundaries of First Amendment rights. In doing so I perform a valuable service to this country by testing guidelines for the protection of all of the citizens of this country.

In order for something to be found legally obscene in America of 1991 it must fail not just one, but all three, prongs of the Miller vs. California test. To not be found obscene, it need only be able to squeak through any one of the three. The courts tend to prefer for something that is obscene to pass than for something that isn't to fail to pass.

The three parts of Miller vs. California are:

A) *Any suspect material, when taken in its entirety, must appeal solely to the prurient interest.*

B) *That said material violates the prevailing community standards of decency.*

C) *That whether or not any reasonable person believes that the material in question, when taken as a whole (specific parts may not be extracted and tested individually) has NO serious literary, artistic, political or scientific value.*

The Supreme Court has upheld further that if ANY one reasonable person believes that the material, taken as a whole, has ANY value in any one of these areas, then it is protected as free speech and CANNOT be obscene.

The Recording, *As Nasty As They Wanna Be,* Goes on Trial.
Federal District Courthouse, Fort Lauderdale, Florida
Skyywalker Records Inc. vs. Sheriff Navarro
March, 1990 Suit Filed/ Ruling June 6, 1990
The Honorable Jose Gonzalez, U.S. District Judge

In the Gonzalez Trial, Skyywalker Records was the plaintiff, and Sheriff Navarro was being sued over the prior restraint isssue. The sheriff's lawyer did not call one single expert witness.

The first witness for the plaintiff side in the Gonzalez trial was Dr. Mary Haber, a well-known South Florida clinical pyschologist and radio talk show host.

Dr. Haber has been a licensed psychologist since 1966. She has been qualified as an expert witness in the area of psychology and has been hired by South Florida courts, on numerous occasions, to establish a defendant's sanity. She was brought in to illustrate that the 2 Live records did not appeal to the prurient interest of Broward's citizens.

She testified that prurient interest was something that she often discussed with her patients to better understand their sexual behavior, sexual needs and sexual relationships. Prurient interest, said Dr. Haber, is whatever turns someone on sexually.

So Bruce Rogow asks Dr. Haber if she knows, based on

experience and research, what turns people on. Yes, she says, she does. It's different things for different people. For men it's mostly visual stimulation like pornographic movies, especially a movie that may feature one man and two or more women. And, she goes on, books and magazines like *Playboy, Penthouse* and *Hustler*. They like graphic detail. Women, she continues, are suckers for the written word and soft sexual fantasy.

It turns out that our Dr. Haber did her dissertation for her degree on the differentiation between audio and visual stimulation and conditions of sensory deprivation, and she found out that people were far more stimulated by visual images than by audio stimulation. She says that she has never had one patient tell her that he gets a stiffie from rap. She says further that she has listened to *As Nasty As They Wanna Be* eleven times and she is of the definite opinion that there is no way that that record could appeal to anyone's prurient interest. She is, in fact, stating the obvious. It's hard to laugh and get a hard-on at the same time.

So in order to have the record declared obscene, her testimony would have to be discredited. Unless the defense proved that she didn't know beans about her field and brought forth a more credible witness of their own who testified that the record did not harden wands, the prurient interest prong of the Miller vs. California ruling fell. That would have been the ballgame— in an honest game.

Mr. Jolly begins his questioning by asking if she has an office in Broward County. No. And she hasn't done any formal polling or sampling as to whether or not the citizens in Broward County might find the record obscene, has she?

He hints that her patients are seeking her help because they are unbalanced. She says that isn't always the case and that most of her patients are going through normal problems like job stress, life problems or even menopause. He asks how many of her patients have sexual problems. She says a hundred or so. He wants to know why she delves into her patient's sex life. She counters that it is part of the evaluation of every sexually mature patient to find out if they're getting any or enough or whatever. I'm sitting in the courtroom smiling, thinking that that's a great

Top left: Even at 8 months people say I had a winning smile.

Top right: Age seven: My mother thought I would be a minister.

Bottom right: When I got out of high school I got a job cooking for the employees' dining room at Mount Sinai Hospital. It was a bitch, but it was money.

Left to right: Mark Ross (Brother Marquis), Christopher Wongwon (Fresh
Kid-Ice), Luther Campbell (Luke), David Hobbs (Mr. Mixx).

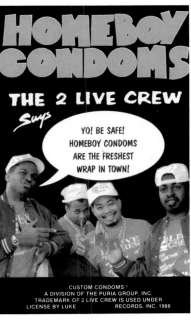

Top left: A point of purchase display sign for the 12" single "C'mon Babe" (February 1990).

Top right: Our first album, *2 Live Is What We Are*, went gold in 1989.

Bottom left: Press pass for the "As Nasty As They Wanna Be" tour.

Bottom right: We tossed "Homeboy Condoms" out into the audience during shows. I always promote safe sex.

Top left: *Move Somethin'* publicity session for our fan club.

Below: Cover shot for *2 Live Is What We Are*, taken before Chris's accident. From left: Mark, Luther, David, Chris.

Bottom: Accepting the Michigan Rap Award in Detroit, January 3, 1990. From left: David, Luther, Mark, Chris.

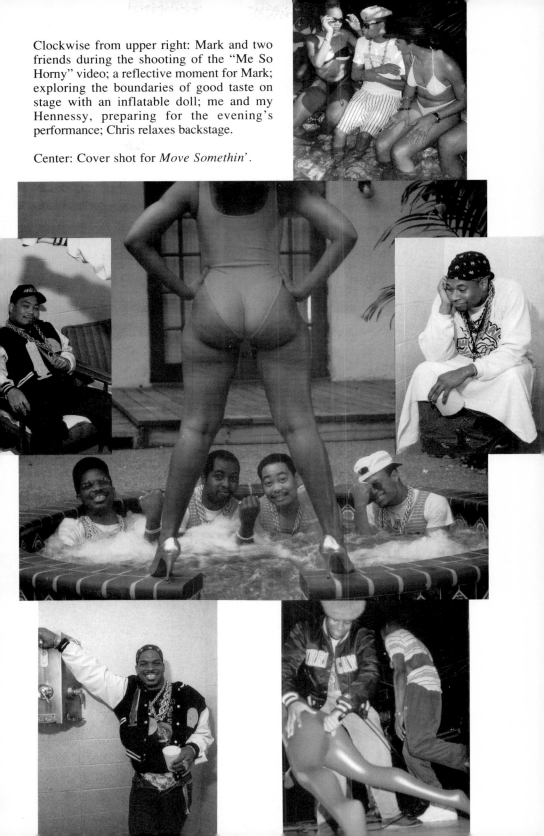

Clockwise from upper right: Mark and two friends during the shooting of the "Me So Horny" video; a reflective moment for Mark; exploring the boundaries of good taste on stage with an inflatable doll; me and my Hennessy, preparing for the evening's performance; Chris relaxes backstage.

Center: Cover shot for *Move Somethin'*.

A Parent's View of Pop Sex and Violence

By CHARLES M. ALEXANDER

Time, May 7, 1990

2 Live Crew, Decoded

By Henry Louis Gates Jr.

Henry Louis Gates Jr., professor of English at Duke University, is author of "The Signifying Monkey."

1990 YEAR IN REVIEW

A NASTY TIME

Startling, 'unbelievable' events of 1990 may be supplanted by quiet stories with long-term impact.

2 Live Crew member Luther Campbell is arrested by Broward sheriff's deputies in June in a dispute that is not over yet.

Rap album ruled obscene

2 LIVE CREW, FROM 1A

2 LIVE CREW CONTROVERSY — A CHRONOLOGY

OBSCENE EXTREME

Frightening message in 'Crew' arrests

By ROB TANNENBAUM

COMMENTARY

Time to ignore filth called rap music

Lewis Grizzard

they wanna be? He says no way

OFFENSIVE: Lawyer Jack Thompson dropped much of a lucrative practice to spend most of his time scorching sinners. He sees it as service to his country.

RAP ROYALTY

Luther Campbell, right, is the king of Miami street music. His company, Luke Skyywalker Records, has redefined rap, producing gold records and giving once-obscure performers a taste of above his success.

By LYDIA MARTIN

Sun-Sentinel

Wednesday, May 16, 1990   25 cents

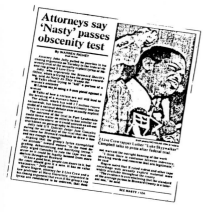

Attorneys say 'Nasty' passes obscenity test

By WARREN RICHEY

2 Live Crew rapper Luther "Luke Skyywalker" Campbell talks to press after federal trial.

In the spring of 1990, most of the nation's newspapers got headlines out of the bust and subsequent trial. I never set out to defend the First Amendment. It just happened that way.

Billboard

Miami's Luke Skyywalker Label Grows, Seeks Distrib Deal
Raunchy 2 Live Crew Endorses Safe Sex

The Rhythm and the Blues
by Nelson George

Speaking Out
By T. Willard Fair   Thursday, March 8, 1990

'Me So Horny' Is For Devil's Children —Only

Left: Photo taken from cover session for "The Estimable Mr. Campbell," a story John Miller wrote about me for Tropic Magazine in *The Miami Herald* (October 1990).

Above: My first daughter, Shenetris (age 9).
Below: Me and my baby Boo (Lucresha).

Above: Boo with her mom, Tina Barnett.
Below: Mamma and me.

way to make a buck—talking to women about their sexual hang-ups.

To further discredit Dr. Haber, Jolly tells the court that she has had a radio show for years. "Didn't you do a weekly show called 'Sexual Fantasy Saturday'?"

"Only one Saturday a month," she counters. So she is only twenty-five percent the deviate the defense was hoping to por-tray her as being. She says that she played the tape for thirty patients and they didn't get turned on. Not one. Jolly hints that maybe they didn't hear the entire tape. She says that they all saw humor in the lyrics and she is telling Jolly and his pal the sheriff that they are twisted if they think the record is a turn-on and they might make interesting subjects to study.

Jolly says that if the record isn't a turn-on, isn't it at least degrading toward women and boring? She agrees to that point. But she has testified that it does not, cannot in fact, appeal to the prurient interest; and being offensive or degrading to one sex or the other isn't part of the test for obscenity.

Lawrence Paull is a record store owner (Larry's Records in Plantation, Florida) whom the sheriff intimidated into taking *Nasty* off the shelves. It was important to show that the store owners and managers were threatened that there might well be a problem, when the record was ruled obscene—making this a clear case of prior restraint.

Mr. Paull stated that the record was a brisk seller and that the threats by the sheriff's people had caused him to remove the records from the shelves. So here's this poor guy shut out of selling what was to shortly become the hottest rap record in the history of recorded sound by some potbellied thugs in brown uniforms. The Navarro "mind police" are attacking records when you can buy crack or prostitutes on virtually any street corner in the county.

Mr. Paull acknowledged, to Rogow, that he was not threat-ened by the deputies personally, as other record store owners had been. He had heard the threat on the television news. So it was news. The sheriff who goes everywhere with six or seven TV cameras stuck up his ass had broadcast his threat to all the record dealers and all of South Florida and hopefully the world.

I was called to the stand to say my name, occupation and the number of copies of the record sold to date. Jolly, my avowed legal enemy, could not think of one question to ask me.

Greg Baker is a music critic for *New Times,* a regional, generally political, muckraking tabloid (based in Miami) with both a soul and a conscience. Greg is a writer whose expertise in rock and roll is widely respected. He is a writer with a great sense of style and humor, and also one of the first critics who had the balls to publish 2 Live Crew's lyrics, which Jim Mullen at *New Times* had the balls to print. Mullen actually has balls of stainless steel when it comes to flying in the face of convention and parboiling local politicos in his tabloid.

Greg Baker, with his shoulder-length blond locks, took the stand in a sports jacket and tie. He is not generally a suit-wearing reporter but this was a special occasion. Though Greg looks like he might just have left most of his short-term memory in the sixties, he's sharp as a fish hook.

DIRECT EXAMINATION OF GREGORY BAKER BY MR. ROGOW:

Q   Where are you employed, Mr. Baker?
A   *New Times* newspaper in Miami.
Q   In what capacity?
A   I'm a staff writer.
Q   Do you have any special area that you cover?
A   Music.
Q   How long have you been working for *New Times* and writing about music for them?
A   Since October 15th, 1987.
Q   What did you do before that?
A   I worked at the *Miami News,* the daily newspaper in Miami.
Q   What did you do for the *Miami News?*
A   I edited their TV magazine, and also wrote about popular music.
Q   How many years did you work for the *Miami News?*
A   Four-and-a-half years.
Q   Have you had any formal training in music?
A   In music, no.
Q   Approximately how many articles have you written about popular music over the past—would you say seven or eight years? Does that cover the *Miami News* and *New Times?*

A   Yeah, I'd say about six years, seven years. Gosh, hundreds; five hundred, six hundred.

Q   Tell us about the *New Times* newspaper. Where is that located?

A   We're based in Miami. The offices are just south of downtown Miami. It's a free weekly publication, supported by advertising and it's distributed throughout South Florida.

Q   Is it primarily an arts newspaper?

A   News and arts.

Q   What's the distribution of the *New Times?*

A   Sixty thousand.

Q   And approximately how much of that distribution is in Broward County?

A   Nine point six five percent.

Q   Of sixty thousand?

A   Correct.

Q   Have you ever written about the Two Live Crew?

A   Yes, I have.

Q   Did you write a feature article about them?

A   An in-depth feature article, yes.

Q   And when was that?

A   That was at the end of August of last year.

Q   What kind of music does the Two Live Crew play?

A   The genre?

Q   Yes.

A   We call it hip-hop, and it's also known as rap music.

Q   What is hip-hop music?

A   It's a sub-genre of rock and roll that involves emphasis on rhythm and lyrics above melody. Generally involves computer-generated sounds, so-called sampling.

    And the phrasing, the inflection and the word structures of the lyrics are its primary selling point.

Q   How long has hip-hop been around as a sub-genre of rock and roll?

A   Well, hip-hop itself has been around about fifteen years. Accepted in the mainstream as a legitimate genre, I'd say about ten years.

Q   Okay. What do you mean by accepted in the mainstream?

A   Well, ten years ago, there was a number one pop song that was a hip-hop song.

Q   What was that?

A   That was a song called "Rapture" by the group Blondie. At that point is when newspapers, magazines, and so forth began writing seriously about it.

That's when you could hear it on the radio, et cetera. That's what I mean by mainstreaming. The first five years of its history, it existed primarily underground.

Q   Underground? By that, what do you mean?

A   I mean where it started in New York, it was at house parties, private functions. There were no record labels involved. There was no business superstructure.

It was simply people creating the stuff on a street level.

Q   Who were those people?

Are there any special names you can relate us to for this beginning of hip-hop?

A   Well, I guess the best known names were people like African Pombada [phonetic] and Grand Master Flash, and so forth.

But a lot of these people aren't known, for the very reason it was a street level name. There were no stories in *The New York Times* about it at that point.

Q   Did they come from a culture within the culture of New York City?

A   Well, a lot of it was happening in Brooklyn. When I was up there and saw it, it was in Manhattan. Just carried over where people go on the street corners and set up and break-dance to a loud rhythmic music.

Q   Were these primarily black people?

A   Yes.

Q   Did it begin with a black kind of instigation in terms of break-dancing and starting the hip-hop concept?

A   Yes.

Q   You talk about break-dancing, what is break-dancing?

A   Well, it's a gymnastic sort of dancing, some of the moves. It added other parts of the body to the dance, other than the feet.

Spinning on your head, flips, that sort of thing.

Q   Is this the kind of thing we began to see on television about fifteen years ago, where there would be some fantastic break-dancers on street corners in New York?

MR. JOLLY: Objection, leading.

THE COURT: Overruled.

Q   Is that what you mean by break-dancing?

A   Right.

Q And hip-hop music grew out of that experience?

A I think the two are interrelated. I think they came along simultaneously. Break-dancing is the dance that you do to hip-hop music, and vice versa.

Q You said that Blondie's "Rapture" was the first kind of establishment show of hip-hop music?

A In crossing over into the mainstream. There was a record label called Sugar Hill before that, that released a number of fairly successful records.

I think it was about 1979.

Q What happened to hip-hop as it developed into rap?

A Well, I think when mainstream society became aware, that it kind of coalesced into a real genre or sub-genre, and people began using it in other ways.

For a commercial, a TV commercial, that sort of thing.

Q You mean the music then began to be used for commercial purposes, selling products; is that corect?

A Yes.

Q And the groups that were doing hip-hop music, then became people on television commercials or radio commercials with their music?

A That, and also just people lifting from it, lifting elements of it and modifying it for their own uses. The emphasis on rhythm, for example, some of the complex rhythm schemes, and that sort of thing, yeah.

Q How about hip-hop in the South Florida area. Where did it develop, and what happened to this New York/Brooklyn hip-hop as it came to South Florida?

A Well, I think it spread across the county to all cities. Here in Miami, I think it would be the same as anywhere else.

You know, there were some street rappers and that sort of thing. Nothing real major happened here in Miami until maybe four or five years ago.

Q What happened then?

A Well, with the start of Skyywalker Records . . . I think that was the beginning of Miami's hip-hop scene, to where there was an identifiable sort of hip-hop that could be associated with this region.

Q Explain to us what Skyywalker Records did that made a South Florida identity for hip-hop?

A Well, the first thing they did was sell two hundred thousand copies of their first record.

Q   And what was the name of that record?

A   "Throw the D." Well, as a record label, it provided an outlet for a number of artists, marketing for their work and so forth.

And it also, I think provided a focal point, something for other hip-hop artists in this community to aspire to.

Q   When you say a focal point, explain what you mean . . . people begin to follow their kind of work and expand upon it?

A   That happens, not just in Miami, nationally that happened. But also just—see, most musicians believe, and usually rightfully so, that you have to go to one of the hubs, New York or Los Angeles, in order to make it in the music industry. When . . . one act or one record label is able to make it in a community, such as Miami/South Florida, it gives it credibility.

And if you're a struggling young musician, you maybe realize that you don't have to go to New York or L.A., because there is good hip-hop coming out of Miami and it's selling well, so I can stay here in Miami and do my work.

Q   When did you first hear of the Two Live Crew?

A   About three or four years ago.

Q   And where did you hear them?

A   I heard about them in all sorts of places. Mostly word of mouth, talking to sources, friends, acquaintances.

Q   Is that part of your work, to learn about new developments in music?

A   Absolutely.

Q   . . . Does it try to keep people up with the avant-garde in music and other arts areas?

A   Very much so.

Q   When you heard about the Two Live Crew, did it encourage you to go out and find one of their records?

A   Oh, absolutely.

Q   Had you heard "Throw the D" before that?

A   I had not.

Q   Did you go out and buy or obtain a copy of "Throw the D"?

A   I eventually did. Before that, I bought their first album.

Q   Which was what?

A   "Two Live Crew is What We Are."

Q   Was there something distinctive about that work, as you had begun to listen and understand the development of hip-hop?

A   A number of things, sure.

Q   And what were they?

A The humorous approach to the music was interesting and new. I think they pioneered that aspect of it, of hip-hop.

And I found a lot of the rhythmic structures and so forth, the use of computer samples, the various aspects that define it as hip-hop better executed than in a lot of the hip-hop I heard from other cities.

Q You talked about sampling. What is sampling?

A That's where a computer is used to store sounds, code them digitally so that they can be called back with the press of a key or a keyboard.

Q Is this a recognized technique in the production of music today?

A Very much so.

Q And how long has it been a recognized and accepted technique?

A A few years now. It's really exploded in the past five years.

Q Has the technology changed and developed to permit more creative use of sampling?

A Dramatically.

Q Give me some examples of the kind of technology used to make this music? . . . Are there certain kind of machines?

A Oh, absolutely, yes. The digital samplers, I mean there's a number of different types, but they all perform the basic function of storing these sounds in digital form.

As opposed to analog recording, where the actual sounds are used, these are not the actual sounds, they're the computer recreating the sounds by the use of a code.

So the sound of the instrument has been through at least one stage of filtering. It has been altered digitally. That allows you to do a lot of different things with it in the timing and pacing of it.

And to do it better than you could through more involved elaborate means. It's made it faster and easier to make complex records.

Q Are the records today complex records that are made using this sampling technique?

A Very much so.

Q Are Two Live Crew's records complex records?

A Very much so, yes.

Q Have you listened to "As Nasty As They Wanna Be"?

A Yes, I have.

Q How many times have you listened to it?

A Probably twenty, twenty-five times, I think.

Q   In listening to it that many times, were you listening for anything special, trying to learn anything from the music?

A   A number of things.

Q   What were they?

A   Well, I wanted to understand the music. First, I wanted to understand the album as a package, then individually within each song I wanted to listen to see if I could determine how they were doing it, to hear the words, learn the words.

Maybe not memorize them, but find the parts of certain songs that I thought were of special value . . . I mean, with music that complex, listening to it once, you don't hear it all.

You simply can't register all of it. I think most music critics—certainly I listen to a piece of music at least ten times before I start thinking about what I want to write about it, to make sure that I've heard it all.

And, also, your feeling towards the music changes with the familiarity. Obviously, the first time you listen to it, it's completely new to you, so it's making that sort of first impression impact on it.

Then as you listen more, you hear certain other things. What you've already heard is now in your mind, creating, you know, a certain reaction.

And I think you can keep doing that with a record for many, many listens. Maybe a hundred listens.

Q   Okay. Is there atonality and dissonance in this music?

A   Yes. Yeah, that's one of the trick scenes.

Q   Does that make it more difficult to listen to?

A   Certainly, yes.

Q   Why is that?

A   Well, any time music surprises you by breaking from what you are trained or by what you're used to hearing or expecting to hear, a traditional musical progression, when that is broken up in some way, it's startling to you.

Simply because it's not what you're used to. And that makes it more interesting.

Q   Does it teach you something?

THE COURT: You're not telling us that dissonance is something new in music?

THE WITNESS: It's not, it's not anything new.

THE COURT: Atonality is nothing new in music, either?

THE WITNESS: No, it's not.

Q   Does the Two Live Crew use atonality and dissonance in different ways from the way they've been used before?

A   Yes.

Q   Explain that, if you would. I mean, are there different sounds?
Scratching, for instance, is that an example of dissonance?

A   Yeah. I mean, scratching's used in a lot of records. It has to be
different. You know, I mean, any time you create something, it
has to be new.

    You might borrow from a lot of things, but the total package
has to be something new. And I think very effectively they
come up with some of these strange noises that do fit into the
song, once you've become accustomed to them falling in this
place in the music.

    But on the first listen, you haven't heard it done that way, so
it's kind of startling. It provoked the reaction.

Q   Is provoking a reaction, something that's important in art
forms?

A   Absolutely.

Q   Do you know Luther Campbell?

A   Not socially.

Q   Have you interviewed him and Chris Wongwon and David
Hobbs and Mark Ross with regard to your article?

A   I have.

Q   Do you know the environment from which their songs come?

A   I don't know it first-hand. I'm familiar with it.

Q   What is that environment, to the best of your knowledge?

A   The streets, the inner city streets.

Q   And which inner streets are we talking about with regard to "As
Nasty As They Wanna Be"?

A   Primarily Liberty City.

Q   Is there anything special about this art form coming out of
Liberty City?

A   I think there are many things special about it.

Q   Tell us what they are?

A   Well, for one thing, there's a number of words that you won't
find in Webster's or American Heritage that are very effective
words, words that I use in daily conversation.

    Learning lingo, I think, is pretty interesting. One of the
extensions of that, one of the great things about this music, is
the humor in it.

    I find it pretty humorous. And in some of the songs I really like the musical textures. I mean, you know, it's not purely melodic, but there are progressions and rhythmic melodies that are pleasurable.

Q   Are you familiar with the Miller versus California standards for determining obscenity?

A   Yes, I am.

Q   Are you familiar with the test that required that a work have serious literary and artistic value?

A   Correct.

Q   In your opinion, does "As Nasty As They Wanna Be" have serious literary and artistic value?

A   Very much so.

Q   And why is that, that you come to that conclusion?

A   Well, as a music critic, from listening to it, it's important music, it's good music.

I mean, there's just a number of valuable things in there, and that's the reason we wrote about it, and have continued to write about them.

Q   You say a number, give us a couple of those valuable things, so we can put a tag on them, not just say a number of them?

A   Well, there's good music in there. I mean, good listenable music. It's excellent dance music. There's a lot of great humor.

Again, I like humor, and I get a big kick out of some of their work.

Also, another thing that I found interesting is when they work in other genres—reggae and the blues, for example—to see how hip-hop musicians interpret those other forms, or genres. I find pretty intriguing.

You know, another thing that's pretty fascinating to do, is to listen to a sampling to see how much of it you can recognize, pick up.

And then, again, to see how they're using that . . . Why are they picking up this Beatles' rift and playing it over, or whatever. It's stimulating listening.

Q   Was this record, "As Nasty As They Wanna Be," made to be played or to have the lyrics read?

A   It was made to be played.

MR. ROGOW: Your Honor, although it's a little late, I'd like to tender him as an expert witness in this area.

THE COURT: In which area?

MR. ROGOW: In the area of music; specifically, popular music.

THE COURT: You may inquire, Mr. Jolly. I presume that concludes your examination?

MR. ROGOW: It does.

CROSS EXAMINATION

BY MR. JOLLY:

Q Mr. Baker, a few moments ago, you offered your opinion that you thought that the tape has serious artistic value; is that right?

A Yes.

Q As a matter of fact, you would even describe that artistic value as being profound; is that correct?

A Yeah, I think so.

Q Would you say, however, you are also of the view, are you not, that there could never ever be an obscene audio recording?

MR. ROGOW: Your Honor, I object. It's irrelevant, and asking for a conclusion of law.

MR. JOLLY: It goes to the interest that this witness has any bias as to his testimony. He's been qualified as an expert.

Plaintiff's counsel—or Mr. Rogow, asked him about his views of artistic value and about the Miller test.

MR. ROGOW: But that's all. Your Honor. He can ask him if he thinks anything would ever not have serious artistic value, but he can't ask him about the conclusion of law as to whether or not anything would ever be obscene.

THE COURT: Sustained.

Q All right. You're a critic; right?

A Yes.

Q You possess no baccalaureate degree; do you?

A No, I do not.

Q Your Associates Degree is not in music?

A Absolutely not.

Q Not in literature?

A No, it's not.

Q Not in humanity?

A I think it's Liberal Arts, I don't know.

Q Okay. But you've never formally studied music at all; have you?

A No, I have not.

Q You're not a musician?

A Very much not.

Q You're unable to read sheet music; is that correct?

A I don't read music, or play an instrument, no.

Q Would you agree with me that you consider your first area of expertise journalism?

A Yes.

Q Are you an expert in classical music?

A   No.
Q   Expert in opera?
A   No.
Q   Expert in jazz?
A   No, I wouldn't say I'm an expert.
Q   So, it would be fair to say, that your characterization as an expert, isn't really in the broad category of music, but it's limited to basically rock and roll?
A   That would be my primary area of expertise, I think, but all music is interrelated, and I am familiar with some of those other forms you talked about.
Q   When you say familiar, what do you mean familiar with classic? Are you any more familiar than anybody else who has ever listened to Wagner?
A   I don't know who I'm more familiar than, but I like to listen to classical music, yes.
Q   Do you find yourself qualified to offer a critical opinion on a classical piece?
A   Yes, sir, I think I could do that.
Q   Now . . . in [the] examination by Mr. Rogow, you said that you discussed dissonance as one of the features of the music; is that correct?
A   Yes.
Q   But dissonance has nothing to do with the lyrical content necessarily; does it?
A   Well, I think it does.
Q   Inherently?
A   I mean, the two are closely related and they intertwine. I mean, a lyric could be dissonant of a scream, for example.
Q   You also mentioned that you learned a series of new words from this particular recording.
    What were some of those new words that you learned?
A   Well, maybe I shouldn't have said specific words, but the way they're put together, phrases . . . For example, "Put Her in the Buck," I hadn't heard that one. And the phrase—the not grammatical "Me So Horny," too; although, I had heard the phrase before.
Q   Where?
A   In a movie.
Q   Which one
A   The Stanley Kubrick film.

Q   Full Metal Jacket?

A   Yeah, that's the one. I might have heard it, and [it] didn't register much on me, but hearing it used musically, it's a pretty amusing phrase.

Q   Would you agree that you consider even the sexually explicit content to have artistic value; is that right?

A   Yes. If I understood your question, I think, yes.

Q   Let me see if I understand correctly.

The line, "Put your lips on my dick, and suck my asshole, too, I'm a freak in heat, a dog without warning, my appetite is sex, because me so horny," you consider that to be a significant artist achievement; don't you?

A   Well, again, you left out the first line of the verse, and I think—

Q   Be my guest, add that first line.

A   "You said it yourself, you like it like I do, so put your lips on my dick and suck my asshole, too—"

Yeah, I think that's pretty good writing.

Q   You think that's pretty good writing?

A   Yes, sir.

Q   As a matter of fact, it's one of your favorite lines in the album; isn't it?

A   I think it's one of the best constructed phrases on there, yeah.

Q   You think it's the lyrical zenith of the album?

A   Boy, there's so many, I would hate to—

MR. JOLLY: I don't have any additional questions.

MR. ROGOW: Nothing further, Your Honor, of Mr. Baker.

THE COURT: Mr. Baker, you're a member of the Two Live Crew Fan Club?

THE WITNESS: I am?

THE COURT: I'm asking you.

THE WITNESS: I don't think so, but I might be, because I'm on their mailing list.

THE COURT: Are you aware of the fact that on the jacket for this cassette, it says our fan club members are listed there. And on the third line is Greg Baker. I assume that's you.

THE WITNESS: That's right. I had forgotten about that, yeah. I never registered to join the fan club, though.

THE COURT: Thank you, sir, you may step down.

Rogow's next witness was John Leland. John Leland is a "hot" critic, who has written hundreds of articles on rap. He was an editor for *Spin* and wrote full-time for *Newsday*. He is undoubtably the world's leading rap/hip-hop critic. Leland is tall and thin, with dark hair, and he wears a tie all the time. He had first testified for the 2 Live Crew in Alabama. They offered to pay him but he refused to take a cent. He didn't want anyone to think he had been bought. Nobody buys Leland.

DIRECT EXAMINATION OF JOHN LELAND BY MR. ROGOW:

Q   Mr. Leland, where are you from?
A   I'm from New York.
Q   Do you work in New York?
A   Yes, I do.
Q   What kind of work do you do?
A   I'm a music critic.
Q   For whom?
A   For *Newsday*.
Q   What is *Newsday*?
A   *Newsday* is the *Times*' mirror paper in New York, and it's actually two papers.
     There's a paper called *Newsday*, and a paper called *New York Newsday*, which is distributed in the five boroughs, and I publish in both of those.
Q   And where is *Newsday* distributed?
A   In Long Island.
Q   What's the circulation of *Newsday/Newsday New York*?
A   It's somewhere in excess of six hundred thousand copies a day.
Q   This is a daily newspaper?
A   Yes, it is.
Q   And where does that rank as compared to other daily newspapers in the United States with regard to circulation?
A   It's in the top ten in the country.
Q   How long have you been the music critic for *Newsday*?
A   Well, I'm one of several, and I've been there since October of '89.
Q   What special area do you cover for music for *Newsday*?
A   ... Well, I'm one of the rock and pop critics, and I cover mostly black music and specifically hip-hop and rap music.
Q   Tell us what you did before you worked for *Newsday* with regard to music criticism?

A   I was a music editor of *Spin* Magazine, which is a monthly music magazine.

Q   What was the circulation of *Spin* Magazine while you were working for the company?

A   Fluctuating between a hundred and twenty-five and a hundred and seventy thousand copies a month.

Q   Is that nationwide distribution?

A   That's nationwide.

Q   Did you have any special area of music criticism for *Spin* Magazine?

A   The same area. *Newsday* hired me really because of my expertise in writing about black music, and specifically hip-hop and rap.

Q   And before *Spin* Magazine, where did you work?

A   I'd been a freelance writer for a couple of years, publishing in a number of magazines.

Q   Publishing what?

A   Articles on music.

Q   What magazines have you published in?

A   Well, I've published in *The New York Times; The London Times; Vogue; The Face; Seven Days,* which Time Warner just bought; *Rolling Stone Review; Musician* Magazine; *Music* and *Sound Output.*

Q   Approximately how many articles have you written over the past ten years, and had published?

A   . . . Well, since joining *Newsday,* I've published about a hundred and forty. So, that really accelerated my rate of writing. But five, six hundred articles, maybe.

Q   Have you received any critical praise for your work as a music critic in this area of hip-hop/black music?

A   Not specifically in this area. In general, I did. Robert Criskow [phonetic], who is the music editor of *The Village Voice*—and calls himself the dean of rock critics—in his summary of the events of the eighties, singled me out and said I was the best post-modern rock critic, the best new critic there is.

Q   Have you ever testified as an expert witness in any case?

A   Yes, I have.

Q   How many times?

A   Once.

Q   Where was that?

A   That was in Alexander City, Alabama.

Q   When was that?

A   I think it was in February.

Q   What was the name of the group whose work you were testifying with regard to in that trial?

A   That was the Two Live Crew.

Q   And what was the name of the record?

A   "Move Somethin' ".

MR. ROGOW: I tender this witness as an expert in the area of popular music, modern popular music, with special emphasis on hip-hop music.

MR. JOLLY: I'll just save it all for cross, Judge.

THE COURT: All right.

Q   What does a music critic do, Mr. Leland; how do you go about your work?

A   Well, my job is to listen to records. Also, I go to concerts, and review concerts. I review records. I interview performers.

I write criticism, think pieces, and also historical pieces.

Q   How did you first get involved in listening to and writing about hip-hop music?

A   Well, I got involved in listening to it a little bit before I started writing about it.

Q   Tell us about it.

A   In 1977, 1978, I was a college student at Columbia College, living on the—sort of the edge of West Harlem. There was a projects down the block from my apartment, and a handball court in the projects.

And that was a tremendous era for graffiti in New York, and anywhere there was a handball court in the City, there was a twenty foot by thirty foot graffiti mural on it.

And so there was a very exceptional one on the handball court near my apartment. And also at that time, the graffiti people and the rap and hip-hop people were all part of the same community.

Q   What community was that; was it a black community?

A   It was a black community. But specifically, a music community. If hip-hop people were to throw parties, graffiti people would do murals or they would do flyers to advertise them.

They were all part of the underground artistic community . . . There were very few clubs for this music, and there were—at that time—maybe one or two records that had come out.

It was a street-level thing, and the main events would be

parties in parks or in block parties. And one day they were throwing a party in front of my house.

A rap crew had set up, and they were on the sidewalk and they had brought a PA system in, and a DJ, who had two turntables, two record players and a speaker system, and a couple of microphones.

And I heard this noise outside my window and I wondered what it was, and I went downstairs and, you know, I'd never seen anything like it.

There was a guy who, with just two turntables and a couple of copies of a James Brown record, was doing these tremendous rhythmic improvisations.

He was cutting up beats, and layering them, and turning one beat and—

Q   Tell us what that means. What do you mean by cutting up beats?

A   A setup of two turntables—the setup for a hip-hop DJ is to use two turntables with . . . a cross fader in between.

The cross fader regulates the information coming out of the two turntables and going to the speakers. It's just a slider switch.

And if it's pressed to the left, the music from the left turntable comes out of the speakers, and the music from the right turntable goes into his headphones.

If it's in the center, both turntables are playing. And if it's pushed to the right, then the music from the right turntable is playing.

Now, cutting up a beat, means finding the most exciting rhythmic spot on the record. Maybe when all the instruments drop out and there's just the drummer playing, and it's going boom, boom, bah, bim, bim, bah [indicating] . . . And what the DJ would do, is he would find the same spot on both records where all the other sounds dropped out, and there was just that one beat—boom, boom, bah, bim, bim, bah [indicating].

And he would play it on one turntable and it would go boom, boom, bah, bim, bim, bah [indicating], and he would throw the fader over to the right turntable.

And with the needle at the beginning of that beat, he would move the turntable forward, move the record on the turntable forward and backward and forward and backward, which is what's known as scratching, and then he would let it go, so it creates a kind of a whicka, whicka, whicka [indicating] sound.

It's a new sound and it is a new music, and it's hard to describe it in terms other than that. So he might go to the left turntable and go, boom, boom, bah, whicka, whicka, boom, boom, bah, whicka, whicka, whicka [indicating], which changes the time signature of the music, and changes the whole feel of it.

Now, on top of it, the people outside were going crazy. There were kids literally dancing on their heads. The most exciting piece of the record is called the break, and out of guys spinning the breaks, came a style of dancing known as break-dancing.

And ordinarily, before hip-hop DJ's, guys would play a record, and they would play the record from beginning to end, and when the record got to that break, people would dance furiously.

And then when the break ended, they would go back to dancing at their regular pace.

Now, with hip-hop, you have these DJ's that were playing nothing but the breaks, nothing but the parts of the record that people danced the most absolutely furiously to.

So he would just push them to dance more and more furiously. And one of the popular break-dancing moves is to get on your back and kick your legs up in air while you're spinning around, and getting such momentum that you go on to your head.

So that your arms are out, your legs are in the air kicking, and you're literally spinning around on your head. And there were kids doing this, and it was the craziest thing I'd ever seen.

Q   Did the music enhance their ability to do this?

A   Oh, the music was what was pushing them to do it.

Q   So that's how you discovered hip-hop?

A   That's how I discovered it, and I'd never seen anything like it before or since.

Q   . . . Where did hip-hop begin?

A   A lot of people think hip-hop began in the South Bronx, which is a bit of a misnomer, it really began in the West Bronx.

Well, people have been killed over this discussion, it's a big deal, this is no joke. People will fight each other to the death to argue this out.

But it started in the West Bronx. A Jamaican DJ by the name of Cool Herc [phonetic] got the idea he would play the breaks of records.

And he played this, and noticed that the kids would gather outside his window. This was around 1968, in the West Bronx.

He noticed that all the kids would gather outside his window. And Cool Herc is this very mild-mannered West Indian guy, with this big beard, about six-five or so.

And he really loved the idea that the kids were gathering outside his windows. And from there, he turned that into throwing parties.

And he put together his sound system, which would be a PA system, and a group of guys to do security to make sure that taking this system out to a poor area, that no one would steal any of his equipment, and he called that the Herculons.

And he started throwing parties at a community center they called the Hevlo [phonetic].

Q Who used to come to these parties—neighborhood people?

A Strictly neighborhood people. No one else would have ever known about them.

Q Was this music recorded; were there recordings out there for sale of this kind of music at the time?

A Not at the time that he was doing it. And, in fact, from the time he started until the time there were commercially available recordings, was about a decade.

Q '68 to about '78?

A '68 to about '78.

Q And what distinguished these DJ's from one another; were there special traits that each one of them had?

A Every DJ had his own style. All the DJ's owed everything to Cool Herc, and they acknowledged him as the master guy who invented this music.

But they all had to develop their own style, and they all had to—more importantly—develop their own record playing.

One of the things that Herc did that made him so popular was he played records that weren't hits of the day. By the time he started throwing his big parties, it's early seventies, and it's the start of the disco.

And there was, at that time, a generation of black kids in the Bronx and throughout New York City that just didn't want to hear about disco, it was too soft to them, they wanted to hear the old James Brown records, and they wanted to just hear the beats of other records.

They didn't want to hear the hustle. Just did not want to hear it. It didn't reflect their lives, didn't reflect the pace of their lives.

So, one of the things that DJ's would do to distinguish themselves from one another . . . would be to have the most exciting records.

You couldn't just play what was in the top forty, what was the hot records at the time, because that's not what the people wanted to listen to, these people wanted alternative music.

So DJ's would go to flea markets and to discount shops and buy records blind, not knowing what they were. Throw away their last ninety-nine cents to buy a copy of some heavy metal record that they thought might have a great beat on it.

And if they had a record that nobody else had, people would go to their parties. And to that end, these DJ's would protect their records.

They would soak them in a bathtub and soak the label off so no one could read what it was, or they would cover the label with masking tape, or they would scratch it off . . .

They were so intense about this, that each DJ had spies that he would send out into the other DJ's camp.

And one of the popular DJ's of the time, African Pamboda, once told me that his spies would go into the other camp's side and they would try to see what colors the label was on a record.

And once he knew what colors it was . . . he could figure out what record company put it out.

And once he knew what record company put it out, all he had to do was go through every record on that record company's roster and find out what it was.

And in the Bronx, on Treemont Avenue, there's a store called Nat's [phonetic] that organizes its records by record company, specifically for people like Pamboda, who wanted to go and find out, hey, I'm going to listen to the records on that mat and find it.

Q   These DJ's were making new music, you said?
A   Entirely new.
Q   Did they have instruments in the traditional way that we think of instruments?
A   A little bit later on, they would play a drum machine in addition to their computers, but in the early going, they just did the sampling.
Q   Is a drum machine an instrument in the traditional sense of instruments that you see in a symphony orchestra, for example?

A   Not in the traditional sense, no.

Q   Does it make any difference that the music that's being made, or that was being made by hip-hop and is being made now, is being made through this sampling technique of using these sounds as you've described?

A   No, because there's a lot of technique involved in sampling, which has to be considered a new musical technique.

Q   And are there new instruments for the modern music that you're reviewing?

A   There are.

Q   And what are those instruments?

A   They're largely computers. First would be the turntable, and popular music for the last twenty years has followed technology.

Once the guitar players learned to make feedback on the electric guitar, it changed the sound of rock music. Made it much louder.

Once DJ's learned to make music by this college technique of placing—really colliding a piece of—a little sample of sound from one record with a little sample of sound from another, the technology followed them.

And people developed computers that could do this a little more simply.

Q   And these are the instruments that you're describing?

A   And these are called digital sampling devices.

Q   You talked to us about hip-hop and its history, the beginning history of hip-hop.

Where does rap come into the picture?

A   One of the biggest DJ's . . . in the South Bronx, and responsible for the movement of the music in the South Bronx, his name is Joseph Sadler [phonetic], also known as Grand Master Flash.

Now, DJ's always had to have crews with them. They would take care of their security. They would protect their equipment and also protect people in the party from getting too far out of hand.

Grand Master Flash used to put a microphone out in front of the turntable with a little rope around it, and guys that were in his security crew or guys from the crowd could come up and talk on it.

And around '76, a man named Keith Wiggin [phonetic], a kid from the South Bronx, he called himself Keith Cowboy or Cowboy, got on the mike.

And when the guys got on the microphone, they'd usually just say hello to their girlfriends or say hello to their friends and stuff; to my girl out there, say ho, or something like that.

And Wiggins was the first person to get on the microphone and talk in rhythm with the beat to the music. And he would say, clap your hands everybody, and everybody just clap your hands.

Or he would say, Jack and Jill went up the hill to have a little fun, but stupid Jill forgot her pill, and now they have a son.

Or something like that . . . He never got very complicated, but he had a very good voice, and his little tiny raps, it might just be, throw your hands in the air and wave them like you just don't care, or everybody say ho, and the audience would yell back ho.

But this kind of focused the attention of the party, and focused the attention of the dancers at the party.

Q   So, rap then is hip-hop with the addition of this—the talking, the rapping, the vocalizing that goes on along with the music?

A   For about eight years you had hip-hop without rap, so you can always have hip-hop without rap. Hip-hop is a style of putting music together.

And then rap goes very well with hip-hop. So it's a particular refinement of hip-hop.

Q   So then we can talk about the genre of hip-hop, because rap just falls into that genre of hip-hop; is that right?

A   Right.

Q   Why is hip-hop important?

A   I think it's a whole new way of looking at music.

Q   A new way how?

A   In the past, you would look at a piece of music as being built out of notes and chords and tones. Those would be the basic building blocks of a piece of music.

And hip-hop throws that out, and says the basic building blocks are little chips of other records, and we'll create an original work of music; not starting with notes and chords and tones, but we'll create them from other records.

The instrumentation is entirely different . . . Instrumentations are, you know, wood winds, percussions, instruments, now they're turntables and electronics . . . In the past, you would think of music as a relationship between melody, harmony, atonal quality and rhythm.

Rap is going to throw out melody, throw out harmony, and reduce music to pure rhythm or focus the music purely on the rhythm.

Q   Do the rap words work to focus the music on the rhythm?

MR. JOLLY: Objection, leading.

THE COURT: Overruled.

THE WITNESS: Yes, they do.

Q   And how do they do that?

A   Rappers will call attention to the beats . . . One of the things they'll do is just say, here's your ticket, hear the drummer get wicked, something like that. And they'll just flat out tell you to listen to the beat.

Or because rap records often have a lot of different beats or different rhythms going on at once, the rapper will follow the dominant beat that they want you to follow for a verse, then they'll slip out of that beat and call your attention to another beat in . . . say maybe the next verse of the next line.

But more than that, they just make you listen to the music a little bit more closely.

Q   When did you first hear a Two Live Crew recording?

A   . . . I was down in New Orleans for the New Orleans Jazz and Heritage Festival. I was in the black neighborhood of New Orleans looking for used record stores, because you can find stuff there cheap.

New Orleans has such a strong heritage of rhythm and blues that you can really find a lot stuff there. So, I'm at a stop sign in a rented car.

There was another critic who is now with *The New York Times* in the car with me. This other car pulls up, and it's like a copper-colored Chevy Nova, and there's four black people in it and they've got the sound system booming.

And . . . there's got to be eight arms and eight legs in the air, and they're just [indicating], and this whole car's bouncing up and down, you know.

And this just incredible music coming out. And we've got our radio going on kind of loud, too, but this is blasting us out of there.

And we just wanted to know what that is. So, I asked them what they were playing, and they go, that's "Throw the D" by Two Live Crew.

The light turned green, and we pulled off, and that was it.

Q   Did you go out and buy a copy of the record?

A   When I got home, I did, yeah.

Q   Were there some new sounds that you heard on that record?

A   By this time, I was very, very deeply immersed in the hip-hop
culture. I knew most of the people involved making it, I knew
most of the people involved in producing it, and distributing it.

And I knew all the records. Any hip-hop record that came
out, came out in New York specifically, but this was something
entirely different to me.

Q   What was different about it?

A   The Two Live Crew just thought of the music differently than
the people in New York did. People in New York thought of it
as taking small bits of records and sort of throwing them at one
another and letting them collide in the most explosive way
possible.

So that two seconds of this record are really exciting, and
then the next two seconds it changes, and those two seconds
are really exciting, too.

. . . And the New York dances grew out of that, and the wild
style of New York dances pushed the New York music to get
even more choppy and explosive, and the music pushed the
dancers to get even more explosive.

Miami has a different kind of dance tradition than New York.
The huge Cuban population is really largely responsible for
disco.

Disco came about when Cuban musicians, Cuban-American
musicians, brought Latin rhythm to rhythm and blues style.
And out of that, came disco, which is a very smooth sustained
rhythmic music.

But Two Live Crew . . . picked up on that and they were also
playing at a tremendous tempo. "Throw the D" is just like that
[indicating], at a time when the New York records were moving
fairly slowly.

So they were working at a different tempo with a different
strategy. They wanted to sustain their grooves and keep people
dancing in a sustained way.

And they were also using electronic instruments, not just
computers and sampling devices, but synthesizers.

Q   Was this a special sound?

A   It was. And the thing that was most striking about it, was where
the New York records ran on the drums—everything was based

on the drums, you know, they would have these lyrics assist the sound of the drum that makes you come to the party—the Miami sound ran on the bass. They tried to pack their records, Two Live Crew's "Throw the D" and their first album entirely, put as much bass as I ever heard on a record before.

Q   . . . Did "As Nasty As They Wanna Be" follow up on these same traditions?

A   With each record, Two Live Crew has pushed that idea further and taken in more influences, also.

Q   What do you mean by that much, taken in more influences?

A   Well, "As Nasty As They Wanna Be," also, besides drawing on these dance music traditions, includes reggae in a really overt way.

It includes the blues in an overt way, and uses pieces of jazz records, as well, and hard rock records and pop records.

Q   This Miami, music, as you've described it, and the bass aspect of the Miami music, is there a special name that's now attached to this kind of music?

A   Yeah, bass music. They call it bass music, because that is the distinguishing vibe of the music.

Q   And is that a uniquely South Florida or Miami sound in this genre music?

A   Yeah, yeah. Southern California picks up a little bit on it, but at the intensity that they do it in Miami, that's really peculiar to Miami.

Q   Let's talk about the bass music in "As Nasty As They Wanna Be".

Is this a good example of the bass music that you've described, the Miami-based music that you've described?

A   Well, the bass music I described is [its] earliest and probably most primitive version. "As Nasty As They Wanna Be" is a great example of that, but it's also something more.

It's also, you know, reaching for a bit more broader appeal than that.

Q   In music, you're talking about?

A   Yeah.

Q   In what way?

A   In what I was talking about before, borrowing elements from the blues, and from reggae, and pop and hard rock.

Q   How many times have you listened to "As Nasty As They Wanna Be"?

A   I think about fifteen.

Q   Do you know approximately how many copies of records it's sold throughout the country?

A   The last thing I saw was an interview with Luther Campbell where he said they sold one point six million.

Q   Among rap music, does two Live Crew have a distinctive sound?

A   Oh, yeah. In fact, a New York group named Stensonic [phonetic], on their last record that came out in the summer of '88, did a tribute to Two Live Crew which they called Miami Bass.

Now, it's not a very good record, because they don't know how to make this music, the New York group, but it's really a tribute to the music Two Live Crew's made.

Q   Has sex always played a role in rock and roll music?

A   It has always played a role in rock and roll, but . . . not just rock and roll. Nelson Riddle, who was the arranger on most of Frank Sinatra's best material, once said, music is sex.

That's the only part of the quote that I remember. But [he] went on to explain that when the rhythms of his songs would approach the heartbeat, that's when they'd have a successful record.

And, of course, Frank Sinatra caused sexual hysteria throughout the country.

Q   How about music itself—not talking about specific people, necessarily—but some examples of sex and rock and roll historically in terms of the music that's been published and sold for the past twenty, twenty-five years?

A   Well, the famous one is people thinking that the way Elvis moved his pelvis was lewd.

And when Elvis appeared on the Ed Sullivan Show, he was shot from the waist up, because his gyrations were said to be simulating sexual intercourse in a sexually explicit way that shouldn't be shown over television.

Q   Are there records that have been published and produced over the past twenty years . . . that have references to sexual activity?

A   Well, it almost gets hard to find records that don't. But right now, the best-selling single record is a record called "Wild Thing."

And that record comes from a line in the Spike Lee movie, "She's Gotta Have It," in which the character says, hey, baby, let's go back to my crib and do the wild thing.

And it's very clear to everyone who listens to that record what he's talking about. The Beatles do a song, "Why Don't We Do It in the Road." What are they talking about?

Jimmy Buffet does a record, "Let's Get Drunk and Screw." What's he talking about?

Q You've heard the lyrics of the songs on the recording "As Nasty As They Wanna Be." Do they detract from the musical value of that record?

A No. No.

Q Do they complement the musical attempt made in the record of the strong bass music and reggae and other forms of music?

A The delivery of the lyrics particularly complements the music. The lyrics themselves work a little bit more . . . complex than that.

I don't think the choice of the lyrics specifically highlights the rhythm. I think the use of profanity, and Two Live Crew certainly uses a lot of profanity, tells its audience that they're in the leisure mode now.

That they're not at their jobs, and they're not in the court, but they're in their room now, or a social mode where they can talk in free ways, and talk in the language that they would use on the street.

Q Is this language shocking to you, the language that you hear on "As Nasty As They Wanna Be"?

A Not shocking to me.

Q Have you heard it in the streets before, as you've done your work in this area?

A I've heard it in the streets, I've heard it in the office . . . I've read it in books, I've seen it on TV. I've seen it in movies.

Q Do you have an opinion as to whether or not "As Nasty As They Wanna Be" has serious artistic value?

A Yes, I do.

Q And what is that opinion?

A I believe it does.

Q Why?

A Because I think that hip-hop represents a really strong musical revolution, and that Two Live Crew have accomplished an innovation within the genre of hip-hop.

Q The innovation being the use of—

A The way they construct their rhythm, the use of a lot of bass.

Q   How often is it that a record sells a million copies in the American music industry?

A   There are about a dozen a year that do.

Q   . . . Let me ask you this: What is an independent record company?

A   Ninety percent of the records sold in this country are sold by a handful of major corporations that have their own distributing companies, they have their own media arms, they're often connected with film studios.

   For example, the large Japanese corporation Sony owns all the music that comes out on Columbia, CBS, Epic, Columbia Master Works, anything that comes out on any of the Columbia labels. And they also own a large chunk of Sony pictures, and they own the equipment that it's produced on, and who knows what else they own.

Q   Are these called the major record companies?

A   These are called the major record companies. An independent company would be a company without any major affiliations.

   It might be anything from a mom and pop record company, to a mom and pop record company that grows into something larger without being bought up by, you know, a large foreign corporation or American corporation.

Q   Is Skyywalker Record Company an independent record company?

A   Skyywalker is an independent.

Q   What are the chances of an independent record company having a product that sells over a million or over million-and-a-half records?

A   They used to be nil. In the last couple of years there's been say one a year.

Q   Is it a rare event in the—

A   A tremendously rare event. Out of the thousands of independent records that are produced every year, it's astonished everyone that in the last couple of years, one has become a platinum album and has been certified for sales of a million copies.

Q   What are the Grammy Awards?

A   The Grammy Awards are a system of honors which the participating members of the recording industry are awarded for distinguished performances.

Q   Do they have different categories of Grammies?

A   Yes, they do.

Q   Is hip-hop a category of Grammy?
A   It wasn't until two years ago. Two years ago, they gave out the first hip-hop Grammy. I think it's a rap Grammy.
Q   A rap Grammy.
    Does that suggest that this is—at least in the music industry—a newly accepted art form?
A   Yeah, because the people who vote for Grammys are the musicians, the engineers, the producers, members of the recording industry.
    And they're deciding to award a Grammy. A Grammy testifies that they've determined that this is valid music . . .
Q   Does inclusion of rap music in the Grammy Awards signify that rap music, as genre, has artistic value?
A   Yes, it does.
Q   And in your opinion, does "As Nasty As They Wanna Be" have serious artistic value?
A   Yes, it does.
MR. ROGOW: I don't have anything further, Your Honor.
THE COURT: Cross examine.

CROSS EXAMINATION BY MR. JOLLY:

Q   Good morning, Mr. Leland.
A   Good morning.
Q   You are a—for lack of a better word—a hip-hop and rap music critic; is that right?
A   No, I'm considered a pop critic.
Q   A pop critic. Do you consider yourself an expert in jazz music?
A   No, I don't.
Q   Do you consider yourself an expert in classical music?
A   No, I don't.
Q   Do you consider yourself an expert in music in any form other than pop music?
A   No, I don't.
Q   And yet, you do not, other than drum scores, you cannot read music; is that correct?
A   That's correct.
Q   You have never taken any course work in rock or popular music where you studied from other people?

A   The only course work I've taken, is in music appreciation, and that was classical music.

Q   And that has nothing to do with the expertise that you hold today?

A   That's correct.

Q   You have a college degree, but it is not in music; is that correct?

A   It's in English.

Q   And other than this case, you have never been to Broward County before; is that correct?

A   No, I haven't.

Q   And you don't have any opinoins about what the people in Broward County may think or not think about the contents of the Two Live Crew's "As Nasty As They Wanna Be"; is that correct?

A   No, I don't.

Q   You and I met for the first time last week when I took your deposition; is that right?

A   That's correct.

Q   And at that time . . . you held an opinion about whether or not Two Live Crew's "As Nasty As They Wanna Be" had artistic merit; is that correct?

A   Yes, I did.

Q   And you had never reviewed a complete transcript of the lyrics of "As Nasty As They Wanna Be"; is that correct?

A   No.

Q   Three or four songs?

A   That's correct.

Q   But you had never heard a complete transcript of all its lyrical contents?

MR. ROGOW: I object to "heard a complete transcript."

THE COURT: Sustained.

THE WITNESS: I can make out the lyrics just fine listening to it.

Q   Nevertheless, you never reviewed a written transcript of the entire content of the album; is that right?

A   No.

Q   And you hold opinions today that this thing has serious artistic value. But, as a journalist, would you agree with me that part of the process of obtaining information is an interview with an artist?

A   That can be part of it.

Q   Did you ever do an interview of any member of Two Live Crew?

A   No, I haven't.

Q   Would you agree with me today that after all of your analysis of a recording or a musical work, in the end, your review about a given work is just one man's opinion?

A   Well, what it is, is an educated man's opinion.

Q   But one man. Could other educated men differ with you?

A   They could.

Q   And the opinion that you hold today, you had already formed at the time that we met last week; is that right?

A   That's correct.

Q   Would you agree with me that at the time that I interviewed you last week, you had not heard the tape "As Nasty As They Wanna Be" in close to a year?

A   I think I said eight months.

MR. JOLLY: May I approach the witness to refresh his recollection, Your Honor?

THE COURT: Just read it to him.

Q   Do you recall that on May 9th, up in the Plaza Hotel last week—

THE COURT: You took his deposition at the Plaza Hotel?

MR. JOLLY: It was absolutely great. I was looking for Iliana all over the place, Ivana, but she wasn't there.

THE WITNESS: Ivana.

THE COURT: Where in the Plaza Hotel?

MR. JOLLY: Mr. Jacobi picked the room.

THE COURT: Well, I'm happy to know that you all went first class.

MR. JOLLY: I didn't even have a back on my chair.

THE WITNESS: Come on, ask me the question.

Q   I asked you this:
       How long ago was the last time that you heard the record. Your response was, must be close to a year now.

A   Oh, okay.

Q   So you haven't listened to it in somewhere between eight months to a year?

A   That was true then, and it's still true.

Q   And you held your opinions at that time?

A   That's correct.

Q   Now, you were a witness in Alabama on the album "Move Somethin' "?

A   That's correct.

Q   That was a criminal prosecution; was it not?

A   That's correct.

Q You . . . testified then that the album "Move Somethin' " had serious artistic value, as well; is that correct?

A That's correct.

Q . . . Would you say that you went into your review of "As Nasty As They Wanna Be" with a completely open mind and you didn't have any prejudice about whether or not this tape might lack serious artistic value?

A Well, I had done my . . . original listening to "As Nasty As They Wanna Be" well before the Alabama case had come up, so that would never have prejudiced my reading of "As Nasty As They Wanna Be" . . .

Q Now, you described, when we met last week, that "As Nasty As They Wanna Be" was buoyant, lithe, dance music; is that correct.

A . . . That's correct.

Q . . . And would you agree with me that you can have buoyant, lithe dance music without lyrics at all?

A That's correct.

Q And without sexually explicit lyrics; is that correct?

A You certainly can.

Q . . . Did you ever hear "As Clean As They Wanna Be," the other version of this tape?

A I heard that.

Q Would you also agree that the description of buoyant, lithe dance music applies to "As Clean As They Wanna Be," as well as "As Nasty As They Wanna Be"?

A I would say that it definitely doesn't, because the rhythms, the raps on "As Clean As They Wanna Be," the delivery of raps, does not have the same kind of conviction, and the rappers' rhythms aren't as strong on "As Clean As They Wanna Be" as they are on "As Nasty As They Wanna Be."

So, with the exception of one song, the versions on "As Clean As They Wanna Be" are not as strong as on "As Nasty As They Wanna Be."

THE COURT: Which song is that?

THE WITNESS: That's the song "Me So Horny."

Q Do the other bass music bands—

And which ones are there?

A There's a guy out of Atlanta, M.C. Shy D.; there's two girls named Latrim [phonetic]; there's a Miami girl named Unket [phonetic]; and a Miami performer named Luanne Love [phonetic].

Q   Do they all utilize sexually explicit lyrics?

A   No.

Q   You commented that the Two Live Crew did . . . effective blues interpretation on their album.
     Would sexually explicit lyrics be essential to blues?

A   Well, sexually explicit lyrics have played a part of jazz traditionally.

Q   Is it essential?

A   Is it essential? No.

Q   And you agree, they do a portion of reggae?

A   That's correct.

Q   Would you say that the sexually explicit lyrics are essential to the section of reggae as performed in the base reggae format?

A   No. You're getting closer to the core. The specific type of Jamaican music that's [being interpreted] on this record is dance hall records, and specific dance hall music called slack music or poonan [phonetic] music, which is generally sexually explicit.
     They use slacks such as poonan, in a way a Jamaican audience will be able to understand is sexually explicit.

Q   But that's not an American music format, is that correct; so American standards won't apply to it if it were played in Jamaica; right?

A   I don't understand the question.

Q   You don't find their vulgar comedy very funny; do you?

A   Not for very long.

MR. JOLLY: I don't have any additional questions.

MR. ROGOW: Nothing further.

THE COURT: Mr. Leland, you told us that "As Nasty As They Wanna Be" sold one point six million copies?

THE WITNESS: That's what I've read.

THE COURT: How many copies of "As Clean as They Wanna Be" sold?

THE WITNESS: In the same interview, the citation is five hundred thousand copies.*

THE COURT: You're familiar with scat singing?

THE WITNESS: Yes, a little bit.

---

*Later on in the trial Rogow noted that the actual number of copies sold of *Nasty* and *Clean* were approximately 1.7 million and 250,000 respectively.

THE COURT: Tell us what that means, what that term defines.

THE WITNESS: That's a jazz singer improvising rhythmic melody without using words.

THE COURT: If we took the lyrics out of "As Nasty As They Wanna Be" and substituted that for scat singing, how many copies do you think they would have sold?

THE WITNESS: All depends on the quality of scat singing. I can't answer that question.

THE COURT: But we do know that "As Clean As They Wanna Be" sold five hundred thousand copies?

THE WITNESS: Based on that interview, yes.

THE COURT: Thank you, sir, you may step down.

In the testimony of Carlton Long, a Rhodes scholar, the defense hoped to show the historical, cultural influences that made the 2 Live Crew's music valid and well inside that white picket fence that protects free speech. Long's testimony was designed to show that this music was being condemned by people who had no frame of reference which would allow them to properly evaluate it. The people condemning the music from a black, poor and urban culture were from a white middle class.

Carlton Long walked to the stand with the self-assurance of a man who is at home in almost any circumstances. Carlton at twenty-nine was employed by the city council of New York and moonlighted as a consultant on black culture. At the time of the trial he was just months short of joining Columbia University as an associate professor of political science with a fresh Ph.D. A native of the rougher streets of Gary, Indiana, he earned that particular degree at Oxford University in England, which he attended as a Rhodes scholar. As a high school student he studied in Mexico due to his command of Spanish. As a Rhodes scholar he had distinguished himself academically and also by his high degree of social commitment. In his opening examination, Rogow established that Carlton was a product of mean urban streets but had been educated in a white, high-class environment.

The following is condensed from the testimony of Carlton Long being questioned by Bruce Rogow:

Q   Have you studied black literature?

A   Yes.

Q   Have you studied the black cultural experience?

A   Yes. In London I made a concrete effort to live in a black (mostly Afro-Caribbean) neighborhood and also in a posh white neighborhood because I wanted to understand what the blacks are subjected to in that country.

Q   Have you ever heard of rap music?

A   Yes, I have.

Q   In Gary, Indiana, while you were growing up?

A   When I graduated high school. That was when rap was beginning to catch on.

Q   Have you ever testified before in any proceeding?

A   Yes, in Alabama. Two months ago.

Q   With regard to what recording?

A   *Move Somethin'* by 2 Live Crew.

Q   Have you heard *As Nasty As They Wanna Be*?

A   Yes. Some sixty times in order to study the cultural aspects of the recording.

Q   Which components did you examine?

A   The lyrics specifically.

Q   What were you searching for in those lyrics?

A   What I attempted to do was to place them into a cultural and historical context. The historical would be inherently political.

Q   Tell me about the cultural context?

A   When I say that I attempt to look at not only what is being said now or how musical lyrics might be expressed today but to look at the trends of African-American expression since the Colonial period.

Q   Why is that important?

A   It is terribly important to understand this in context if you want to see where it came from. Trends and influences.

Q   Do white people and black people hear this music the same way?

A   Not at all.

Q   What are the reasons for that?

A   The music has a certain cultural context. It involves a number of traditions, which are themselves indigenous to Afro-American culture and point all the way back to an African past.

Q   Can you give us some examples of that?

A   Several, in fact. One important tradition would be Doing the

Dozens, then Boasting and also Call and Response. All of these are traditionally black in origin and go back to Africa or to earliest slavery.

Call and Response has been traced back to West Africa. In this tradition a leader would introduce a theme or an idea to a group and they would all respond, and that response would be an affirmation or an agreement on the original statement that the leader introduced. There was an example of that Call and Response in the movie *The Color Purple* when the lady was calling out to the people in a church service and they were responding in a song called "Speak to me Lord." It was a very emotional scene.

The Judge says that this is nothing new or black but is common in church services everywhere. As in the common prayer book, he says.

A   Yes, but in the black culture it is apt to be an emotional, impromptu response. When the theme is introduced the leader does not know exactly what will come back.

The Judge says that's Jazz.

A   When I say S, you say E; when I say X, you say SEX. And he [Luther] changes the form of Call and Response by having the two sides playing against each other. The girls say, "All fellows eat pussy!" and the guys say, "All hos suck dick!" Then he incorporates the Miller Lite beer theme and says, "Is it less filling?" and the response is, "No, it tastes great!" and so forth and it moves from debate, as in the commercials, to the dynamic between two groups. And it is a fun thing for the participants and it brings them together, in effect, bonding them.

The Judge says this is not peculiar to black churches but also holds for white church services. Dr. Long explains that this particular form of Call and Response is an urban street tradition adapted from black church services. The obvious difference is that the 2 Live Crew's Call and Response is secular.

Q   You mentioned "Doing the Dozens"?
A   Doing the Dozens is definitely a black thing and dates back to

slavery. It is a word game that deals with insults. It was a tool to toughen up people's skins to insults. It's also a game that hones mental skills and is based on one-upmanship. Black kids and adults like this and see it as a game. According to Reginald Jones, who wrote *Black Psychology*, it serves as a group survival skill.

The Dozens were designed as a defense for the society of slaves, who were treated as subhuman beings, and given rigid social codes by their owners, which were not to be violated. When Emmett Till, a retarded fourteen-year-old black child, referred to a white woman as Babe, he was murdered. The social code said that you would swallow back insults and that you would not look white people in the eye and that to show further that you were confused, or unsure, you would shuffle from one foot to the other while being addressed by whites.

Q   Is Doing the Dozens represented in this recording?

A   Yes, throughout. "My mamma and yo mamma was talkin' a little shit—My mamma called yo mamma a bull-dagger bitch." The section about Abe Lincoln, "Abe Lincoln was a hell of a man, jumped through the window with his dick in his hand," is as well because of the irreverence for the man who is credited with freeing the slaves. The only time you would alter the dozens is when someone you were playing with had a dead mother or sister or whatever because the goal is not to cause real emotional pain.

Q   You mentioned Boasting as another tradition incorporated into the music.

A   Boasting is a way to inflate yourself. To enhance your image among your peers. It might look like arrogance on the face of it, but if you are stuck in a position of being impoverished or disadvantaged it is terribly important to be able to elevate yourself to a level most people take for granted.

Q   How about sexual boasting?

A   This is important, especially if you are not well off financially. Sex is the great equalizer and for those without any great deal of status it gives a sense of being a man. This is not only a black thing but exhibits itself in white society as well. This appears throughout the albums of 2 Live Crew. I remember a diamond ad in *The New Yorker* that said something like, she married you for better or worse, show her how it's going with a diamond. 2 Live would say, "Want a rock, then suck my dick!" It amounts to the same thing but with a street spin.

Q Is it important to try and understand these traditions in trying to understand the recording?

A Yes. Because all of this is a code and you have to try and get into the code to understand the tapes of 2 Live Crew.

Q Is boasting humorous?

A Incredibly humorous like the dozens. You might say, "Those are some sorry-ass shoes." The response might be "Your mamma didn't think so last night."

Q Can not understanding these traditions impede the understanding of this music?

A Definitely.

Q Is there anything of political importance here?

A Definitely. There's a section where they talk about Georgie Porgie being a man and not a boy. That goes to the heart of the civil rights struggle and the demand to be called a man and not a boy. Just the fact that they have chosen to express themselves as they have is political. They are saying, "I am a man and I'll talk as I please and you have to either accept me as I am or not at all."

Q Does the music have entertainment value?

A Definitely. It's funny and good rap music.

Q Does the music have serious literary value?

A As poetry it is very good. I have taught poetry workshops. The work is filled with personification, alliteration and rhyme.

Q Would street people know these terms?

A Some of my friends at Harvard would not necessarily know them.

Q In terms of looking at the material, does it matter if the words are profane, indecent or shocking?

A No, absolutely not. In fact, in one song, "The Seven Bisos," they invented a new language.

Carlton Long finished by saying that the tape has serious literary value, serious artistic value, serious social value, entertainment value and cultural value. He also responded to Rogow's question as to his fee for appearing in court. Five thousand dollars.

In the cross-examination phase, Mr. Jolly got Dr. Long to say that he had been a witness for 2 Live in Alabama some few weeks earlier at twenty percent of the fee. He also explained that he had written an article for *Newsweek* on rap and rappers getting a bad rap. He further explained that *Nasty* does not chronicle the "black" experience but one small subculture within that group.

That was really it for the defense side.

The following pages contain Bruce Rogow's summation.

MR. ROGOW: This case, of course, has two parts, and I'll just address at this moment the part that Mr. Jolly just talked about . . . Mr. Jolly uses a lot of words, and words are powerful, but none of the words that he uses are relevant to what the issue is before this court: abomination, street talk, is not what it's about.

All it is about is the three-part Miller test. It's all about . . . community standards and the prurient interest, a narrow kind of question of what are the community standards, and does this have a tendency to appeal to the prurient interest . . . If it's obscene, I concur that it's not protected. But it's not obscene until the government proves it is . . .

I think that we have an advantage in this case, and the advantage is that we start off with the constitutional protection.

The Constitution is a restraint on government power and the First Amendment is restrictive on government power. So for the government to take this tape and render it obscene, they've got a heavy burden to carry under the Constitution . . .

First, the appeal to the prurient interest. I think it's important that we start with what Roth says. It says sex and obscenity are not synonymous.

Obscene material deals with sex in a matter which appeals to the prurient interest . . . The word obscene signifies that form of immorality that has a tendency to excite lustful thoughts. . . .

You certainly don't have any evidence from the State's side, from Sheriff Navarro's side, with regard to either community standards or prurient interest.

And then we come to our case . . .

[We introduced material other than the Two Live tape] basically for two purposes. One, to demonstrate what is out there readily available in the community.

Most important, the tape from Bob News, which is right across in the Copper Kettle, just a short throw from the courthouse, right here in this community.

Doesn't mean it's wonderful stuff, that's not the point of it. The point is, in this community, that kind of material is readily available.

And the magazines introduced to the Court were also readily available. So it was presented for that purpose, to show you in a larger picture what's available in the community, to help you try to judge the community standards.

And it was also provided to demonstrate things that do appeal to the prurient interest. And what were they? Visual things.

And Dr. Haber testified that in her experience as a psychologist, in the work that she's done, that it is the visual that excites people.

THE COURT: Men, she said.

MR. ROGOW: Yes, and women read it . . . [There is] no evidence, no evidence at all, that a recording is anything that would in this community, for the average person, tend to incite lustful thoughts; and, therefore, the prurient interest . . .

Remember, under Roth and these cases, obscenity is not indecency, obscenity is not "fuck the draft" in the courthouse, under Cohen versus California.

I remember what the court said, well, that's political speech . . . Of course, it's interesting, when I read . . . what Justin Harlin said about sex being such a big force in human life, that he put it on the same level as . . . political speech.

In fact, most people would rather talk about sex than politics. So, what you have is speech that is known in this community, and in every community; but let's focus on this community and the evidence in this case.

We had a tape of *Eddie Murphy Raw*. Purchased where? Blockbuster Video, the family video store. This is evidence of the community standard.

We played that part of the tape. Your Honor heard it, the same words that are used on the Two Live Crew tape—and I don't need to repeat them—are used by Eddie Murphy on this video tape that any family person can buy at Blockbuster Video stores.

You don't have to be an adult to rent that, you can go in and rent that any time, and that's sitting there on the shelf in our most esteemed video store in the county.

Now . . . that's the evidence in this case, Your Honor, with regard to community standards.

And if anything, the evidence in this case is overwhelming that the community standard of the average person in this community is a tolerant one. And there's nothing the matter with that.

What other evidence is there of community standard? There is evidence from the Broward Sheriff's Office . . .

As the court will remember, in that file, there was not one complaint, one piece of material, evidence, letter, thought, anything else, from anybody in Broward County complaining about "As Nasty As They Wanna Be."

The only thing from Broward County that's in that file is a letter from a lady in Cooper City, that says, protect our First Amendment rights.

Is that relevant to the issue of community standards? I think it is . . .

As to prurient interest, [there is] no evidence at all that this—under the Roth standard—appeals to the prurient interest.

We sat in this courtroom, we listened to the tape, and it's interesting what we heard. . . .

Is there anything in there that appealed to the prurient interest by any evidence in this case? I don't think there is.

Dr. Haber's testimony is that her experience shows that this is not the kind of thing that would.

And, again, I disagree with Mr. Jolly. What is he saying—that because she's a psychologist and she treats people, that all these people are deviants, that only deviants go to psychologists?

That's a mischaracterization of the evidence and of her testimony. Average people go to psychologists, and these are average problems, and she talks to them about sex, because psychologists do talk about sex.

Because, just as Roth says, it is the great primary human motivating force. It makes sense that Havelock Ellis and Masters and Johnson deal with sex, because both psychology and the law recognize that sex is an important force in our lives . . .

Now, there's a second [part], of course, to the community standard test, too, about whether this would be a patently offensive description of sexual conduct . . .

Something can depict or . . . define sexual activity in patently, obviously, offensive ways, but that doesn't make it obscene, because [it's] got to [satisfy the Miller criteria] on all three fronts . . .

Whether or not it's patently offensive, obviously offensive to the average person, I'll tell you the truth. Judge, I don't know, and I don't welcome your job.

Because these words have followed me ever since I got into this kind of business of trying to figure out what they mean; the average person, what the average person finds to be patently, obviously, offensive . . .

But I'm not going to argue about whether or not it's descriptive of sexual conduct. It is. No question about it. But, of course, there's nothing the matter with that, because that's what the cases say, sex, you can talk about sex.

You know, I remember, thinking about it this morning, cunnilingus, fellatio, masturbation, pederasty, why these—

THE COURT: That's from *Hair*.

MR. ROGOW: That's right, *Hair*. And the name of the song, "Sodomy," twenty-five years ago, Southeastern Promotions versus Conrad tried to take that out of commercial use.

And not only did they sing the song, Judge, but they sang it naked.

Patently offensive? I don't know, but I'm not going to fight about patently. I'm not conceding it, but I'll leave it to you to figure that one out; but I am going to fight about serious literary artistic value . . .

The evidence in this case is absolutely overwhelming that this has serious artistic value.

Greg Baker, the *New Times* music critic . . . had an understanding of hip-hop music.

. . . [And] that Leland really is the country's expert. Baker is a local expert, but [Leland] does the job, this has artistic value, he knows about the beat, the breaks, the scratches, about the purpose of the music, about mixing, about sampling, about fading, about making new music.

And you know, all this is a real challenge . . .

I never knew about these things before I got involved in this. I have no idea what the court knew about this kind of music.

But that's why the test is the evidence in the case. And the evidence in the case is, this is music, this is new music.

Mr. Leland's testimony about the Grammys just recognizing rap music two years ago is a very clear piece of evidence about how new the music is.

THE COURT: This isn't a case about rap music, though.

MR. ROGOW: It is a case about—

THE COURT: You think rap music is on trial here?

MR. ROGOW: This rap music is on trial.

THE COURT: Oh, this rap music.

MR. ROGOW: That's right, this rap music. But it's got to fit into a context, Judge.

I mean, this is not just being dropped from the sky with a bunch of dirty words, this is being done in the context of a developing genre of music.

And that's why, again, Mr. Jolly's wrong, hip-hop is relevant to this, and rap adding to hip-hop is relevant to this. And "As Nasty As They Wanna Be" adding to rap to hip-hop is relevant to this, it's relevant to the question of whether or not this has serious artistic value . . . And one of the things we all have to learn, I think, in dealing with anything that comes into our lives in a new way, is to place it in a larger perspective, to understand it for what it is, where it's come from, and perhaps to where it's going . . .

We had [Baker and Leland] come in, and they were not shaken on cross-examination, their testify is unrebutted that this music has serious artistic value.

And Mr. Long, the cultural value, this is part of what I was talking about before when I say you have to see this, anything new, and understand where it's come from and what it is.

This is street music . . .

And remember, Judge, the test for serious artistic value is not a community test, either, and it's not a majority test, it's under Pope versus Illinois, whether or not a reasonable person would think that this has artistic value.

Mr. Leland is certainly a reasonable person. Mr. Baker is a reasonable person. They represent, presumably—because they've been hired by these newspapers that have some substantial distribution—they represent the thought of reasonable people.

And so the testimony in this case, from reasonable people, is that this has serious artistic value. And that's why when Mr. Jolly says, take it off all the streets, he's missing the point all together . . .

This is not a majority rule issue. [It] doesn't have to be a whole lot of folks that find serious artistic value in something, but it has to be a reasonable person that finds it . . .

I think what's happened is that there's been a confusion here between indecency, between shocking words, between concerns for people, which are legitimate concerns.

The confusion between that and the First Amendment standard takes me right back to Officer Wichner. He didn't have the foggiest notion about what the First Amendment standards were.

Miller versus California; not his job, he doesn't have any idea about it. I think it's wrong, Judge. It is his job.

847.11 of the Florida Statute, that he's enforcing, uses those Miller standards. Says them almost exactly. He didn't know anything about it.

What he got caught up with was having that tape transcribed and looking at those words, reading those words. And that's another mistake in this case.

These words were not made to be read, they were made to be played. If Skyywalker Records, Inc., and the Two Live Crew wanted these words to be read, they would have had a lyric sheet.

There's no lyric sheet there. These words were not made to be taken out of context, to have six songs typed up—and mistyped, too, in the transcription—and then read and dwelled on word for word to see the shock value of those words.

That's not what it's for. It was for dancing, it was to strengthen the beat, it was to make it work. And you heard Mr. Leland testify that "As Nasty As They Wanna Be" is serious art, it has the beat.

And the "As Nasty As They Wanna Be" record is the one with the great beat. That really is the one that is much better art than the clean recording that Your Honor inquired about . . .

So there's been confusion here about what the test is and how you apply it. I don't say that this is an easy matter for lay people, for sheriffs, for deputy sheriffs.

It's not. It hasn't been an easy matter for the Supreme Court. But the Supreme Court laid down the guidelines for us.

And we came to this court ready to follow those guidelines, and although it wasn't our burden to prove that this record is not obscene under the Miller versus California standards, they have utterly failed to carry their burden.

And we carried our burden without any kind of hesitation under at least clearly two of the three Miller standards.

But, of course, all we have to do is win on one and this record goes home.

Does Your Honor want me to argue the other [issue]?

THE COURT: Yes . . . The plaintiff has asked the Court to enjoin the sheriff from conducting ex-parte probable cause determinations of obscenity, among other things.

I think I quoted that right.

MR. ROGOW: Your Honor, I want to be clear about what we sought in the complaint.

THE COURT: It says: "This action also seeks to enjoin the defendant and his deputies from arresting persons who sell "As Nasty As They Wanna Be" to persons over the age of eighteen, and to enjoin him and his deputies from seeking ex-parte probable cause determinations of obscenity without the opportunity for a prompt subsequent fair and reliable adversarial hearing to determine whether presumptively First Amendment protected material is obscene.''

MR. ROGOW: Yes, and . . . Paragraph C in the prayer for relief, is very important, Your Honor, because it brings it all together.

Declare that the procedures used by Defendant Navarro to chill and restrain the sale, distribution, lending, giving, playing or otherwise disseminating productive protective First Amendment materials violates the First Amendment and the due process clause of the Fourteenth Amendment, and permanently enjoin him from utilizing such processes.

The first issue is, is there a prior restraint by this kind of procedure. And I think first we have to talk about the evidence which describes the procedure . . .

Here's the evidence. Officer Wichner goes to the judge, Officer Wichner gets a probable cause order. Officer Wichner and deputies throughout the county canvas the record stores in the county and give them a copy of the probable cause order.

And look at it two ways, in the light most favorable to them, advise them that if they sell the record, they could be subject to arrest; a felony for minors, a misdemeanor for adults.

Or, as one of the memos in the file says, [threatens them with arrest] if they sell this material. And, of course, we had the testimony of Adrianne Heinz who got just that impression, that that's what was told to him.

And the survey testimony from Emily Douthhitt who says that thirty-four, I think it was, of the forty-one stores she called—the other ones being Christian book stores or book stores that never carried it—said, can't sell it due to the ordinance . . .

And so these people respected that court's probable cause finding and recognized the power of the sheriff's department to enforce that probable cause finding.

And up to that point, it's okay, everybody did right. But after that, the sheriff had a duty to make sure that there was the trial for obscenity. There wasn't.

So there's been confusion about this from the start. Confusion and misunderstanding what the procedures are. Confusion and misunderstanding that talk about sex and four-letter words and indecent language, is not obscenity under the Miller versus California standards.

And that's why we're here before you today. We're here before you today to tell the sheriff, to tell the community, that the First Amendment does mean what it says; it means the government shall make no law restraining free speech, except under Roth versus United States, if it's obscene.

But in order for it to be obscene, the government has to prove all three of these Miller tests. They didn't use the procedures that were proper, and they didn't have any proof to meet all three tests.

And for those reasons, there ought to be:

A, a permanent injunction enjoining the sheriff from engaging in this kind of procedure;

And, B, a declaratory judgment declaring that "As Nasty As They Wanna Be" is protected by the First Amendment.

THE COURT: Thank you, Mr. Rogow.

When Rogow finishes his summation, I'm all smiles. It looks like I'm getting my money's worth. Allen Jacobi, my entertainment attorney, smells victory and smiles at himself for having the foresight to have gotten me to hire Mr. Rogow. Jacobi is certain that the case is airtight. He looks at Mr. Jolly and smiles like a Cheshire Cat.

When the two sides gather to hear the ruling there is little electricity in the air. Me and my group are waiting for the judge to finish so we can put this behind us. Jack Thompson, Nick Navarro and Mr. Jolly are all standing there cowering like dogs. Judge Gonzalez starts by slamming Navarro for not taking the record to court sooner (nineteen days passed before Rogow had filed the suit). We the plaintiffs square our shoulders and tighten our ties in righteous indignation at the dressing down the sheriff is getting from the judge. Then Gonzalez drops a bomb on us.

The sheriff was found to have used prior restraint and had to pay some twenty-five thousand dollars to the plaintiff in attorneys' fees and lost revenues. But instead of freeing the record from the cloud hanging over it so that we could get the money river flowing again in Broward, we were thrown a curve ball. *Nasty* was declared obscene by Judge Gonzalez. His court order held within the federal district covered by his court, in effect halting sales of *Nasty* in all of South Florida. Gonzalez decided that the recording was legally obscene. Anyone selling it in South Florida could now be arrested and prosecuted.

So set for defeat was the sheriff that he didn't even show up in the courtroom until the final day of the trial. When Gonzalez ruled against the record, Mr. Jolly, Navarro's lawyer, and Navarro seemed every bit as shocked as everyone else. In fact Jack Thompson was the only person in the courtroom who seems to have expected the verdict.

The Gonzalez ruling was a sunbeam breaking out from the dark clouds for the conservative fundamentalists and the sheriff was going to take off his clothes and lay right out in it. He saw this as a signal to gear up for a war with the rappers. From where he was sitting it looked like it was going to be an anti-pornography turkey shoot.

As soon as the Gonzalez ruling was released, saying among other things that *Nasty* was "music for the loins and not the intellect," storm clouds began gathering. The very day after the ruling, a record store owner named Charles Freeman called the press and vowed to sell the record. Freeman, the black owner of E. C. Records of Fort Lauderdale, was arrested for selling the record. Some store owners continued to stock and sell the record even after the Gonzalez ruling came down of June 8, 1990. Some, like Gordon Chin of Uncle Sam's Records of Pompano Beach, sold it even after Charles Freeman was arrested. Freeman's problem was that he confronted Sheriff Navarro on television. Navarro took the challenge and showed up at E. C. Records the next day with a phalanx of newsmen, so that he could arrest Freeman on the air. Freeman would later be convicted and fined a thousand dollars. The judge in the case would order Charles to donate the grand to an elementary school's music program.

The repercussions from the Gonzalez ruling were immediate and deafening. While the *Miami Herald* had in fact previously written that the lyrics were too profane to publish, only a few other newspapers and magazines had published lyrics from *Nasty* before the ruling. One was the newsletter put out by Tipper Gore's organization. *New Times* writer and music critic Greg Baker had used lyrics in an article he did on 2 Live Crew before the controversy. Before the Gonzalez trial, the press was mixed in its defense of the group. There were very few members of the press that loudly questioned whether this record was worth a trial. More than a few thought the record was sexist, misogynistic, vile, vulgar and filthy. Before the trial there was a great deal of criticism in the press from newspapermen as widely divergent as George Will, the conservative columnist from *Newsweek*, and Tom Wicker, the liberal *New York Times* columnist. After the Gonzalez trial, the press closed ranks and became overwhelmingly favorable to the group, universally condemning the authorities and the censorship forces.

Once it was pointed out by other papers in other regions that this assault on *Nasty* was a threat to the First Amendment, the *Miami Herald* quickly got in line with almost every other member of the media and defended 2 Live Crew's right to exist and create their music. In the process the media began a merciless assault on Navarro and Martinez.

As the shock waves radiated outward from the Gonzalez trial, Sheriff Navarro and Governor Martinez must have wished they hadn't listened to Jack Thompson. Martinez, a Republican, was horrified to see his popularity plummet after joining Thompson in attacking 2 Live Crew.

As Bruce Rogow later wrote in *The NOVA Law Review*: "The 2 Live Crew cases involved 'low' language, 'high' law, race and show business and so naturally the case generated a solid wall of publicity." The fact is that there are several file cabinet drawers filled with articles from all over the world that were collected by Luke Records' Debbie Bennett, furnished by the publications and mailed in by fans and supporters worldwide. This library of clippings represents only a small fraction of all the articles written on the subject.

After the Gonzalez trial it became obvious that the state had not proved the record obscene. In fact just the opposite was true. Whether or not it was universally popular (or even slightly popular) music, the fact remained that Bruce Rogow and his witnesses had proved, to the satisfaction of everyone who had covered the trial, that the record flew past not just one, as required, but all the three prongs of Miller vs. California by a wide margin.

Rogow proved, or certainly seemed to prove, that *Nasty*: 1) provides information about a poor, mostly undereducated, segment of the black urban culture and its attitudes about sex and other subjects; 2) in its content sustains a continuing tradition that has historical roots and is culturally significant; 3) is an important variation of rap, a new and valid musical form, 4) is literature; 5) does not violate prevailing community standards; and 6) does not appeal solely to the prurient interests.

It has been suggested (by some attorneys) that Gonzalez found the recording obscene to see what the U.S. Supreme Court would rule because it had been so long since the last obscenity guidelines were established. Although Judge Gonzalez is seen as a Liberal, a Jimmy Carter appointee, it isn't surprising that he wasn't the sort of man who could rub shoulders with *Nasty* without getting shit on his face.

In order to rule as he did, Gonzalez had ignored all of the expert witnesses, and since Navarro didn't have any expert witnesses, the judge had, in effect, made himself the expert witness for the state's case and declared it obscene. Regardless of the fact that Luke Records is almost certain to win on appeal, the judge, himself a resident of Broward County, let the people of Broward know that he agreed with his fellow member of the South Florida Cuba Club, Nick Navarro.

The fact that the judge considered himself to be a music expert or music lover was probably the greatest danger we were facing. It is obvious in reading the transcripts that Gonzalez sees himself as an expert on music. In his interactions with music critics Greg Baker and John Leland, he made the court aware that he was conversant in the terminology of music and that he thought he knew quite a lot about music. A judge like that could take the 2 Live Crew lyrics, and the sampling, as desecration of music. This might just explain why the judge made himself the only expert witness whose opinion mattered to the court. My personal opinion is that Gonzalez had to rule against the home-boy, Narravo, on the complaint, but threw Navarro a bone and slammed the record company for suing in the first place. What did it cost him?

Bruce Rogow was in shock when *Nasty* was ruled obscene. Naturally Bruce had thought the case would be a slide-through. We should have won. The defeat made no sense. Rogow prom-

ised me that we would go immediately to the Eleventh Circuit
Court of Appeals in Atlanta. The grounds for the appeal were
obvious: Judge José Gonzalez had seriously overstepped his
authority in ruling *Nasty* obscene against an overwhelming pre-
ponderance of evidence to the contrary.

I listened, but even knowing that Bruce was right, I felt about
as mad as I can get without losing it completely. I went off on
the sheriff and the judge on the courthouse steps, and called the
Gonzalez ruling toilet paper. My last words, as I stood beside
my car surrounded by a crowd of my supporters, were addressed
to Jack Thompson, who stood nearby talking to reporters. I
said: "Jack, you need to get some pussy!" For the first time that
day, Jack Thompson was total speechless.

8 Morality Police

Friday, two days after the Gonzalez "toilet paper" ruling, we played in Dade County, on Miami Beach at Club Nu. The show there was fairly uneventful. The house was packed and it was hot. There were cops everywhere, in and out of uniform. They had already told us that they didn't have any interest in arresting us for playing to adults. They all said that Navarro was an asshole. They had fun and were laughing and most of them had 2 Live Crew tee-shirts over their shoulders. I signed some autographs for those of them who asked for their kids. As usual, we played a clean show for the kids and then an X-rated show for the adults.

Friction had been building between me and Navarro for the weeks before we played there. He couldn't touch us in Dade County but he was huffin' and puffin' and shoutin' at us over the county line. Then after the Gonzalez deal he went fuckin' crazy and started making a ruckus all over the place. Navarro can't pour piss out of his shoe without having a TV camera crew filming it for the six o'clock news. Me and him both had been

posturing and neither of us was going to back down. I didn't
know this owl-eyed, snow-peaked old fool. Our insults were
being passed, by the media, from me to him and from him to
me, almost faster than we could react, and they were having a
six o'clock news wet dream between the two of us. They kept
stirrin' the shit up and we kept coming to the surface.

I knew that I was within my rights and he was probably acting
like an asshole because he needed to drum up some votes by
attacking some shit to help cover up his latest scandal or
whatever. He stood up and said that anyone who broke the laws
in Broward County would be arrested. Anyone who knows
anything about Broward County knows that it is ten times easier
to get a blow job from a hooker in front of the sheriff's office
than to get a decent haircut. His deputies spend half their time
investigatin' and arrestin' each other—unless the sheriff is leading the cops or a *Geraldo* film crew on a drug hunt, busting
houses that it turns out the neighbors have been complaining
about for months or years. Give the good sheriff a camera crew
and he'll make up that ugly fuckin' face with cold cream packed
under those eyes, suck in that fat-assed gut and do his supercop
job. When Charles Freeman was arrested he had to cool it forty-
five minutes, staring at Detective Eugene McCloud's ugly face
waiting for Navarro to come by and arrest him personally. Some
camera crew—Channel 10, I think—was late getting on the scene
and Navarro waited, in a car down the street, for them to get in
position. Once they were all there and had the tripods all set up
and shit, here came Navarro to arrest a Charles Freeman who
was about to fall the fuck to sleep. Navarro looked like he had
been asleep.

Navarro had said on TV that if one song from the LP *As
Nasty As They Wanna Be* was played in his county, the band
would be arrested and jailed for violating the obscenity laws of
the State of Florida. He basically said for us to stay the fuck out
of Broward County and if we did pass through to keep our
mouths shut. The Miami Beach people and the police chief made
it clear that this wasn't their fight and they didn't want none of
it. Besides most of them are Jewish or Cuban and they did not
want to be seen to be oppressing any freedoms. Jews and most

Cubans know all too well what freedom is worth. So at Club Nu I taunted Navarro and led the crowd in a "Fuck Navarro" chant. Then, I did a "Fuck Martinez" thing. Fuck Navarro, fuck, fuck Navarro! and Fuck Martinez, fuck, fuck Martinez! All these people screamin' that shit at the top of their lungs. The walls were shakin' and shit. Even the cops were screaming Fuck Navarro! See, that made the concert a political rally. Bruce Rogow had said that political rallies are protected, so I asked him what constituted a political rally. He said "Fuck the Draft" was considered protected speech. So I said, can I say "Fuck Martinez"? He said, "Say fuck anyone you please that holds office."

The following night, June 9, 1990, at the Club Futura, which is just inside Broward County, we happily repeated the political chants into the mini-cassette recorders that were sticking out of the deputies' shirt pockets and purses and shit. The crowd was like maybe five hundred and mostly eighteen to twenty-five, I think. Motherfuckin' cops were everywhere and they were very easy to spot because they were old and shit and dressed like they had run through K Mart in the middle of the night, grabbing shit off the racks with the lights out. Like undercover cops always look, like hicks come to the city for the first time. They also kept making eye contact with each other, and nodding at each other and prowling about with their arms crossed, and they talked into their pockets and shit. Just like cops. Cop-clowns. You would think that cops in plain clothes should be kind of hard to spot, right? Also, we recognized McCloud as the fat detective who had stood around with Charles Freeman when he was arrested on TV, and he had this tape recorder stickin' out of his shirt pocket with the little green light burning. That blonde bitch that later testified at the Futura trial, looked like a old drunk ho. I think she was drunk and tryin' to dance and look sexy. And we weren't sure if she was a cop or some old drunk that had stumbled into the club to pick up a man and we were laughin' at her while we were playin'.

The crowd was even louder in its political chanting there in the good sheriff's backyard. The cops all just stood there, in their outfits, and glared at us like we were raping nuns.

We knew we would be arrested that night at Club Futura. There was no way I could back down and call myself a man and I was pissed but it was funny. I'd be tryin' to watch TV and I'd see that asshole sheriff with them big ole eyes that looked like they had tea bags glued under 'em saying he was going to do this and that to us. The man looks like a worn-out Captain Kangaroo who's a lot more interested in that drama shit, and his image, than fighting crime. But hey, if that's all it takes to keep Broward County voters happy, who am I to tell them they could do better?

Club Futura was smaller than Club Nu and it is in the middle of fuckin' nowhere near Hollywood, Florida. The crowd had a blast and was laughin' and singin' along with the lyrics and shit. People were there for one of three reasons: to have a really good time, to watch the arrests, or to have several drinks on the county's tab and gather evidence for the fuckin' arrest. They had fourteen fuckin' detectives but two, with three sets of handcuffs, would have been plenty. If the sheriff had come in and said, "Y'all boys meet me down at the jail," we would have. We knew we weren't breaking the law so we had nothing to worry about. I had the bail money, somethin' like eight thousand dollars, in my pocket 'cause I didn't know but they might arrest the dancers and all that shit along with me.

We had started with the PG show for the shorties and then cleared the place and performed an X-rated show for the adults. Policemen stood and checked IDs at the door and no one under eighteen was let in, period. No one under eighteen even tried.

After the show was over there was something like thirty deputies around the place and across the road. They waited until me and Chris Wongwon a couple of miles away in the limousine (they said later that they didn't arrest us at the club because they were scared of a riot) before they came flashing up with their lights on. Everyone of them was followin' us and nobody followed Mark Ross and David Hobbs. The cops naturally must have tipped off the press to where they were going to pull us over, and there were plenty of media people there. Even the guy from *Newsweek* was there. They must have come with the cops because no one was following us when we left. Then they hooked us up with handcuffs and the guy from *Newsweek*, Spencer Reiss, told me that he thought the woman driving the van they stuck us in was with us. She was a deputy but he thought she looked like either a ho or a Move Somethin' dancer with our group.

Thanks to the press, America saw the Skyywalker emblem on my tee-shirt as I was led to the police van. The truth is that I was wearing a jacket over the shirt during the show but the cops had taken it off me when they cuffed us. George Lucas's people saw the "Skyywalker Records" logo across my back and it cost me a great deal of money since I was technically violating the court order not to use the name again.

Me and Chris were booked that morning, June 10, 1990, at like three o'clock a.m. The sun was up when we got out. Chris was handcuffed behind his back even though his left arm is like a wet noodle from a car crash. These deputies were all over the place like they had done something really important. There must a been a hundred of them, before it was over, comin' over and lookin' in the windows like we were the first black men in handcuffs they had ever seen, and they were all slapping each other on the back like catching a white limousine going thirty-five miles an hour was something that they had never been able to pull off before. I consider that I have a good relationship with most cops. I use off-duty policemen to help me at my clubs and any events I have, and most cops that stop me say, "Go on, you have had enough trouble." Most of these Broward deputies were doing what they were doing because they had been ordered to. I mean the language in any cop car is worse than one of our concerts. Cops know how to cuss and talk about sex a lot better than we do.

So then we were booked and we knew that we were in for a fight. The score was two to one with Navarro. But I still knew if we could get to a jury trial, that Bruce Rogow would smoke the fuckers, and I was ready for my turn at bat.

9

The Broward County Obscenity Trial, October 1990

"Censorship is to art what lynching is to justice."
—*Henry Louis Gates*

The 2 Live Crew misdemeanor obscenity trial was followed, day after day, by most of the free world. As the main defendant, I had my face reproduced on virtually every newspaper, news magazine and television station in America and Europe for weeks. For the two weeks of the trial, the streets around the building were packed with television trucks, radio news wagons, fans, fundamentalists, curious attorneys and sightseers. The media understood that the trial's impact on obscenity could well equal the impact that the Scopes Monkey Trial in rural Tennessee decades earlier had had on education. The chief adversary in both landmark trials was the same general group of people: white, middle-class, religious fanatics.

The obscenity trial of Florida vs. Luther Campbell, Christopher "Fresh Kid Ice" Wongwon, and Mark "Brother Marquis" Ross was more than a trial for an obscene performance given in some small run-down club on the outskirts of Broward County. The trial told the story of worlds and of cultures in collision. It was "important" because in it the religious right targeted a specific creative work by a major artist. The trial spotlighted the conservative white faction and that group's fear and misunderstanding of the growing black urban population.

The Broward County trial is a story about one group trying to impose boundaries on the behavior and language that it will tolerate from another group, and to do so without taking basic cultural (and racial) differences into account.

Jury selection gets off to a bang of a start when Judge June Johnson reads the information to the first twenty-five prospective jurors. This reading of the charges (which will not be published in any of the local daily newspapers because of the language) brings me to my feet right away, yelling: What the fuck is this shit! With that said, I walked right out of the courtroom with a shocked Bruce Rogow on my tail.

This is what Judge Johnson was reading:

> Luther Campbell, Mark Ross and Chris Wongwon as live persons did knowingly conduct, perform or participate in by words and/or by conduct, an obscene show or performance which was obscene and which included but was not limited to a rendition of "C'mon Babe," and a rendition of an apparent version of "Me So Horny," said renditions consisted of verbal depictions of sexual conduct, to wit sexual intercourse, deviant sexual intercourse, as defined by Florida Statute 847.001 and actual physical contact with a person's unclothed buttocks, examples of which are: "Let me stick my dick in your behind," "I'll be fucking you and you'll be sucking me, lick my ass up and down lick it till your tongue turns doodoo brown." And in the course of said performance did simulate an act of deviant sexual intercourse as defined in Florida Statute 847.0011, examples of which are: Placing the face of a woman into or in very close proximity to the groin of one of the performers, Luther Campbell, and through the acts of another performer, Mark Ross, uncovering and exposing to view the breast of another female.

I did not then understand that what I had heard read was just the charge and not trial evidence. I had been assured that the jury would not hear the lyrics read in isolation, out of the context of the tapes that would be introduced as evidence. Unfamiliar with courtroom procedure, I freaked out, thinking I had been ambushed by a system that I didn't understand or trust. Bruce Rogow pulled me into an empty judge's chamber to explain what had just happened. Then he coaxed me back into the courtroom. When we returned, Mark and Chris are sitting with their attorneys, Allen Jacobi and Randy Strauss, staring at the judge who is still reading the information. There is a look of discomfort and confusion in their eyes.

Jury selection is an art. Rogow isn't happy with the system, which he feels excludes young people and especially blacks, since the juries are selected by voter roles. Though some 13.5 percent of Broward County is black, only 8.5 percent of Broward's voters and potential jurors are black. There seems to be a shortage of young people and blacks (people who would best understand what we do, and fans of rap music in particular) in the potential jury pools.

In the Charles Freeman trial, Rogow had challenged the way juries are selected in Broward County trials, but that judge had ruled against him and Freeman's jury had consisted of six affluent white women over forty. To those women Charles Freeman might as well have been a rapist-murderer who had been captured behind the Broward Country Club after slitting the throats of their very closest friends. Freeman never had a snowball's chance even with Rogow sitting beside him. In Freeman's trial one of the juror's residences was appraised at $3.6 million. These people were light years from understanding rap or the culture that spawned it.

Prosecutor Leslie Robson wants to know why the jury has to be slanted toward African-Americans for the 2 Live to get a fair hearing.

Is this bitch from Mars? I ask.

Judge June Johnson agrees that it might well be a concern but asks if she might withhold her judgment till after the jury pool has been examined. By now, thanks to the media, everybody who hasn't been living on the moon knows that middle-aged white people from affluent backgrounds have no real solid grasp of black urban music. Especially ethnic music that talks about fucking doggie style, licking assholes and sucking on skin ween-ies.

Leslie Robson isn't actually from Mars at all. She was born in Hong Kong and raised in England. She hardly seems the foam-ing-mouthed, right winger on a mission from God to cleanse Broward County of the black, devil-heathens who talk about fucking and sucking like it is something completely normal, and sometimes comical. There she is in her business suit, whining across the courtroom. Nothing pleases her. Within minutes everyone in the crowded courtroom is saying, "Shut the fuck up, fool!" with their eyes or under their breath every time she opens her mouth. After her first four hundred objections, even the judge looks like she would rather be bending sheet metal in a Boeing plant than listening to Robson.

Robson's associate, Pedro Dijols, is a nice enough looking young man. He is well dressed, intelligent and all that. He is also black—Puerto Rican really, but, most importantly, he looks black to the jury. Pedro is from New York but attended law school in Florida. He denies that he was "volunteered" for this case because he is black but nobody in America believes him for a moment. His specialty is DUIs (driving under the influence) and he has a damned good conviction rate in that arena. Robson never seems to let Pedro ask questions. Until later, that is, after she collapses in the lady's bathroom one day during the trial, and Pedro has to take over.

The entire case boils down to whether the obscenity laws have been breached. Rogow will say over and over again that according to Miller vs. California, if any one reasonable person says that the material (the tape of the performance) meets even one of the four criteria then it is not obscene. Dijols and his buddy Leslie Robson will say that obscene is in the eye of the beholder and their eyes are beholding a big, nasty evil. Robson, who looks like she is smelling something unpleasant even when she smiles, looks like someone who could be driven to sleepless nights knowing that people are saying such things in Broward County. Dijols looks bored mostly, except when he is manning the sound boards and directing the "evidence" (tapes) at the jury. Dijols's nature is competitive enough that he will try and win this case up to the last minute.

Robson does get four songs from *As Nasty As They Wanna Be* introduced as evidence and played for the judge before prospective jurors are brought in. The judge wants to hear them and asks, "Are they singing or talking?" Rapping, answers Rogow. The members of 2 Live Crew, who have heard the lyrics before, smile when the judge looks at them. "Would one hear this sort of music in Vegas?" she wonders. Rogow assures her not. I have this picture of Wayne Newton, standing in front of an orchestra, running through a medley of rap's greatest hits and sliding from "Me So Horny" through about twenty rap tunes and closing with "Ice, Ice Baby."

Pedro Dijols spends the first part of the trial looking like he is strictly table dressing for the media. "Look Bubba, it *was* a fair trial. Hell, they was prosecuted by one of their own kind!" Later Dijols will say that as soon as he heard the state's evidence he knew the case was a suicide mission. That is proof, he will say, that he volunteered for the case. In his defense, even in the face of certain defeat and looking the buffoon on an international stage, he does his best to play a convincing role. It is his first obscenity prosecution, and considering the drubbing he will take from the press, surely his last.

Leslie Robson does not imagine it might be possible to lose. You see in her eyes that she expects us to be beaten to the full extent of the law. When she looks at Mark, Chris and me, sparks fly from her eyes.

The prosecution, desperate to let the jury hear just how nasty and perverted and twisted the 2 Live lyrics are, insists on getting a transcript of the poorly recorded concert in the hands of the jury to help them decide if the performance is as obscene as Leslie insists it is. There were eight deputies inside Club Futura that night and each was required to make a transcript of their tapes. Eight deputies spent a week doing this while muggers mugged, purse snatchers snatched, scammers robbed the elderly, crack dealers dealt, and killers killed. Not one of these transcriptions will be admitted as evidence. They will languish forever in a dark property room with the four-by-six-foot blow-ups of the lyrics of the songs which cost hundreds of dollars each but will also never be introduced into evidence. If you don't have a case, make it as big as you can.

The state will try, time and time again, to get these lyrics on paper in the jurors' hands. It is as though the full shock value will be lost unless the jurors can run their eyes over these hideous words. Suck, fuck, asshole, dick, etcetera.

Robson is like a pit bull on pep pills with the transcript issue. She mentions it numerous times in an attempt to pave the way for how pathetic the tape quality is going to be. Every time Robson says transcript, Rogow yells, "Move for a mistrial, Your Honor!" He insists that the record is not on trial. In fact the record was already judged obscene by a federal judge, as Robson tells the court on more than one occasion. Judge Johnson does not seem to find Robson amusing. Neither does the audience. Nor do members of the jury, who have taken to staring at the ceiling or into their laps every time she opens her mouth.

Leslie Robson and the prosecution save their biggest ploy for last. Robson moves that the good judge recuse herself from hearing the case. Why? Because she went to NOVA University and Bruce Rogow was teaching there. In fact, he taught her. The state says that this will prejudice her. You can hear a pin drop as Judge Johnson thinks the motion over. The good judge has been accused of favoritism, of, if you will, being a bad judge. It is a big gamble and might backfire. With a lot of judges it might have. Judge Johnson insists that she doesn't remember Rogow's course, particularly. She says she has a far closer relationship with Pedro Dijols as he tries most of his DUI cases before her bench. Johnson says that she doesn't particularly want to try this case, but will certainly not step down. "That's that," Johnson says. But Robson manages to get a Writ of Prohibition, an emergency order that will stop the trial until the matter is heard before another judge. Judge Johnson says fine, let's go now; and everyone in the courtroom, and I mean everyone in the courtroom (plus some people who are in the hallways and decide this is worth seeing), goes upstairs and crowds into the hallway outside another judge's chambers. But he has gone for the day and everyone looks embarrassed for both Robson and

Johnson. It is about this time that I start to wink at Leslie Robson whenever she looks in my direction. People who had been feeling that there must be a method to Robson's madness, are now beginning to wonder.

The next day, the other judge upholds Johnson's decision and the jury selection begins in earnest. The state has seemingly run out of stall tactics. Now the prosecution is really panicking because soon it will have to show its hand in front of the world.

The *voir dire* (French for to speak the truth) phase of jury selection begins with questioning from both side's attorneys to determine each potential juror's fitness in this case. Theoretically, at the end of the questions, the opposing attorneys should know whether or not the individuals will help or hurt their side.

Pedro Dijols asks whether or not the jurors can "stomach" talk about anal sex and oral sex.

One matronly lady replies, "Why yes. Well, I hear worse than that every single day!"

"What do you do?" asks an astounded Pedro. At the prosecution table Leslie sits with her mouth open wide.

"I am a school teacher."

"School. What grade?" asks Dijols.

"Kindergarten," she replies with a perfectly straight face.

Another man, a motorcycle gang type with tattoos up both arms, says that the prosecutors are fascist Nazis for persecuting 2 Live Crew.

One older black lady goes on about police brutality in Broward County. One black man is a "fan" but says he's never heard the music.

There is a man that Rogow likes. He is an elderly black bellhop. He says that we aren't guilty. So Rogow wants this guy on the jury. So he says, "Well, the law is funny and sometimes following the law is hard. It's like when you have some bags to get up to a room. I mean, they look light but when you try and lift them you find that they are heavy and don't you say to yourself, well, it's a hard job but then you do it because you put all your effort into it. Well the law is like that. It's hard work but couldn't you do it no matter how hard it was? Just like your job. Couldn't you put all your effort into following the law here?"

The man thinks for a moment and says, "No, they're not guilty and that's that!" And so he goes.

When Rogow asks the prospective jurors if they think that oral or anal sex is morbid or shameful, they all say no. This amuses Rogow because both are illegal under the Florida Sodomy Laws. When asked by a foreign television crew if sex is illegal in America, he says, "In America only good sex is illegal." Sex is only dirty when you do it right.

I look into the eyes of the prospective jurors and feel I can get a fair trial from these people. Rogow later says that I was right about a couple of jurors that he wanted excluded but relinquished when I insisted that Rogow let them be seated. I feel strongly that any normal person will decide with me that my music is comedy, regardless of the graphic language, and as such is protected by the First Amendment.

Robson's voice might well be likened to a vintage air raid siren, shrill and monotonous. Dijols, as if under her wing, becomes tiresome and abusive. He browbeats the potential jurors until they agree with him. At one point Pedro says, "Do you believe that Ms. Robson or I work for Navarro? Do any of you think we are against democracy?" I raise my hand silently. Pedro asks, trying to annoy the press in the audience, "Does anyone, except the people in the audience, believe that the U.S. Government should be overthrown?" Leslie, seemingly pleased with Pedro's enthusiasm, and sentiment, silently nods. The jurors look at each other like maybe they missed something.

The jury that is selected consists of a sixty-year-old Jewish mother of an entertainer, a seventy-six-year-old former sociology professor who once taught at Howard University in the sixties, the fortyish principal of an integrated middle school, a twenty-six-year-old diesel mechanic who is a fan of Jim Morrison, a black grandmother who lives six blocks from two large adult book stores (located across from the sheriff's substation) and the foreman, who is gay.

The prosecution is up at bat first with its star witness, Detective Eugene McCloud. McCloud is large and black and has a thick ebony beard. He stares out of a set of thick glasses like his brain is gearing up slowly for the next series of words that will usher forth from his mouth. Detective McCloud is a fourteen-year veteran who held Charles Freeman inside his E.C. Records store after he played "Fuck Shop" over the PA system for McCloud and the TV cameras, until the good sheriff arrived to make the arrest, personally. McCloud is a good deputy. He follows orders without asking any questions of his superiors. Not one of his superiors will be in the courtroom to help him when he is on the stand for two and a half grueling days.

McCloud's time on the stand is mildly entertaining as Rogow leads him around through the intricacies and nuances of the case that he has been instrumental in creating. McCloud has attended seminars on pornography and obscenity, but he has no idea what prurient interest is. When Rogow cross-examines him he is evasive and hostile. He has no idea how many topless bars or adult bookstores there are in his county. He does know that Solid Gold and Pure Platinum are the best known strip clubs in Broward County and that bare-butted women dance there. He knows that there are two adult book stores within spitting range of the sheriff's substation where books and videos depicting any sex act you can imagine will be found. He won't discuss them, due to the possibility of compromising "ongoing" investigations.

He admits that the deputies were given sixty dollars in cash for tickets and alcoholic beverages. He says that each of the eight deputies was carrying a concealed mini-cassette recorder. McCloud's recorder captured the best quality because it was in his shirt pocket. Detective Werder also got a recording, judged to be of high enough quality to be played in court. When handed the recorder to show the court how it works, McCloud has to have help from Pedro Dijols to switch it into the record mode. McCloud admits that he could have used a much larger recording device and gotten better sound quality, though, he says, even a crystal clear studio quality recording would not have made any difference to the substance of his case. I will say later that the detectives could have brought a large reel-to-reel recorder or videotaping equipment to get the concert as several TV stations did, without any objection from us. I would have preferred to have an accurate, high-quality recording. In the end, not one TV crew that was there that night would turn over one second's worth of footage to the sheriff's department for trial purposes. They all said it was erased by accident.

McCloud says there were around thirty deputies involved in the case, fourteen in the actual arrest. The highlight of his appearance is his performance as an interpreter of the lyrics in question, taken from the tapes, which have been played for the courtroom before. Pedro Dijols mans a mixing board and giant speakers are aimed at the jury. Their faces are frozen in a blend of horror and boredom as the music alternates between a blast, roars and screeching sounds. Poorly recorded is a description that does not begin to do justice to the police tapes from that evening in Club Futura. When the digitally enhanced tapes (thousands upon thousands of dollars worth of experiments in rerecording) are finally played, they sound like they were re-corded from the window of a speeding car passing the club that night. The detective listens for a few seconds and then, looking at his transcription which he has been handed by Pedro, he tries to recite the lyrics. "SCREECH MUMMBLE MUMMMBLE SUUUUC!"

"Yes, Mr. Dijols, I believe that was 'all whores suck dick,' " he says proudly. "And 'all fellows eat pussy!' "

"All *hos* suck dick!" I whisper so the jury can hear the correction.

The humor picks up again when McCloud dances for the courtroom, depicting the "sort of hunching" dance that he says the audience was participating in. The jury roars along with the courtroom but into their fists. Later they pass a note to the judge asking if they might be allowed to laugh out loud if something is funny.

Werder is no better. She sits with the earphones on and parrots the lyrics. "I believe that was 'I'll be fucking you and you'll be sucking me,' " she drones in her squeaky Minnie Mouse voice. Robson and Dijols and McCloud and Detective Werder will all use as many of these verbal horrors as often as possible. The effect is that the words become ordinary. Our defense attorneys cleverly allow the prosecution to say "fuck" and "suck" and "asshole" and "hard dick" as often as they wish.

Bruce Rogow never uses one of the four-letter words. Not once does Rogow take one step down the low road. He says "fellatio" or "oral sex" instead of "blow job" or "suck my dick." He says "anal sex" instead of "fucked in the ass." He is a master at blunting the sharp edge the words might have held if used in moderation. The courtroom is filled with vulgar, foul-lyric-spouting people, and they are all sitting on the side of the courtroom farthest away from Mark Ross, Chris Wongwon, and me.

Werder has this vacant look in her eyes and the head band of the earphones is at her chin. Like McCloud before her, she seems to highlight how silly this trial really is. These people are supposed to be adults. They are supposed to be police officers protecting the citizens of Broward County from criminals. And here they sit, day after day, making complete fools out of themselves, entertaining the world press with incompetence that sets new standards of official ineptness. These experts on obscenity just seem to have dirty minds and to know very little other than that the sheriff sent them on a fool's errand.

Rogow's cross-examination of the detectives plows them under completely. The even odds for acquittal in Las Vegas are now three to one for a clean walk. Navarro, who has kept up with every minute of the testimony, is reportedly furious at the detectives' performance. "They killed us!" he is reported to rave after Werder's cross. Later in the bathroom, a disgruntled Dijols is having a conversation with an attorney from his office. "It certainly isn't my fault if my fucking witnesses have no credibility!" he yells, his words reverberating through the tiled enclosure.

The defense, with a dozen experts ready to testify, decides that it will call only two. Anything more would be overkill, Rogow says. "We have either won or lost already. No real sense dragging this out."

John Leland, music critic for *Newsday* via *The Village Voice*, *SPIN*, and an impressive string of articles for *The New York Times*, and Dr. Henry Louis Gates of Duke University, one of

America's leading black scholars, are selected. Leland has testified for 2 Live Crew three times before in trials. He is clean, lean, self-assured, and credible. He is a leading expert on rap/ hip-hop music, having studied it almost since it started.

Henry Louis Gates is a Rhodes scholar who received a degree at Oxford in English Literature. He has taught at Yale, Cornell, was at Duke at the time of the trial and has since moved to Harvard where he is a professor of English Literature. His testimony will effectively close the door on doubts about 2 Live Crew's music having literary, political and artistic value. "Skip" Gates was initially asked to testify because of an article he wrote for *The New York Times* entitled "Decoding 2 Live Crew." In that article he placed 2 Live's music in the black historical and cultural perspective. The prosecution will make much of the fact that he was paid thirty-five hundred dollars to testify because they cannot discredit him. The Gates testimony is a highlight of the trial and as he speaks the eyes of the jury light up. Dr. Gates puts the whole thing into a perspective that makes sense. Suddenly, none of what the prosecution said during the trial means anything. It is obvious to everybody that not only is the emperor (the plaintiff) without clothes; he has no idea where to find any.

DIRECT EXAMINATION BY MR. ROGOW:

Q   Dr. Gates, have you ever testified as an expert witness before, in court?

A   No.

Q   Are you being paid a fee for your testimony today?

A   Yes, I am.

Q   And how is that fee being computed?

A   At two hundred fifty dollars an hour.

Q   When you make your speeches around the country, what is your rate for making a speech at the universities that you described?

A   Three thousand dollars an hour.

Q   Have you listened to the tape recording that we provided to you of the performance of Two Live Crew at Club Futura on June 10th, 1990?

A   I have, two and a half times.

Q   And have you listened to the recordings of the songs, "Me So Horny," "Fuck Shop," "If You Believe in Having Sex" and "Come On, Babe"?

A   I have.

Q   Dr. Gates, when did Two Live Crew first come to your attention?

A   Two Live Crew came to my attention when a *New York Times* reporter . . . John Pirellis, [phonetic] called me.

Q   As a result of the telephone call from Mr. Pirellis, did you write anything with regard to Two Live Crew?

A   Well, yes.

Q   What did you write?

A   I went out and bought the tape. I told him I couldn't respond to his questions because I hadn't heard the tape. That wouldn't be honest. I bought the tape, listened to it that night a couple of times, thought that I had an interpretation that might be unique, and the next morning decided to write what is called an op. ed. page for *The New York Times*.

Q   Was it published?

A   Yes, it was.

Q   What was the name of that piece?

A   "Decoding Two Live Crew."

Q   What was the thesis of that piece?

A   Well, the thesis was, in a nutshell, that what we saw was not what we got. That there was a meaning hiding beneath the surface of the obvious meaning of the lyrics.

   What was going on was much more complicated and was quite different than what people were claiming was going on.

Q   Dr. Gates, what is "signifying," when you wrote your book *Signifying Monkey?*

A   Signifying is a very old and venerable tradition. It is often confused with games called the "dozens."

   It involves great teasing, cajoling, renaming people. Often it involves the use of lewd language or off-color language. Often it involves graphic descriptions of sexuality, but it is such a highly refined practice that it is taught now in many university courses.

Q   Is rap a form of art?

A   Oh, absolutely, it seems to me it can be defined as art.

Q   Does it detract from being art because the words that are used are four-letter words?

A   Oh, no, not necessarily. The greatest literary tradition in English literature . . . people such as Chaucer and Shakespeare, Greek literature, Western literature, has always in its vernacular . . . included a lot of lewdity, a lot of verbal puns, sexual puns, curse words, et cetera. So this is very much a part of the art of Western culture.

Q   Are we to take the lyrics literally that were heard on the tape?

A   Well, there is very little art that should be taken literally.

Q   What do you mean by that?

A   Well, imagine a pond full of fish. From a hundred yards away, you look at that pond, you see the surface of the pond. It looks like that's what the pond consists of, what's on the surface.

So if you see mosquitos floating or lily pads floating, et cetera, et cetera, it appears to be the contents of the pond. But once you get up to the pond and maybe jump in it, you realize there is a lot of life under the surface. That's the way art works.

There is always a surface value and there is always a sub-value, a content underneath that surface. In fact, the technical name for this is the difference between surface content, what's on the top, and manifest content, what's underneath.

Q   What's the manifest content of "Fuck Shop," "Come On, Babe," "Me So Horny," "If You Believe in Having Sex" and the performance that you listened to on that cassette tape?

A   . . . I have to back up a little bit. These are songs that have taken one of the worst stereotypes about black men, primarily, but also about black women, and blown them up.

Q   What are the stereotypes?

A   The stereotypes that have been most commonly associated with black men in Western culture concern the fact that we are oversexed and hypersexed individuals in an unhealthy way.

Q   How did that stereotype evolve?

A   It evolved, as nearly as we can figure, from the sixteenth century when Europeans were "discovering" Africans and stealing African human beings and making them slaves. They had to find ways to justify their enslavement . . .

It would be the way that men used to treat women. Men used to say because a woman is not smart enough, she is meant to cook or to have sex with. So women had to overcome that stereotype.

How do we overcome that stereotype? I think one of the brilliant things they embrace is that stereotype.

Q   What do you mean?

A   Well, they represent the stereotype over and over again, in such a graphic way, namely to exploit it. You can have no reaction but to burst out laughing.

You realize how ridiculous this all is. That's why we all laugh when we hear the performance. I thought one of the healthy things, listening to it, as I said, was hearing the reaction of the audience.

There is no cult or violence there. You can't hear any danger at all in the background. What you hear is great humor, great joy, the boisterousness. Why? By showing the black man as nothing but the refrain in "Me So Horny, all I want to do is make love," that was the litany of these four songs.

They are being written and sung by young virile black men. Everybody understands what is going on. Even if they don't understand it as a literary critic, they understand it on a subliminal level. Their response is to burst out laughing, to view it as a joke, a parody.

Parody is one of the most venerable aspects of any literary tradition. It is certainly very important to Afro-American culture and literature.

Q   If you took them literally, would you be missing the point?

A   The whole point is . . . the lyrics of these songs are metaphors. They are not to be taken on a literal level. They are to be taken on their figurative or metaphorical level.

CROSS EXAMINATION BY MR. DIJOLS:

Q   Sir, you don't have any degrees in music, do you?

A   No, sir, I don't.

Q   And when were you first contacted to testify in this case, sir?

A   I can't remember the exact day, but it was within two or three weeks after my *New York Times* piece was published.

Q   And who contacted you?

A   Mr. Rogow.

Q   We have already agreed you haven't testified as an expert before, is that right?

A   That's right, except for the deposition that you took, et cetera, but I've never been in court before.

Q   And you don't have any knowledge as to the Broward County community standards, do you, sir?

MR. ROGOW: Objection, beyond the scope of direct. I did not tender he was an expert.

THE COURT: Sustained.

Q   Are you as familiar with other rap artists as you are with Two Live Crew?

A   No.

Q   Have you ever met with any of the members or spoke with any of the members before today?

A   I met Mr. Campbell at lunch two days ago and just shook his hand, but we didn't get a chance to talk, unfortunately.

I wanted to get his autograph for my daughter, but I wasn't able to.

Q   That's understandable.

Let me ask you this. You haven't had a chance to talk to them about their intent or their ideas or their motives behind writing these things—

MR. ROGOW: Objection, intent has nothing to do with it.

THE COURT: Sustained.

MR. DIJOLS: This goes to the fact of the music. He just gave an opinion as to the music without knowing their intent or motive. He should be allowed to answer that.

THE COURT: Maybe you can formulate the question in a better way.

Q   When you met with Mr. Campbell the other day, were you able to discuss the ideas behind writing this music?

A   As I said, I only introduced myself and said hello. I wouldn't mind that opportunity, though.

Q   You based your opinion on their music without discussing any of the aspects of their music with them?

A   No, because—could I tell you why?

Q   I'm sorry, sir. You will have a chance on redirect.

THE COURT: He can say no and then explain his answer.

Q   The answer was no?

A   Well, because of something that is called the intentional fallacy in aesthetics theory. What that means, you are not supposed to ask an artist, if you are a critic, what their intent was. You are supposed to tell them what the effect is that they have achieved, because . . . always when you create a work of art, what you get out of it is much more complicated and often quite different than what you think you have put in.

Even if an artist says, "This is what I intended," this is irrelevant. It is interesting.

No critic would use the testimony of an artist as their final bottom line in their summation of a work of art.

Q   You have discussed a lot of terms. Most of the terms you discussed were literary terms, the history vernacular, if you will, and other terms you stated here.

Obviously, you are dealing on the literary aspect of the work?

A   Yes, but—

Q   Okay. And . . . you are an expert on black literature?

A   I am an expert on black literature and visual images and oral images of black people.

Q   I believe your words were that this is great virtuosity?

A   Uh-huh.

Q   This is great sense of historical vernacular language?

A   Uh-huh.

Q   This compares with some of the great classics in literature?

A   Uh-huh.

Q   Okay. Let me ask you this, sir.

Where is the literary value when they say, for instance, "I was the first to make you hot and wet. I wet you, you never tell your parents. You said it yourself, you liked it. Put your lips and suck my asshole."

Can you point out the great literary value there, sir?

A   Well, it is very difficult for a critic. You have to take a work of art as a whole. You can't—

Q   Haven't you been talking primarily about literature? The words—

A   Yes.

Q   So let's concentrate then on what we have been talking about today, sir. The words—can you point out, what I just read—

MR. ROGOW: Can he answer? He is arguing with the witness.

THE COURT: You need to pause, Pedro, so he can answer.

Q   If we can deal with what you have been talking about today, sir. The words that I just read to you, can you just point out the great literary value in that line?

A   When I say the words, I mean the words with a beginning, a middle and an end, one must take a composition as a whole. You can't just excerpt a stanza and insert an interpretation of that. That's not allowed by the rules of my game, the rules of literary criticism.

I could say without, I think, violating my own integrity as a critic that those lyrics are part of what I alluded to earlier; the fact that you name these sexual images over sexuality in such a graphic way, they are blown up.

In fact, the more scandalous, the more shocking, the more it fits the theory.

Q   When we are—come on. One of the songs that was performed at the concert, where they sing, "Together as one we will be, I will be fucking you, you will be sucking me then licking my asshole, lick it till your tongue turns doodoo brown," that's great classical literature?

A   I never said it was Shakespeare.

Q   We'll get to Shakespeare in a second. You've obviously compared them to Shakespeare?

A   I didn't compare the rhyme scheme of that song to a sonnet out of Shakespeare.

Q   Why don't you?

"I will be fucking you, you will be fucking me, lick my ass, lick it till your tongue turns doodoo brown," that was performed at the concert.

Can you just point out the great literary value there?

A   I think the last thing I said before you asked this question, the more shocking the visual image, the more the effect because it is so absurd. That is the effect this achieved in that particular stanza.

Again, it is very hard for a self-respecting critic to try to analyze literature, to take it out of context the way you just did it.

Q   Let me ask you this. In that line, would Shakespeare have written anything about the words fuck or suck, anything like that?

I'm sorry, I kind of misstated that.

A   I didn't say he used those words.

Q   You compared them?

A   He used a lot of four-letter words and has a lot of risqué lyrics, what are called Anglo-Saxon phrases.

Q   Was fuck, suck, pussy any one of these things?

A   No, he would have used the other words. But words, and it is important to say, which would have had the same meaning in the same lewd way for the language community.

We have to understand language is not a statistic. It doesn't stand still. The younger generation calls what my generation called signifying under the name of dissing. It is true with sexual acts as well. Many of these words were in Shakespeare's time.

Q   You have heard the tapes two and a half times?

A   Yes, sir.

Q   You have heard one of the songs, "Do-Wah-Diddy"?

A   Yes, sir.

Q   And you have stated in front of the jury this is parody, this is humor also?

A   Yes.

Q   Where they said basically, "I saw this fag sitting at a bus stop and do-wah-diddy dum diddy I do, I said you sissy mother-fucker, you ought to stop singing," and they go on to say, "And spreading AIDS."

Sir, where is the humor of making fun, obviously, of homo-sexuals with AIDS?

A   I don't think that's what that does. If it were to be taken literally, it would be disgusting, in my opinion. But I can't take it literally.

One of the sad things about black culture is that—

Q   Sir, I'm sorry—

A   I'm trying to answer your question.

MR. ROGOW: Your Honor, also he just went through a quote and he asked him where is the value and he tried to explain it.

THE COURT: Go ahead.

THE WITNESS: One of the sad things about black culture is it is tended to be sexist against women and "homophobic," meaning, anti-gay.

I think what the lyric does is dramatize one of the worst aspects of black culture as you would do in the same Archie Bunker motive. It is called to be not homophobic.

Q   These songs by Two Live Crew, as nasty as they are, what you are saying is this is part of fighting for black rights?

A   Oh, absolutely.

Q   This is part of fighting for equality?

A   Absolutely.

Q   So, basically, you are kind of equating them with other great black leaders such as Martin Luther King?

A   I didn't equate them with any individual, you asked me.

Q   Well, this is fighting for black rights?

A   But there is a difference [between] leading a civil rights march and exploiting the stereotype—

Q   Where is the exploitation—

MR. ROGOW: He is answering, your Honor. Let him finish.

THE COURT: Please. Go ahead.

THE WITNESS: There is a difference between engaging in a civil rights march through Selma and recording an album which makes a statement.

One can say they are similar in one way, but they are very different in another that seems obvious to me.

Q   Let me ask you this.

If this was written by whites, would this be less or more artistic?

A   That is not a proper question. It is not a proper question because race of the artist doesn't make something inherently better or worse. It doesn't make something more or less artistic. That's ridiculous.

Q   Well, you have been talking about black artists for the last hour.

A   I have, but black art is made by black people.

Q   So if this material is written by whites, it is less or more artistic?

A   Whether it would be effective, [depends on] how good it is, how [well] it was put together, but white people can write about black people and they can do it well. And black people can write about white people.

There are no general rules about that to start with, that would exclude a white person from making a valid statement about a white person.

Q   You can compare Two Live Crew . . . to other great blacks such as James Baldwin and Ralph Ellison?

A   . . . Sure, but compare means to measure one against the other.

Q   In your opinion, they are just as good then?

A   They are different. One works in the novel form, the other works in the rap form. It is very hard. It is like comparing a good apple and a good orange.

Q   So when they say, "I want to fuck because my dick is on bone, you little whore, you will drink my come and nothing more," that's basically comparing them to Ralph Ellison and James Baldwin?

A   You can't do it that way. It is basically saying they are engaging in a parody trying to exploit these images of black people.

Q   And it is the effect of these words, a parody?

A   The effect of the words is brilliant parody.

Q   You didn't see the effect on the audience, did you?

A   I couldn't see.

Q   Based on this tape, you were able to make an opinion?

A   Yes, what I heard was what I said I heard. I heard a joyous response from the audience.

Q   Okay. And basically your interpretation of the effect is not of their music, but of the refrain of the audience, nothing more than that?

A   How to characterize it is what's called call and response. That's an inseparable relationship between the performer performing and the audience responding. It is like a hand and a glove. There is no response without the call.

Q   You have to agree that many people laugh for different reasons?

A   People [may] laugh because they are embarrassed.

Q   Many people could have been laughing at that performance for many great reasons, if you will?

A   Absolutely.

Q   And in your opinion, this is how you will break the sterotype, by basically singing a whole lot of fucking and sucking—I mean, rather let me repeat that.

"A whole lot of fucking and sucking at the fuck shop."

And "Please come inside, make yourself at home, I want to fuck because my dick is on bone," this is breaking the stereotype?

A   You have no choice but to laugh at it when you hear it.

Q   This is advancing black culture?

A   In my opinion.

Q   This is acceptable to the black community of Broward County?

A   I have no idea.

Q   You've never written a critical analysis about other contemporary black artists, have you?

A   No.

Q   You stated a few minutes ago, you felt that this tape was not giving you a full picture, yet you still made an opinion or gave an opinion?

A   Based on what I heard.

Q   You are basically getting paid two hundred fifty dollars an hour?

A   Yeah, it's a loss, but I am.

Q   I understand that.

No further questions of this witness.

REDIRECT EXAMINATION BY MR. ROGOW:

Q   Could you give us a better opinion of the performance if you had seen the dancers dancing on stage?

A   Beyond the words dancers on the stage, I didn't know there were dancers on the stage. I think I could have given a complete account of the performance if I had seen it. The visual part is a very important part.

Q   Could you have given us a better opinion if you had seen the audience's participation?

MR. DIJOLS: Objection, calls for speculation.

MR. ROGOW: He opened the door. I didn't ask the question.

THE COURT: Overruled.

THE WITNESS: Yes, I could.

Q   Would you have given a more complete opinion if you had seen the disc jockey who was spinning the records and adjusting the records?

A   Yes.

Q   Could you have given a more complete opinion of the performance taken as a whole if you had seen the lighting that was going on during the time of the performance?

A   Certainly.

Q   Could you have given a more complete opinion if you had seen the dancing that was taking place on the stage by the performers?

A   Yes.

Q   Is the opinion you gave the best opinion you could give, given what you had to work with?

A   Yes.

MR. ROGOW: I don't have anything further.

RECROSS EXAMINATION BY MR. DIJOLS:

Q   All of these so-called missing parts, you still believe that this is brilliant work? You were still able to give an opinion as to their brilliant work?

A   I think I have stated that clearly before.

The ceiling in the courtroom is a checkerboard of suspended fiber panels and fluorescent rectangles of light high above two rows of hard wood benches. I pass the hours looking up at this ceiling with my legs extended and my hands folded across my belt buckle. People are talking and joking in small clusters. The Saturday bailiff has shoulders that roll toward his shiny, black shoes and eyes like lead shot. He has spent years standing at doorways. He is paid seven dollars and fifty cents an hour. Not enough to be required to take any shit. The female bailiff, whose hair is slicked back tightly against her scalp, yawns into her fist every few seconds.

The reporters and photographers, representing the world press, have a pool running on how many hours the jury will stay out of the courtroom. The prosecutorial staff, who will be cited in *The Miami Review* for gross incompetence, are sitting at their table looking confident.

Bruce Rogow, my defense attorney, sits on a bench in an expensive Italian suit with his legs crossed, laughing and telling stories to reporters, while reflections of the fluorescent tubes dance across his bald head. My former entertainment attorney, Allen Jacobi, with the disrespectfully hip hair and terminal tan, is flitting around from one group to another nervously cracking jokes and only half-listening when someone speaks to him. Photographers circle like jackals, shutters clicking and whirring.

It is a Saturday lunchtime. There are camera crews setting up a wall of cameras in an abandoned courtroom down the hall. They are positioning their flood lights, measuring light waves, checking each other's eyes and teeth and exchanging compliments. TV commentators smile and do their hair in small mirrors.

We three defendants are sitting on a bench in the hall fending off fans, reporters and eccentrics who have faked their way in. Al Goldstein, a famous man who is fat, wears pull-on Vans sneakers and shorts, and creates graphic pornography, has been here all week. His tabloid, *Screw,* shows half-tones of naked people with their private parts touching and their tongues exploring each other. It is a "suck and fuck" magazine that makes no aspirations to be anything else. "These guys are a disgrace to obscenity. I should be on trial here!" Goldstein says to anyone who will listen. His proof is a stack of his tabloids that he is constantly passing around the courtroom from a large brown envelope.

When the verdict is delivered, the prosecuting attorneys will have to call their boss who in turn will have to call the sheriff. Since, according to the red-faced sheriff, this is a tiny misdemeanor trial, blown all out of proportion by the world media, he feigns lack of interest, but the hundreds of thousands of dollars this trial cost him say differently. In fact the sheriff, who usually moves from flood light to flood light like an obese moth, has been suspiciously absent from this trial. Veteran trial watchers say he will appear as if by magic if the verdict swings his way. Today, Las Vegas odds on the trial are nine to one against conviction.

The real reason that the sheriff has distanced himself is that public opinion is heavily against the state on this trial and a majority of Broward County residents are shocked at the wasting of tax money. And it takes a lot to shock the residents of Broward County.

After two hours, the courtroom is alerted that the jury has reached a decision. Within ten minutes, every seat is taken, the aisles are filled. We three defendants stand and face the jury. The foreman hands the court clerk the verdict on a white sheet of paper. I feel my legs quiver. The attorneys stand at parade rest. The crowd is silent. The jury stares at us. The electricity builds and the photographers prepare to launch themselves into the center of the room for reaction shots. My mom, in a wheelchair at the rear of the courtroom, has closed her eyes and is praying, silently.

The defense had said that if one reasonable person thought that the music passed the Miller vs. California test then the work could not be adjudged obscene. The prosecution had interpreted the law differently, asserting that if one reasonable person thought the work failed the Miller vs. California test it could be adjudged obscene. The judge, after reading the law carefully, had instructed the jury as follows:

> The value of the material: In order for you to find that this material is obscene you must first find that taken as a whole it lacks

serious literary, artistic, political or scientific value. IF ANY REA-
SONABLE PERSON WOULD FIND THAT THE MATERIAL
HAS SUCH VALUE IT IS NOT OBSCENE even if it appeals to the
prurient interest in sex, and even if it depicts or describes sexual
conduct in a patently offensive way.

If it has serious literary or artistic effort, or if it attempts to
convey scientific information or political points of view, it cannot
be obscene.

The jury so instructed stayed out long enough to take a vote
using their hands. That done, they ate a pizza, after which they
returned to the courtroom and delivered their not guilty verdict.
Although it was expected, Chris, Mark, and I welcomed hearing
those words. Every group embraces its own terms and meanings
and one cannot be allowed to persecute another.

Bruce Rogow was elated and said; "Censorship cannot survive the human desire to know and to judge things for one's self.
No law, judge or jury will ever eradicate that irrepressible
instinct. We could have a thousand obscenity trials, but words
and thoughts about sex will never be limited to a missionary
view. Prurient interest, openly offensive descriptions of sexual
conduct and serious artistic, literary, political, or scientific value
should be discussed some place—any place—rather than the
courts."

After the trial, I hosted a major barbecue at my home overlooking the PGA golf course. It was the first time in over a year
that I felt free to do business again. My life had been turned
upside down by a group of people who were still little more than
shadows to me—voices on the radio and stern faces on a
television set.

I do not like that such a large group of people were so intent
on silencing me. I am still angry, even as I am congratulated by
my friends, fans and family. I am angry to think that had I not
been wealthy and convinced that I was right, I would probably
have been forced to fold my tent like so many others had to do
over the years.

I am convinced that I was singled out because I am a black

man who was getting rich and had become a role model for young people who appreciate my raw sexual message, my honesty and the anarchy in my music.

Would I do it all over again? I already am.

10 The Five Worst Songs on Earth From *As Nasty As They Wanna Be*

There are many versions floating around of the lyrics to *As Nasty As They Wanna Be*. Everybody has transcribed them, from the Christian forces at Focus on the Family and Tipper Gore, along with every other crusading right-wing fanatical group, to the Broward County Sheriff's Office which made numerous transcripts from the record and the tapes of the Club Futura performance, to every member of the media who covered the trial and had to make his, or her, own copy. In fact, the only people who never got around to transcribing these lyrics is the 2 Live Crew. No official lyric sheets exist as none were ever made by the authors who never thought it particularly important, since we know the words. We perform them from memory. The following are the lyrics from the four songs generally cited as the most offensive by the "experts on pornography," though this could probably have been decided with a coin toss. This particular set was transcribed by John R. Miller who had to wait until his children were asleep to accomplish the task. The lyrics may just be accurate.

ME SO HORNY

What do we get for ten dollars?
Everyt'ing you want.
Everything?
Everyt'ing!

Chorus:
Oh, me so horny—oh, me so horny
oh, so horny, me love you long time
oh, me so horny-oh, so so horny
oh so horny, me love you long time

Sitting at home with my dick on hard
I got the black book for a freak to call
picked up the telephone to dial the seven digits
said, yo this Marquis baby, are you down with it?
I arrived at her house, knocked on the door
not having no idea what the night had in store
I'm like a dog in heat, a freak without warning
I have an appetite for sex 'cause me so horny.

Girls always ask me why I fuck so much
I say what's wrong baby doll, with a quick nut
'cause you're the one and you shouldn't be mad
I won't tell yo mamma if you don't tell your dad
I know he'll be disgusted when he sees your pussy busted
won't yo mamma be so mad if she knew I got ya ass
I'm a freak in heat, a dog without warning
my appetite's for sex 'cause me so horny.

You can say I'm desperate, you even call me perverted
But you'll say I'm a dog,
when I leave you fucked and deserted
I'll play with your heart just like it's a game
I'll be blowin' your mind while you're blowin' my brains
I'm just like that man they call Georgie Puddin' Pie
I fuck all the girls and I make 'em cry
I'm like a dog in heat, a freak without warning
I have an appetite for sex 'cause me so horny.

It's true you were a virgin until you met me
I was the first to make you hot and wetty-wetty

You tell your parents we are going out
never to a movie, just straight to my house
You said it yourself, you like it like I do
put your lips on my dick and suck my asshole too!
I'm a freak in heat, a dog without warning
my appetite's for sex 'cause me so horny.

PUT HER IN THE BUCK!

There's only one way to have a good time
fuck that pussy and make it mine
lay a bitch on the bed flat on her back
hold her legs up high, make the pussy splack
you can put her in the buck by sittin' on the sink
wrap her legs around you, now take this dick
dick, dick, dick—Now PUT HER IN THE BUCK!

It's a position in sex that's done by the masses
it ain't the sixty-nine or what you learn in class
it increases the intensity of a fuck
legs up high known as the buck
it's the only way to give her more than she wants
like a doggie style to get all the cunt
'cause all men try real hard to do it
to have her walk in front and we try to abuse it
a big stinker pussy can't do it all
so we try real hard just to bust the walls.

PUT HER IN THE BUCK!

I'll break you down and dick you long
bust your pussy and break your backbone
I'll go between them legs that's open wide
pushin' this dick from side to side
legs to the ceiling, now I'm feelin' the feeling
when I bust a nut your ass will be screaming.

PUT HER IN THE BUCK!
(*sounds of sex and orgasm to music*)

TWO LIVE CREW

DO YOU BELIEVE IN HAVING SEX (Lyrics)

If you believe in having sex, say hey yea, fuck you (rept.)
If you believe in having sex, say hey oh, fuck you (rept.)

When I say S you say E
When I say X you say SEX S-E-X (Sex)
S-E-X (Sex)

Let's Go!
To the ladies from this Mother Fucker (rept.)
To the fellows from this Mother Fucker (rept.)
All whores suck dick (rept.)
All fellows suck pussy (rept.)

Yo fellows, how many fellows gonna get some pussy when they
    leave here tonight? (talk)
Say all gonna get some pussy (rept.)
Yo ladies, how many fellows aint gonna get no pussy because you
    all aint fucking that shit (talk)

Say you aint gonna get no pussy, because you aint got no money
    (rept.)

Yo fellows, how many fellows take a girl to hotel and she tells him
you aint getting no pussy and all that shit like that?
What you ought to tell them fellows is: Say, take your grubby
    asshole beef (rept.)

Eat my pussy, eat, eat my pussy
Eat the pussy, eat, eat the pussy

Yo! where are my white boyfriends at? (rept.)
Fucking . . . you wanna get your cock sucked, bring it up to me.
Say suck my cock and I'll eat your pussy (rept.)

Is it less filling
No it taste good (audience)

Less filling
Taste good

Say pussy is less filling and it taste great and I could do some right
    now. You all might not understand.

C'MON BABE

Female voice: Fuck, baby! Oh me! OH FUCK ME! Deeper,
harder, harder, oh God I can't stop, I can't, come inside me baby!
Come on me. Oh come in me. OHHHH! Fuck me!

When the party's over we can get together
go to my house and fuck forever
and do whatever comes to mind
let me stick my dick in your behind
so pour me a glass of Dom Perignon
and suck my dick until I come
soft as your body to the end you kiss
come on baby, we can do this.

No need to act stuck up, pretty as a vidie
got a funky disposition and you think you're witty
lots of people saying things like this
it's called criticism and not a dis
I only get compliments when they are due
now I'm gonna tell you all the truth
you claim to be a virgin, I mean the purest
it'll be different baby, 'cause we can do this
Love's the key to end all your woes
you'll be my bitch and not a dirty ho
together as one we will be
I'll be fucking you and you'll be sucking me
then lick my ass up and down
lick it till your tongue turns doo-doo brown
don't try to be slick and give me a kiss
come on baby, we can do this.

Bitch it's time to spend the night
let's walk the beach in the moonlight
holding each other like lovers do
but the pussy's wet, I know what to do
making love, holding you near
screams and moans is all I hear
quick as your tongue so dick the lips
suck it bitch, 'cause you can do this.

Let's get it going on, let's act a fool
listen and learn, I'll take you to school

you say you don't fuck on the first date
then fuck you bitch, I ain't gonna wait
'cause my dick is hard, my back is strong
I'll find another bitch to get it on
'cause now is the time so stop the bullshit
come on baby, we can do this.

As you move your body the shit you say
will make any man want to stay
'cause being with you is all I ask
and fucking you will be my task
my lonely nights will be filled with fun
no more clubs and sex on the run
just suck this dick and here I lay
you can do this, so come on babe.

Bitch you said you was gonna give me some
now you want to start acting dumb
you want to play cat and mouse
when I catch you I'm a stick my dick in your mouth
now stop the teasing and start the pleasing
just fuck me good until I ski
bitch stop fakin', I mean now quit it
Come on baby, we can do this.

Step to me and go to your knees
suck this dick, put me at ease
do something special you know that I like
smoke the head and please don't bite
slow and easy, I'll hold the seat back
up and down as I climax
steady in motion I have to say
we can do this, so suck it babe.

Old lady's voice:
"I think that type of sexual activity is disgusting!"

THE FUCK SHOP

There's only one place where we can go
where the price is right just to fuck a ho
it's always popular with the girls and the guys

for all of my money it's the best buy
Ten dollars—two hours is the time of your stay
it's more than enough time to say
each room has a bed and also a sink
so you can wash your dick after fucking the pink
but be careful of the things that you use
'cause you can get arrested for sex abuse
so as you hit the door and the panties drop
A whole lot of suckin' and fuckin'—At the Fuck Shop.

Please come inside and make yourself at home
I want to fuck 'cause my dick's on bone
You little whore behind closed doors
you would drink my come and nothing more
now spread your wings open for the flight
let me fill you up with something milky and white
'cause I'm gonna slay you rough and painful
you innocent bitch, don't be shameful
break out the ice cubes and the hot water
this is the second half and not the second quarter
I'll fuck you till you sleep and you'll sleep like a baby
and in your dreams you will say I'm crazy.

Chorus:
In the Fuck Shop, that's where it's at
In the Fuck Shop, the place to splack
In the Fuck Shop, where all the boys go
In the Fuck Shop, fuckin' all the hos.

11 After the Verdict

Prosecutors, officers and politicians are all sensitive to public opinion. Even Sheriff Nick Navarro, after the 2 Live Crew performance trial, seemed in a hurry to be done with the mess he was in. At first it had been a good smoke screen for Navarro, whose department, with one of the country's largest budgets, was plagued with the old standard problems and scandals of any department its size. Little things like runaway corruption, rigged bids, favoritism, bribery, child molestation, incest, extortion, prostitution, pimping, drug trafficking and the like. To many of the people in South Florida, Broward County looks more like another banana republic run by a dictator fronting for business-men. While Navarro orchestrated his professional life like a continuous media event, any short-term gains in media coverage and in popularity were to be lost as the motives for the prosecu-tion of the 2 Live Crew became clearer. One Miami Beach councilman wondered how a man who was supposedly pro-human rights could justify arresting black men whose worst crime was swearing to a musical beat in a club filled with adults who had paid twenty dollars to hear it. The plain fact was that I had pissed Navarro off and he was out to get me. Period.

Questions were asked about the runaway costs of the trial. No matter what Navarro said he just looked foolish, arrogant and petty. The excuses he offered did not work their usual magic for him. It got so that he would not appear in public forums unless it was agreed beforehand that there could be no questions or jokes on the 2 Live trials. Navarro, who is more than a little image-conscious, didn't like being made to look like a short-sighted and vindictive old fool who would waste the taxpayers' dollars on a personal vendetta. He had continually referred to the trial as a "2 bit nothing" trial, while pouring up to $300,000 into it.

It says something important that out of the tens of thousands of prosecutors, police and public officials across the country, only a handful took any action against *Nasty*. Those who did take action, like the prosecutor in Lee County, have a history as overzealous, antipornography crusaders and did so for a quick grab at some easy headlines. The reason that the majority of the officials didn't act against *Nasty* or the "live" performances of 2 Live Crew is primarily due to two things: first, their awareness of the teeth in Miller vs. California and its power in protecting speech, music and art, and second, the possibility of negative publicity. Had the Broward trial gone against the 2 Live performers and passed through the appeals successfully, there surely would have been an avalanche of trials all over the country. When prosecutors saw the raw costs in both cash and political popularity, they decided not to join Navarro on the spit.

Both Sheriff Navarro and Governor Martinez undoubtedly wish they hadn't listened to the fundamentalists led by Jack Thompson. More recently, Navarro has collected almost $50,000 from morality-minded individuals who believe his cockadoodie tale of needing campaign funds to fight an opponent that the dark forces are sending against his candidacy. That opponent has strangely failed to materialize, incidentally.

Most people think the censorship issue sank Martinez's gubernatorial reelection bid. But in all fairness, his administration had already been perceived to be a rudderless vessel that was taking on water, big time, from his anti-abortion stance, and his lack of direction. Taking the moral high road against those "naughty nigrahs" was just one of a long list of things that exploded in his face. The 2 Live Crew issue simply made him look inept and pathetic one last time.

In the heyday of the 2 Live phobia, even President Bush and Vice President Quayle took swipes at the music while campaigning for Martinez in Florida. Bob Martinez was made the country's drug czar after he was annihilated in his bid for reelection.

By the end of the trials Navarro and Martinez certainly wished that they had never heard of 2 Live anything.

During the trial, Jack Thompson interfered with the proceedings to the point that Judge June Johnson threatened to find him in contempt and file charges against him with the Florida Bar. Moments after the acquittal was announced, Thompson launched a frothing attack on the judge, the prosecutors and the jury. He faxed "evidence" that the foreman of the Broward jury, David Garsow, had been a homosexual, defense "plant" who had lied to get on the jury in order to get us acquitted. Thompson's malicious fax attack on Mr. Garsow set a new low-water mark for public behavior. When the fax hit the *Miami Herald,* the entire newsroom fell silent as reporters and staff read the sheet of paper and shook their heads in disbelief. The prevailing opinion, as voiced in *New Times,* was that the fax showed how desperate, sick, disjointed from reality, unchristian, cruel, perverted and completely twisted Mr. Thompson actually was. With that one act uttered in anger, Mr. Thompson lost any shred of credibility that he might have had.

Below is the affidavit Thompson sent out into the selected pressrooms throughout the country.

Affidavit
Comes now before me, the undersigned authority, John B. Thompson, who, upon being duly sworn, states:

1. I am over eighteen years of age, a resident of Dade County, Florida, and licensed to practice law by the State of Florida.

2. On Wednesday, October 17, 1990, I was told by an employee of Key Biscayne Presbyterian Church, where I regularly attend and

am a member, that David Garsow, the man who became the foreman in the recently concluded criminal obscenity trial involving 2 Live Crew and presided over by Judge June Johnson, had in fact not attended Key Biscayne Presbyterian Church for more than two years.

3. David Garsow, during voir dire, testified under oath that he not only attended Key Biscayne Presbyterian Church but that he was also currently singing in the choir. I have verified by speaking with both assistant State Attorney Dijols and (Miami) *Herald* reporter Dexter Filkins that that was indeed the testimony of Mr. Garsow: Mr. Filkins reported in the *Herald* that sworn testimony the day after it was offered in open court.

4. Mr. Garsow has now admitted to *Ft. Lauderdale Sun-Sentinel* reporter Barbara Walsh that he has not attended Key Biscayne for years because of his homosexual life style and discomfort over biblical teaching at Key Biscayne church that active homosexuality is not condoned by God in scripture.

5. Mr. Garsow apparently also testified during voir dire that he is a graduate of the University of Miami. This also appears to be a lie, based upon interviews the affiant has recently conducted, with those who have known Mr. Garsow for quite some time.

6. I informed Judge Johnson of the apparent perjury of David Garsow at approximately 12 noon on Wednesday, Oct 17, through her assistant Marty. I also informed, through an intermediary, the Broward Sheriff's Office of his apparent perjury. The B.S.O. confirmed, in a discussion with the pastor of K.B. Presbyterian Church, Stephen W. Brown, that Mr. Garsow had misrepresented his involvement in the church.

7. I also informed assistant state Dijols, one of the prosecutors in the case, of the apparent perjury of Mr. Garsow and in keeping with the incompetence shown by the prosecution of the case Mr. Dijols concluded that Mr. Garsow's status and alleged devout involvement in a particular church was irrelevant!

Mr. Dijols failed to appreciate the significance of a juror so motivated to get on this jury and assist the defense that he would apparently lie about his affiliation in order to disarm the prosecution and make himself appear to be a juror favorable to the State's position by his alleged phoney Christian affiliations and activities.

8. Further investigation of Mr. Garsow reveals, based upon corroborated evidence by a number of witnesses that have known Mr. Garsow for quite some time, that Mr. Garsow is "a pathological liar."

9. The undersigned has spoken at length with a Dade County Court Judge and has asked him what he would do if he were given the information Judge June Johnson was given at the time she was given it. This Judge unequivocally stated that a mistrial must be declared given the vitiating influence a juror is motivated a) to perjure himself, and b) to seek a leadership position as foreman has upon the fairness of a verdict. This Dade Judge noted that seating an alternate in such a situation would be unacceptable given the reality that jurors and alternates despite admonitions to the contrary, invariably communicate with one another verbally and otherwise through a trial thereby conveying opinions, attitudes and predispositions.

10. On Friday, October 19, the undersigned officer of the court hand-delivered to Judge June Johnson further informing her of the apparent perjury of the juror and offering to make himself available for sworn testimony to prove the perjury and therefore as far as the affiant knows Judge Johnson did absolutely nothing with this information. She certainly did nothing to contact the affiant in order to insure the fairness of the jury.

11. The Associated Press has carried on its wire service that Judge June Johnson has been provided information as to the apparent perjury of the juror and has done nothing with that information.

12. Since the verdict was handed down to further corroborate his keen personal interest in the outcome of this case, has repeatedly and eagerly held forth to the media about how "funny" and "harmless" the music of 2 Live Crew is.

13. The fact that a homosexual who engages in the bizarre sex acts described in 2 Live Crew's "Music"—anal sex, oral sex, licking excretement from the anus of a man (described in "Me So Horny" and reflective of the widespread homosexual practice of "rimming") is far from likely to find such representations obscene.

14. It appears, based upon what the affiant knows to be the truth, corroborated by the admissions now of Mr. Garsow himself, and a third party, and highly reliable witnesses, that Mr. Garsow did

perjure himself to be a "Mole" for the defense in this case and lead this jury, as its foreman, to a defense verdict.

15. As an experienced litigator and as an officer of the court the undersigned affiant, John B. Thompson knows by training and practice that such apparent and egregious misconduct by the foreman of the jury indicates an overwhelming amount of evidence that the State of Florida did not receive a fair trial in this case.

One does not need to be a lawyer to know the massive influence a foreman has upon jury deliberations. A jury foreman who perjures himself or herself clearly is an individual who will do what is necessary to attain the "right result." Such a juror might even contact the defense, particularly during a protracted jury selection process, to signal the defense of his intentions.

The undersigned affiant does not know that it occurred in this instance but the affiant does know that when he brought up the subject of the apparent perjury of David Garsow on the television set of the local CBS affiliate last evening, Professor Bruce Rogow, 2 Live Crew's defense counsel, inexplicably walked off the set never to return.

16. As a matter of law, this phony acquittal must be set aside.

17. It is the affiant's intention that all necessary parties, including administration and appellate judges, along with the Florida Supreme Court, will be provided this affidavit and other information in order that the jury system might not be further subverted and so that this acquittal, apparently obtained through perjury might be vacated.
Further affiant sayeth not.
(Signed)
John B. Thompson

Jim Mullen, editor of *New Times,* was one of the multitude of newspapermen who received that fax. He was so repulsed by this "typical" Thompson attack that he decided to respond. (Before this he, like most editors, had felt that there was no sense stirring up a madman with a law degree when ignoring him seemed the best method of silencing him.) He interviewed David Garsow and wrote an article containing the fax and the Garsow response. The article, which appeared in the November 6, 1990 issue, was entitled "Jack Thompson and the Truly Obscene."

In that article, Mr. Garsow said that he had not attended his church for six to eight months, since he had shared with the minister (in confession) that he had tested HIV positive. The minister insisted on taking this confession to the congregation for prayer for Garsow's recovery instead of dealing with him on a one-to-one basis as Garsow felt would be best. The result of this appeal to the "Christians" at Jack Thompson's church was an issuing forth of anonymous letters from members of the church asking him not to come back.

Garsow said that when he was asked if he had a religious affiliation, he had responded that he was a member of Key Biscayne Presbyterian Church. He said that he was not asked the last time he had gone to his church. Garsow went on to say that he does not tell lies under oath because it would hardly be worth jail time to sit on any jury. He said that he was very careful about what he said and how he said it.

Thompson said that Garsow had lied about his degree. Garsow denied that he had lied about that. He did, in fact, graduate, in 1988, with a music degree.

Garsow pointed out that he didn't ask to be foreman but five of six voted him in. He also said that they could have all voted the instant the jury retired but felt they would take the time to cover the law. And that there was never any time that he could have influenced anyone on the jury.

Garsow expressed interest about Thompson's knowledge of homosexual acts. "I'm glad that he's so up on terms. No one in everyday society would know what 'rimming' was. Not even every homosexual knows about rimming." As for Jack's statement about knowing Garsow's sexual practices he said: "I'd like to know when was the last time he was in my bedroom in order to know what I do, or don't do, and with whom. Why does he need to resort to such low, underhanded tactics?"

Thompson usually has "information" to support his accusations but he never shares the names of the accusers. "If he has this information, why doesn't he give names? If anybody is going to take him seriously you need names to verify."

Garsow concluded by saying that this attack from Thompson had made him ill but that he was going to forget it. So, as usual, Thompson was safe because no one wants to get into a legal scrape with an attorney, especially an attorney like him.

The following are excerpts from the faxes that Jack Thompson sent to the *Miami Herald* when they refused to print his allegations.

John B. Thompson
Attorney at Law

IMMEDIATE PRESS RELEASE—OCTOBER 27, 1990

Yesterday, Friday, October 26, The Miami Herald solidified its position as the leading censor in America . . .

The most recent casualty of the Herald's heterophobic effort to control and censor the news is the Garsow story, which story reveals the intersection of the homosexual agenda and the obscenity lobby's agenda . . .

Please call for details. You won't read them in the Herald, whose homosexuals have yet to learn that the truth cannot be contained in a corporate condom.

Copy: The homosexual-laden and censorial Miami Herald.

John B. Thompson
Attorney at Law

Dave Lawrence
Chairman and Publisher
The Miami Herald
One Herald Plaza
Miami, Florida

Re: *The Herald's Homosexual Agenda*

Dear Mr. Lawrence:

. . . You may have no idea how willing even some of your editors are to talk about the censoring of the news that occurs at your paper as a result of the staggering number of homosexuals that work for you.

Maybe you need to administer a polygraph to your underlings to see who is talking to me and others. Some at the Herald are fed up with the homosexual bias and with your lack of leadership in presiding over the censoring of the news to please the perverts at One Herald Plaza.

The October 29 censored article . . . is yet further proof of the Herald's bias. The homosexual aspect of the story was killed, as were other salient facts in order to make me appear ridiculous. One has to pick up this week's New Times to find out that Garsow is not only gay but also that he has AIDS.

As to Mr. Garsow's possible problem here, please refer to the book by Dr. A. E. Wilder-Smith, *AIDS Fact Without Fiction*, which, at page 130, states that "AIDS dementia," which befalls 90% of AIDS victims, is often the first symptom of the malady. It is marked by memory loss, inability to reason, mental chaos.

Gee, sounds like the Herald editorial board, as well, without the viral overlay. Mr. Garsow has been described by those who know him as "a pathological liar."

Please be finally advised that on November 7 I am appearing live on Pat Robertson's nationally-broadcast *700 Club* to discuss 2 Live Crew and the Miami Herald's cover-up.

Pat and I can't wait. You censors want a war. Fine. You've got one. All I'm going to do is speak the truth. Good luck with the stuff you traffic in.

Best,
John B. Thompson

copies: Others

John B. Thompson
Attorney at Law

Dave Lawrence
Chairman and Publisher
The Miami Herald
One Herald Plaza
Miami, Florida

Dear Mr. Lawrence:

Please be advised that yesterday I had the pleasure of appearing on [Christian Broadcasting Network's] internationally-televised "700 Club" and was interviewed by Pat Robertson.

I told the world, among other things, of your paper's continuing cover-up of the 2 Live Crew alleged perjury, of the sabotaging of your paper by its huge number of homosexual employees . . . and of the Herald's status as "the most anti-Christian paper in America." Amen.

I am going to continue to hammer your paper with the truth in various fora, and I would strongly suggest you make the hammering stop by beginning, for the first time in a long time, to see to it that stories get printed fairly and accurately regardless of whose toes get stomped.

You can begin that task—since you are the paper that saw fit to report Gary Hart's sexual philandering and his blackmailability—the overwhelming testimony suggesting that Dade County State Attorney Janet Reno is a closeted lesbian and a drunk whose prosecutorial decisions are determined by these alleged personal problems. Governor Martinez's Special Prosecutor was provided *sworn testimony* regarding these allegations, and you were told months ago that he was.

The Herald appears to treat Reno as an icon because of the gays that hold your paper hostage. Prove otherwise.

If you at the Herald think you can forever hide the scandals in this community of which your paper has, by its ongoing censorship, become a part, then think again.

And if you think you can discredit me by augmenting past false defamations of me with future ones, then: Go ahead, make my day.

I have more power at my disposal than the Herald. Why? Because God is a lover of truth, and your paper has repeatedly assaulted it and Him. He has more circulation.

Jack Thompson

copies: Significant others

The *Herald*'s response, after passing them around for a belly laugh, was to put the faxed letters and the press release in the nearest trash can. Any other action would have been like poking a blind man with a sharp stick. "Idiots are best left alone" is the official policy where Jack Thompson is concerned.

Judge June Johnson was furious that Thompson had continued

his attacks on her rulings and her integrity and certainly toyed with the idea of slamming him from the bench. But in the end she too chose to ignore him, which undoubtedly served to make him feel vindicated and filled anew with righteous vigor.

Jack Thompson, who seems willing to try anything to nail me, also collected a rag-tag group of desperate individuals (all of whom I had genuinely tried to help on more than one occasion since those Ghetto Style years) that were ex-hanging buddies of mine from my old neighborhood in Liberty City. According to one of them, Thompson spent several months trying to talk them into suing me, through him, for a healthy share of my fortune. He almost had them convinced that I had screwed them out of a fortune that was rightfully theirs since they had hung out with me while I was beginning to amass my fortune.

By way of illustration, as this manuscript was going to the publisher a story broke about a man in Milwaukee who hated homosexuals so much that he strangled at least a dozen and a half young men. The point is that he kept the bodies around the apartment and fucked them in the ass before he cooked and ate their decomposing flesh. Most recently, Thompson sent a fax to Doug Morris, the president of Atlantic Records, attacking the label on the eve of the release of *Sports Weekend, As Nasty As They Wanna Be Part II*, the 1991 release by 2 Live Crew. He compared Atlantic to a Wisconsin serial murderer, saying that while the murderer had done his work against society for free, Atlantic was charging for it. The fax was incoherent and even more perplexing than most of his other attacks.

The Florida Bar has received numerous, serious complaints that do not speak well for Mr. Thompson's mental stability and have talked often of what an embarrassment he is to that body. The bar has held hearings into his sanity and competence. When last investigated by a psychiatrist and a psychologist, Thompson was declared sane enough to practice law in Florida. Several attorneys have questioned that opinion.

It is interesting that the vice-mayor of Fort Lauderdale, who recently ran on a drumbeating, Bible-thumping, antipornography, antinude dancing platform, resigned after it was reported (on July 29, 1991) that he had been a customer of a prostitute. A prostitute whose pimp, her husband, just happend to be one of Sheriff Navarro's best deputies. The news reports said that the devoted husband dutifully watched and made blow-by-blow notes from his perch in the closet.

Polls show that Americans believe that there is enough censorship to go around already. We have many forms of institutional censorship in place, including the FCC censoring the airwaves (though they do not have the legal authority to do so) and publishers and producers censoring what they allow in their respective media. They are careful to keep their material in a comfort zone that will be acceptable to the majority of end-users. But parents want censorship forces to do what they aren't willing to do themselves; be watchdogs that regulate what influences their children are exposed to.

Rap music sprang from New York's street-wise "hip-hop" culture the same as graffiti and break-dancing. Rap fosters separatism and created a new and exciting language of black codes and street lingo designed to exclude outsiders. It is a window opened onto the black urban ghetto and it is revitalizing modern music, fashion and dance. It is also directly reflective of the anger festering under high unemployment and a cycle of abject poverty. Rap is intense and can be very frightening to outsiders. Political rap groups like Public Enemy and Professor Griff are as intimidating as the Black Panthers or the Black Muslims were in their time. But what is being expressed is what is being said, thought and felt within those hard-street communities. Because it is powerful and honest music it has become extremely popular with kids of all ages. Many people feel that primarily because it is becoming popular with white kids, it has been singled out for persecution by their parents, who fear the message and especially the old prospect of race-mixing on a mental, but especially on a physical, level.

Jack Thompson was a good enough enemy, but we are ready for the big guns. Jack never made the ranks of the heavyweights because his personality sucks and he comes off too unstable. The man ain't shit and it's time for him to move over and let someone with some spark and flair take us on. Jack don't know shit about the obscenity laws. He attacks Bruce Rogow but Jack couldn't hold Rogow's underwear.

12 The Interview on Sex, Violence, Drugs, Women, the Music Business, Blacks, Cubans, and Whatever

The following are excerpts from conversations between Luther Campbell and John Miller between August 1990 and September 1991.

Q   You have been widely criticized for the way you depict women in your songs. What are the distinctions of women in your world? In your music?

A   There are women who are housewives, girlfriends, hardworking businesswomen, mothers. Women who deserve respect. Then there is the woman who is out to steal someone's husband. The sleazebag, the whore, the ho, the big stinker pussy. That's the woman I sing about. People know that she exists. People know that she neither demands nor receives any respect. The songs about this woman should teach girls that virtue is rewarded with respect and lack of virtue and moral standards are rewarded with contempt and disrespect in my world and in yours too. Goodness and hard work are rewarded with respect. Love is repaid with love. I have had people tell me that their daughters, cousins, whatever, have heard the songs and said that they didn't want to be a woman like that woman we sing about. The kind of low woman who gets pregnant simply to capture a man and get her lazy ass a meal ticket would also go in that group. The woman who screws the boss to cement her position at work.

The point is that this woman in Phoenix you wrote about, this ho, exists in all women either on the surface or buried on some level inside. These people in the Phoenix story have lived the fantasies that we all have in those private moments. Masturbation fantasies or whatever. It's human. All of it is. Sexual fantasy is universal and bridges all social, economic, racial barriers, and people of different languages and cultures. Whether or not you engage in those fantasies is up to an individual, but the thoughts are there and the distance between thought and action is shallower in some people than others. And all men have a bit of these men within them. People will say this is not true but they know in their hearts that it is true. If there is anyone with none of this within them, I have yet to meet them.

I believe that women are beautiful naturally, and born pure and chaste. They are the creators of our universe. They, women like my mother and your mother and other hardworking, decent women, should be honored. Hos are different. They get contempt and are put down. Hos are for sex and whatever. People can say my music exploits women but they don't want to admit that a ho is a ho the world over and there is a little ho in all of us.

Q   You have categories for physical characteristics: pretty, fine, beautiful, etc. . . . Can you run those down and explain them?

A   Yeah. Well, pretty means a woman has a face you enjoy looking at. A woman may be pretty to you and not be to me, but if I say a woman is pretty then I mean that I like looking at her face.

Now fine means that a woman has a body that is exciting to look at. She may not have a face but a body that does it. You know?

A woman can have a pretty face and a fine body and still be ugly. Beauty is in the inside. I have women friends that are not physically what you would call beautiful but inside they are beauties. They care and are giving and are good people. Beauty is the only thing in a woman that really matters. It lasts long after the butt goes flat and the breasts point down and wrinkles take that face. Rarely do you find that combination of all three but that combination is what all normal men seek, most all their lives. A lot of men marry a face or a body and wake up in Hell.

Q   You say "bitch" a lot. That draws the ire of feminists and a lot of other people. "Bitch" is a very derogatory term in white culture. Like just a cut above referring to a woman as a "cunt."

A   Well in your culture I see white women wearing tee-shirts that say "BITCH" across the front, or some "BITCH" bumper stickers. Of course they don't really think they are bitches. It's a joke to them.

Q   Like you never see a truly beautiful woman in a Foxy Lady tee-shirt. Always a . . . whatever, but well, never a fox.

A   [Laughs] Yeah, but when I call a gal a bitch it isn't necessarily derogatory. See, I can call a woman or a man a bitch. A man that acts like a woman can be referred to as a bitch. A good friend can be called a bitch. Some nigger you hardly know can be called a bitch. It's one of those words that slides around every corner and can fit whatever way you feel about some . . . bitch. [Laughs again]

Like, I hear you say "boy" to people. You say, "Okay, boy, I'll see you later." You don't mean that like porter or inferior or nothing. You say that to white people and black people. It's a term with many meanings to many different people. Like bastard, honey, asshole, or kid or even bitch. It will be perceived by one person one way and another, another way. But I will say bitch when I think it applies. You may not like me calling you a bitch any more than I like you calling me boy. Chances are I won't slap you because I understand where you are coming from and I know it's just a word and you are not disrespecting me.

Most of my friends would beat the shit out of you or dislike you anyway.

Words are just words. Interpretations are personal things. In Spanish you give someone from Cuba a compliment and the same phrase spoken to say a Mexican or a Spaniard will be an insult. Don't dwell on what I say, watch what I do. You see?

Q   I was on the road and I noticed you bring out the freaks . . .

A   Sex freaks, yeah. It's something that happens. Like the golf club lady. And she was beautiful, not like you wrote. How can a white man tell if a black woman is beautiful. She was a ho, but she was a good one and she was into a good time. What you gonna do?

Q   Freaks. What was the freakiest experience you can recall?

A   Well, we had this girl that wanted us to shit and let her . . . can I say this? Eat it. But you know, sometimes you have to draw the line somewhere. [Laughs] Did you believe that?

Q   I never know.

A   That's right, John. You never will know either.

Q   You have been called a pornographer, the Great Satan, Lucifer Campbell, and a role model for the Antichrist by the right wing.

A   I have been called worse but that's just due to the fact that these fundamentalists don't get enough sex and don't want anyone else to either. There's nothing wrong with fucking and talking about pussy, the way we talk about the shit has been around since the dawn of time. God wouldn't have invented something as wonderful as pussy if he hadn't wanted people to talk about it. Hey, God, good work! This culture may condemn us and others but the language we use on our albums and the message will be with man as long as man walks the earth. Not ten million zealots, ten million members of NOW or ten million anything else can change that. It's human nature. We didn't invent anything, we just repeated it.

Q It all boils down to sex and dirty words. They are powerful . . .

A Little motherfuckers. Powerful motherfuckers. It's like sex . . .

Q Speaking of sex. Can you give me a little of your sex history?

A Oh shit! [Laughs] But no dates or names, alright?

Q No Problem. So take me back to your first . . .

A Okay. Well, it was about the time that I saw the hair starting to grow on my dick and I thought, it's time to fuck. My dick, Thompson. Well, see, I was twelve and a lot of girls liked me 'cause I had long hair and I wasn't ugly or nothin'. My brothers had girlfriends and stuff. I didn't want to be no virgin. I wanted to be able to discuss it intelligently.

The first girl was this girl who lived down the street and she was this dark girl and she had an odor problem. I fucked her in this house down the street. I had wrestled with this other beautiful gal for months and had sucked her tits and stuff but I had to settle for fuckin' the gal with the odor. It wasn't that bad. Ain't never stopped fucking since.

I used to fuck girls in my van in my backyard. I slept in it a lot 'cause I was getting pussy. I used to park on the street but cops would say that I couldn't fuck there so I would park in my own backyard.

When we used to be on the road I would fuck three girls a night. I had clap so many times that I would just go in the back door at the doctor's and get my shot. I think I counted to sixty-seven or something before I lost count. Just clap though. Since '86 I have always, always used a condom. Or two condoms.

Q You are known for freaky sexual encounters. But with a couple of exceptions you seem to have normal long-term relationships.

A On the road we attract freaks for some reason. Maybe it's the music. They follow us like hornets. They encourage you to do strange shit.

Q   It might be better to masturbate than . . .

A   Whoa! This is freaky. I have never masturbated. I have never had to and I just couldn't, well, you know, do myself. It's just a psychological hang-up. Like I know it's normal and everybody does it including priests but, hey. But check this out, if Pee-wee Herman had been me, he wouldn't have got arrested.

But speaking of freaky sex. The first time I saw women fucking each other this guy brought them over. Five years ago. Eating and fucking each other. Mark was there and when he saw that, it scared the shit out of him. Mark is the kinky one on stage but he is very straight. I was laughing so hard that I couldn't get it up. It was time to be in but I just laughed. They wanted dildos and were pissed that we didn't have any. They made this other guy go get some baby oil. Everybody had oil on them. They were eating each other's pussy. I ain't never eaten no pussy. I let Thompson eat the pussy for me. I named my dick Thompson because it's probably the only good pussy Mr. Thompson ever gets.

One night I was fuckin' a woman and this guy was fucking this woman in the bed and this guy's gal said, "I want some of his dick!" and he left the room. I fucked mine and fingered his. My gal got jealous and we went into the bathroom to finish up. This gal was on the sink with her legs up in the air. It was wild. In the Buck!

Q   You say a ho doesn't deserve respect. Isn't it just possible that some of these women are doing it out of necessity—because they have to?

A   Be a ho? No! No! She isn't doin' it because she has to. She's doing it because it's in her blood. It is in people's blood to be fucked up sometimes, you know, like it's in some people's blood to be good. Some people are going to be, no matter what happens, they always gonna be a nice, kind, loving person unless something really fucked-up happens to make them say, "Hey, the world is fucked up!" A lot of it is how a person is raised. Hos are raised like that most of the time. It's men and women too! People will get pissed when I say this. But If you are raised in a single-parent family, and I seen this shit a million times, where there ain't much money, the mother be fucking different men and be fucking the man and he'll be giving the kids a couple of dollars and say, "Be happy, here is money." The man fucks the mother and she tells him, "Give me some money!"

Then what happens, the daughter grows up and starts hanging out and the mother says, "Don't be fuckin' with them men unless they gonna spend money on you and give you some money." That's the shit that goes on in single-parent family poverty homes in the projects. That's a survival thing 'cause that check don't do nothin'. That's the natural born thing that happens. It feeds on itself and the projects grow bigger every year. A pyramid. A few guys come around and they do it. They have three or four children and they can't work because they got little ones and no one to watch them. Then the babies have babies and the mother becomes a grandmother and baby-sitter. She has to provide for her kids. It is a natural thing.

Q   So a woman is treated like she acts, or she acts like she is treated?

A   Let me just say that of all the types of women that I have messed around with in the old days, and even when I was free and hung out with women that were loose, I have always approached every girl or lady that I have met like they were pure virgin until they told me otherwise by saying something or suckin' my dick. Act like a woman and I'll treat you like a woman, act like a ho and I'll treat you like a ho. I happen to like freaky, exotic sex but I have never forced anyone to do anything they didn't want to do. A ho will tongue your asshole but it would never occur to me to ask a woman to suck my dick, that's for hos. It takes all kinds to make the world go around and somebody got to be the garbage cans of this universe.

I tell women all the time who try and act like hos and aren't, to get an education or a job and find a nice guy and settle down and have a life. Being a ho is a dead-ass-end street. Better yourself. I have saved a lot of girls with encouragement. I can take any girl and show them the projects and the hos and explain to them that having these babies and staying here is the end of the earth. Anybody in their right mind knows that.

Q   What do you feel it's going to take to break the circle of black poverty? This thing you were just describing . . . I mean you did it . . .

A   Easy. You ready for this? It's easy. It would take more black men being real men. Black men always runnin' around saying somebody oppressin' him and depressin' him and that . . . all that pressin' shit. But the truth is they don't take no responsibility. They don't take care of the kids they father. And I use the term "father" loosely. If they would show some respect for the women, then the mother won't have to be there and lose her life. These men brag about how many babies they father like they were bragging on how many cars they own. Like it's something to be proud of. That's fucked up. Do they take care of their babies? Fuck no! Two men in ten may take care of their kids to some degree and one will be a real father. Black men act like hanging around and doing nothing but keeping their itches scratched, whatever that may be, is more important than molding the life of a child they fathered. They do not show responsible behavior because it is work on their part. Who cares whether the reason is that they're not taught how to be responsible or they're lazy or stupid or selfish? The net result is the same. That is the cycle that has to be broken. Blacks will never come into their own until they learn that betterment of their entire people is more important than self-gratification. Look at the Jews or the Palestinians or the Germans or any group.

These men act like having a dick is something special and that it takes some sort of talent to shoot a load into a hot pussy! Every day of the year these woman have these babies with these men. For these men to be responsible they have to be the ones to say, "Hey, I'm gonna use a condom or hey, are you on the pill? 'Cause I don't think it's time for us to have no kids." Just as smooth as he talks her out of the pussy, just as smooth as he give her some money to have sex or give her the stuff that makes her fuck him . . . just be responsible. The men are ruining these ladies' lives. Destroying their chances. It's sad. It's like, if I can't have nothin', then don't nobody get nothin', if I can help it. It's that fucked up.

Q But the women have to take some responsibility . . . to break that cycle.

A Absolutely. They need to take it up too. "Hey, I want you to use a condom or I'll take the pill. I got a life to live!"
I tell my nieces and I'll tell my daughters that a lot of guys will just run around sayin' I got this and that and then you gonna be pregnant and have to take care of some kids. And without no education you'll have some shit five-dollar job and you won't have shit. You'll be another statistic. So do you want the "Project Road" or do you want the role of being a success. The project road is just a bunch of motherfuckers fucking you and all and who would want a bitch that's been jumped up and down by every Tom, Dick and Harry. No man worth a shit wants a ho or someone with a bunch of kids that don't look alike. If you want a good man, behave yourself and carry yourself in a respectable way and you will get a good man and have a life.

Q You just had a baby with Tina Barnett, who is not your wife but your live-in girl friend of two years. What makes this baby different than your other daughters?

A Well, even though I love my first daughter Shenetris beyond words, it's different in that this baby, Lucresha, is the first I worked to have. Before it was "Congratulations, asshole, you're a daddy." I was trapped by the mother who wanted a baby as a means of having a meal ticket and told me that she was on the pill and lied about it. It's that old cycle of, you support us since it was your sperm. Well, I have always supported her, my baby. But just having my baby don't give a bitch rights to life on easy street. I would have taken her and raised her right but the courts say I am on the road too much even though it would have been far better for her to live with me in a big house with people that care instead of in the projects with siblings that are from different men. Well, I pay for everything for her, good school and everything but I can't have her but a couple of weekends a month. That's the law. It isn't right. So I pay and pay and get none of the rewards and her mother lives in a bad place because she won't do better for herself. I love women that have the desire to better themselves.

But even Boo [Lucresha] wasn't my idea. But with Tina I have said don't use that baby as leverage against me or I'll throw you out and the baby too. I won't put up with a bitch thinking that because they have my baby they own me. What you get of me is what I decide to give. I care for Tina but I'm going to live my life exactly as I want to.

I want my children to have the best but they are going to have to earn their way to getting more than a start from me. I'll make opportunity available but I won't give a child anything they should have to earn. No child of mine is going to be lazy and get anything from me. I have worked every day of my life and believe me when I say nobody has ever given me anything. Anything.

Q   You have two children. Two daughters. Some say three. Devania Branch says three.

A   Well, I have three biological daughters. According to a recent blood test on me, Lutheria Branch seems to be able to make a convincing claim that I am her father.

Q   A convincing argument? What's convincing?

A   Ninety-nine point something percent certain. There's a little slack there.

Well, see, my first child was with a lady I met in the kitchen at Mount Sinai Hospital, Terry Brimberry. We had a thing and we had Shenetris nine years ago. She has custody and I get her weekends and a month in the summer.

Devania and I were hanging out a long time. But when I was on the road I found out that she was running around on me. She . . .

Q   How did you find out?

A   I tapped my own fuckin' telephone. What, you wanna hear the tapes? When I got back I had a nice interesting recording to listen to. The bitch had no shame. So I got rid of her. For the years we were fucking, we never used any birth control. After I threw her out, I ran into her once and we did the whatever and POP goes the weasel. It seemed like more than nine months to me. Tell me I waddn't set up! Until this day I can't believe it. So then she says that she built [Skyywalker] records. It's that greed and easy lawsuit thing. I mean, the bitch wanted a hunk of the company. I think that the kid may just be a fallback position for her. She knows she ain't gonna get no real money in this here lifetime, unless she gets it from me.

Then there's Tina. We been together a few years. Two and change. Boo wasn't planned, like I didn't say, hey let's have a baby or anything. She got pregnant. I wasn't thrilled with all the shit flying around in my life and all that. This was during the obscenity trials and all that. But I love my little Boo. I love kids, what can I say? It's the female adults that I have the problems with. But I take care of my children. I am a responsible father.

Q   Will you ever get married?

A   As I have said to you before. There is only one lady that I have met on earth that has all of the qualities I would wish for in a woman and that woman is married. To my father. A woman like my mother. You find one in this fucked-up world, I'll marry her. There ain't a woman out there that can see past my bank book. If there is I ain't met her.

Women are attracted to men on a superficial level. When I was a shorty, girls ignored me because I was a little kid. Then when I started playing football, girls were attracted to me during the season. After the season I couldn't get shot by a girl. When I started playing DJ, there were girls that were attracted to me because I was the center of attention on that level. Later when I started making money, there were girls that were attracted by that. No, I am flattered but never fooled. I can feel when a woman likes me for me. Tina does. She is the only woman that has convinced me of that. Now women fall all over me but I never give them a chance to get inside. They want to go face down in return for a drink or a trip to a club, okay. But that's all they'll get. Women are attracted to me on TV or on stage or to my Rolex or something that's superficial, and it shows in their eyes. Sometimes they try to impress me with how little they are impressed with what I have, that's entertaining.

Q   Trust comes hard for you. It took me a long time to get to where you and your people would talk to me. It was like a stone wall.

A   Well, trusting strangers who want to dig into my personal life and find out shit about me that nobody knows is weird. See, where I come from people know to mind their own business. You ask personal questions. The truth is that we had you figured for a cop and you was getting information to make a case. So until you got down with us and at least let the girl in Phoenix do what she did, we didn't trust you. I mean, you wouldn't believe the shit the cops have done to try and bust us. The city of Miami sent plainclothes cops to follow us around California with video recorders and I know that because they played the tapes for me. They were out in California following us from venue to venue and at the hotels and everything. It was nuts. So when you came out of nowhere and you had done a piece on the Klan and Skinheads and you had done the Martha Mitchell piece and been involved in the Watergate and all that we just figured you for a Fed or something undercover. Who else but a Fed would have been interested in doing a thing on the Klan and those Nazis. Oh, we checked your ass out and we couldn't find much that made sense as to why you would be interested in me and my personal life.

Q   I was interested in why you are like you are and not in the controversy as much as how you handled it mentally.

A   Yeah, see, that shit is crazy. I mean, nobody else ever asked who I was when I wasn't Luke. It was like who I really was wasn't relevant. It was fucked up. Well that's why you did the book and not somebody else that had asked to do one. Because you had wormed your way into information that wasn't available and my people thought you were okay. I also thought it was important that you could add a white perspective to this thing . . . sort of explain things from a different place. And are you ever from a different place . . . Mars.

Q   I wanted to ask you about your relationship with your family.

A   It's okay, I guess.

Q   Well, I was wondering about the relationship with your parents. I mean, I understand that you and your father haven't always seen eye to eye. Your cousin Shawn told me that your father always told you that you were a loser.

A   Well, let's say it this way. My father is a strong-willed person and so am I. Let's just say that he liked Brannard and Stanley more than me and it was obvious to me and everybody else. Let's say that he would take a belt to me and, although I am not going to say that he abused me, he sure wore my ass out. Now my mother and I were real close. I don't know whether he maybe thought she was spoiling me, he said so all the time, and maybe he was trying to balance the books on me. But I thought at the time that he didn't like me. In fact he spanked me until I was old enough to stand up and say, "Hey, if you don't like me, I don't think you should be hitting on me." And he never hit me again. But I don't hate him and I don't think he hates me. We get along now that I am a man and especially since I did make something of my life. A lot of people don't get along with their fathers as they grow up.
Do you know something I don't know?

Q   Your brothers were such overachievers. Did that have anything to do with the friction?

A   Possibly. My half-brothers and I are not close and we never were really because they were so much older than I was. But I respect them and what they have done with their lives. But I don't have anything in common with them but my mother and some photographs in books.
Stanley was a genius. He still is. He made the highest grade point in engineering school in history or some shit and he was a Navy fighter pilot. Now he is flying corporate charter. The truth is he is too fucking smart. But we are not real close and that's a long story but I love him. Stanley is close to Mamma. Brannard

and I were closest in age. They're okay. They may or may not like what I have done but I could give a shit. They have all done well for themselves. I was always in trouble growing up and my father couldn't deal with it. I guess you could say that I have always been the black sheep of the family, more or less. I didn't always fit into the Campbell scramble the right way and my parents spent many a sleepless night because of me. Daddy did say that I would never amount to a hill of beans but I think he said that because he was hoping I'd prove him wrong. I think I have done that and we have ironed our problems out.

Q   You have a very close relationship with your mother?

A   Yeah. She's my mother and she has always found a way to accept me for what I am and never asked me to alter my life for her. She has never withheld her love. When the stuff started up about my music, she was my biggest fan and staunchest supporter even though she didn't listen to the records. I don't think she has ever listened to my music. She knows that what I do is comedy. She says, "Luke is Luther's job." It's in the proper perspective in her eyes. My old gal is one of a kind.

Q   Most of your close friends are athletes. Do most of the black athletes you know come from solid families?

A   No. Most black athletes come from broken families. They have a drive that separates them from the other kids. They make it by turning the bodies into weapons. Finely tuned engines that purr and perform in a superior fashion. The drive is to get out of a bad life and very few that are truly talented do. Most get crushed and discarded. The average athletic professional career . . . NFL, NBA, etc. . . . is just three to six years of earning real money. Then they had better have set up the rest of their lives or they are dead because they are cast off by the team owners and coaches and their fans like used rubbers.

Sports is an easier way out and you are controlling your destiny. The majority of these guys come out of big, single-parent families but they happened to be good at high school and then college. The colleges only want these athletes. They talk the shit about educating them but they don't. Those guys are

out there playing their hearts out for no money, while the fuckin'
bookies are betting millions, the networks are getting a show
and paying the NCAA these big dollars, filling up these big
stadiums and getting all this money. The schools are making out
like robbers because they don't pay the athletes. They are
getting the same TV money the NFL is getting but the NFL
pays millions and millions in salaries . . . oh shit! The NFL
profits are peanuts compared to the schools'. The schools don't
even have to educate the motherfuckers, they just feed 'em and
pass 'em for four years. Most athletes are intelligent as anyone
but if somebody says just do what you love and we'll handle the
rest you let 'em. These handlers make the athlete think the game
will take care of the athlete forever.

Well, the athletes that get hurt or don't make the cut up the
line find that their benefactors don't know them if they can't
produce. So these athletes that made a fortune for the schools
are cast off. So they got no formal education and can't play.
Whose fault is that? It's on the guy to make it but it's more on
the schools. This big football player is treated as a dummy. The
teachers treat him like a dummy even though he wouldn't be if
they didn't treat him that way. It's a scandal. He is the provider
for the school but he don't mean shit to them. He isn't expected
to do shit but play. If they are stars they can do whatever the
fuck they want to do. Shoot guns on campus or whatever.

The fact is that athletes are exploited by everybody. What
can be done? Well, they can start by using their clout to make
sure that they are treated right. To see that they have a good
education in case they don't make a billion dollars for the NFL
or whatever. They should also get a slice of game revenues in a
fund that they would get when they graduate or get sidelined
and a guaranteed full four-year scholarship even if they get
knocked out due to some injury. I guarantee you, if all the
college athletes stuck together they could get whatever they
want.

I am for paying college athletes a set salary as a percentage of
what the sport makes for the school.

Like if musicians would stick together against the shit in our own industry. I guess the fence in my own backyard could use some repairs too.

Q   What's wrong with the music industry, besides the fact that it's built on greed, dishonesty and lies and deceit . . .

A   Easy now. What's wrong with the music industry is what's wrong with black people in general. Black people control the charts, the major bulk sales, the money, and yet still the black people will not support their own. They don't want no black managers, they run to a Jewish manager. Like when you and I are together on the road people assume that you are my manager. Blacks don't want to be on no black label.
Berry Gordy made his money when he created those artists. Did you ever see when the black artists did great on a white label and then call when the contract was up and say, "Berry, why don't you bid on my contract? I'm gonna shop around because it's smart to, but since you are a black man, I owe you a shot at the thing." Fuck no! Like these rappers. This little kid, a rapper at the Black Music Expo, twelve or so. He said, "Y'all on that panel saying black this and black that. Y'all got Luke there. How come y'all ain't on Luke's label. Luke's label is one hundred percent black. The only one. So y'all singing all this black shit on white-owned labels!"
Not one rapper has ever called me and said I want to negotiate with you 'cause my contract is up and I'd rather see my money going into a black company than a Jewish company. Black people don't want to work together. Like Michael Jordan signed a lifetime contract with NIKE when he could have got with a black outfit, 'cause all the shoes come from Korea anyhow, and he could have helped a black company. A black man wants to spend his money in a white establishment because he thinks if something is from a white store the service and quality will be higher. That's crap. Black stores stock what there is a market for. Why would a black store owner stock Armani suits at one thousand dollars a pop when the brothers are going to buy those suits from Bernini or whatever? So the brothers say they can't get the quality from the brother's shop when he doesn't stock

something he can't move. If they would support black business then the businessmen could cater to them.

Lately I have seen a few guys go black. Hiram Hicks who manages Keith Sweat and New Edition and a lot of guys is really a top talent manager. Before they had Jewish or white managers. That don't better our race, does it?

Q   What is happening with rap today? The majors are signing a lot of . . .

A   What's happening with rap? Rap music is making money. So now the white people want in on it and they want to cut us out. Same as always with every form of black music. Of course there are a few white people that can rap worth a damn but they will simply water down the medium until it fits the general audience. The white audience doesn't really know what good rap is, anyway. It has to be hammered into a small area, a narrow band of interest to appeal to the white audience. It always happens that way. Rap messages are too anarchistic for white America. They don't want to be frightened, they want to be sung love songs. So we have Vanilla Ice.

Q   Back to the music. . . . You invented the Miami Bass Sound?

A   Yeah. Rap was happening but it really wasn't catching on here like it needed to. So I watched and I noticed that people had to work and change their dance steps to keep up. Well, I experimented with a steady beat throughout the entire song, a constant boom-boom, you know, or what ever, but you could dance to it. See, disco was still a valid form of entertainment but over-saturation killed it. It was so big it had to go to make room for something else but the club scene never really stopped and the club music still gets reaction.

So it's better for us to keep rap pure and not to let it get too "Hollywooded" 'cause that will kill it. It's like milking a cow till it drops instead of milking it over the course of a natural life. I ain't gonna change my music. If I sell ten thousand records instead of two million then that's okay. All this stuff is in cycles but the pure stuff like jazz or rhythm and blues or country or classical maintains its audience for decades. And rap is urban music, and when the little white kids and Madison Avenue and Hollywood find the next thing, our fans that hung with us in the old days will still be willing to listen to our new stuff. So going big and mainstream is fine. If you approach those dollars like an athlete approaches those career bucks and invest, then you won't be standing there with your dick in your hand when it goes back to the one hundred thousand units from ten times that. The big bucks for us ghetto rappers will be big for a short time. So my advice is to harvest while you can. Make hay while the sun shines.

If I lose everything I have, financially, tomorrow I will just rebuild it in another direction. Like I said, money can't buy happiness. But it can buy a lot of rounds of golf.

Q   You said that white America would move you out?

A   Well, now suddenly we can't get insurance for our concerts. It serves as censorship as well as clearing rap for the white promoters who see the financial rewards. White promoters can get insurance at reasonable rates. We know that we are going to get our faces pushed into the mud as they climb over us toward the money wagons. We built rap from scratch, it's ours but soon there will be all these white kids blending rap with rock and roll and heavy metal and you won't be able to recognize it from pork and beans.

Right now the labels are signing up dozens of rap acts for their curb appeal and seeing which ones catch on and which fall away. We are all expendable to these guys. To get the big bucks they have to "whiten" the music to get the white kids into the concerts and buying the records. The records have to go platinum or at least gold or they kill the whole deal and find another lambada or something. They took rock and roll and rhythm and blues and they're doing it with rap. But hey, there will always be an underground audience. That's my audience and I know they will always be there. This other audience is fickle and they'll pump in the big bucks, then they'll be off into salsa bump and grind or some shit.

Blacks who were able to dictate fair contracts with the majors are finding that as the medium is diluted they have less and less pull in the marketplace. Do what we say or get the fuck out and we'll replace you with another rapper off the streets. So now, just when we were able to get good money they are playing the low percentage game again. You are going to see a lot of rap's pioneers ending on the streets with shit to show for their efforts, but the managers and record company officials will be driving their Mercedes.

We put out good rap and the little jitterbugs will find the records. The powers that be try to destroy the radicals. Me and Too Short and Public Enemy. If we were on the same tour, there wouldn't be a tour. The insurance would be five dollars per concert ticket sold. The insurance is a game of racism. The rock and roll groups that had people maimed or killed at their concerts can still buy insurance when they tour. They probably pay thirty-five cents per customer for insurance. We have never had a serious injury or a death at any of our concerts but we can't play because we won't bend over for white America. Oh, whatever you do, don't let the blacks congregate and when white kids show up, oh shit! The truth is that if blacks were allowed to go to concerts all the time there wouldn't be problems when they did get around to allowing us a venue. These kids see so few concerts that they get nuts when they do get out. We are bad kids, we are worse because we are black kids and we are getting ours. We are taking ours. They made the rules and we won't live by them because they don't have nothing to do with us.

Hey, I am black and I don't think that matters. It certainly ain't getting in my way. If I want something, I go get mine.

Q   Blacks are getting into film again.

A   Yeah, in Hollywood they say Spike Lee is a great director. For a black man. The critics always say he's black. You would assume that he is history's first black director. Now think about that.

He's a credit to his race, I guess that can be said in many different ways. No matter what he does, they ain't gonna let him forget that he's the Charlie Pride of movies. They all seem amazed that a black man could direct a film. Spike attacked me and called me an ignorant brother. Relax, Spike. I am not your enemy and we are both black and attacking me is pointless. These guys in Hollywood ain't gonna think you are white because you are too cultured to be black any longer. I am a black man. I am so black that nobody will ever mistake me for a white man.

George Jackson is the producer of *New Jack City*. He came to me and asked me to do something with him for that movie. I thanked him five times if I thanked him at all. He was great. Spike Lee wouldn't come to me and say, "Hey man! This is a black movie and we want you to put the sound track out on your black label. Let's negotiate." Oh no! Chances are they'd get better distribution and make more money for themselves. And they must know that. Not Spike Lee, Robert Townsend or John Singleton asked about the possibilities of getting a black label to do the albums for their movies. Not that I know of. And I like those dudes and we could have dealt. We won't have no black film houses until a Berry Gordy of the movie industry comes along. The blacks in film still have to dance to a white tune. I am the only black person distributing my own product. Atlantic presses. All my tapes are in my warehouse. Luke Records is the only black-owned record company of any size. Black people built this company. I own it! They press my music and send it out. It's efficient to have it in one place. I pay the plants to press my records. One-stop shop.

Q   The guys from Atlantic Records . . .

A   You want to talk about my deal with Atlantic Records? Shit. Okay. Well, the record was selling and an attorney I won't name and one of my ex-employees hooked up this Atlantic meeting. They said, Oh, we want to get back into black music. We were the original major that supported black music with Aretha Franklin and these others. And we believe that you are being persecuted because the fundamentalists are getting the record chains to toss your records out. If you had our power behind you they would not throw your records out. We have clout. Why Luther, we would tell them take 2 Live or you get no Atlantic product. And that bullshit, there. Well, it turned out that they couldn't get the chains to take the record and even more pulled out. Someone said recently that if Salmon Rushdie had been a musician, and the fundamentalists were the Iranians, that Rushdie's head would have been waved from the rooftop as soon as the first picket line appeared outside the record company's office.

They sat there with their thumbs up their asses and made excuses by the score but the fact remained they didn't do shit. The record is only available from stores that have balls, period. Freedom-loving stores that understand that once this ball gets rolling, and people like Jack Thompson and Bob DeMoss, James Dobson of Focus on the Family and Pat Robertson and those people get the ball rolling, you will be listening to numerous remakes of *The Sound of Music* and they'll make Donald Duck wear pants and marry Daisy Duck on TV. See, people who understand know that Nazi and fascist countries started with an innocent ''let's just take off the radical, far-end shit'' censorship and grew to the point where they were censoring the fuckin' population with gas chambers and bullets. The Jack Thompsons don't think they are Nazis, they just see themselves as big superior beings. They have this image of themselves as Christ whipping the money changers out of the Temple and not men in black uniforms smiling as the books they don't think we need to read are heaped on the fires.

The point is that Atlantic lets these guys make punks of them and the record store owners get the same thing and they take it because they do not believe in freedoms, their own included.

Q   Record store owners. A strange breed. We were talking about Charles Freeman the other day. The record store owner that was arrested and convicted in Broward County of selling *Nasty*.

A   Yeah. Freeman is a trip. He got arrested the other day for drug trafficking which was supposedly going on for a long time. I don't know anything about that there but I can tell you that people have said that he did and he didn't. It has nothing to do with the 2 Live stuff because it isn't even a Broward County deal.

See, he called here and wanted some of our people to go check on his wife. They said what? Call her yourself. My people don't know his wife and they are busy. There never was any connection between Freeman and us. He sold the record because he wanted to. We had told him that we didn't want one person to go to jail or get arrested because they were selling the record. We said that we would take care of it, ourselves.

But Charles did what he did and he spent one hour in jail. One hour. He got on talk shows and that there and his name was everywhere and there was talk of movie deals and all this and that and I was happy for the cat. But then he sent a stack of his personal bills for me to pay! I had helped the store clerk in Alabama and had said I would support that guy's family if he went to jail, but I was not going to give Freeman money to pay what amounted to his old bills that he incurred before the trouble. The man sent me bills from three separate American Express Cards he had and overdue rent payments and all kinds of shit. Of course I didn't pay it. If he wasn't a businessman why was I supposed to give him thousands of dollars. And the press acted like I had abandoned him. That's shit. I sent him my attorney, Bruce Rogow, for his trial. He was making his own statement which was, "This is America and I'll do whatever the fuck I want." And he took the consequences. He actually made money in the wake of the arrest, hand over fist. I don't know where the money went. I talked with the record distributors and the money he owed them was forgiven. He had to pay C.O.D. on delivery, but so what?

Charles Freeman is a nice guy and I don't have anything against him. But he is a man and he has to make his own bed. That's all.

In this life we all make our own beds and then we have to sleep in them.

Q   This old pal of yours called me the other night and he was saying that you had double-crossed a lot of your old friends.

A   My philosophy is that if someone makes me money that's great. But I ain't into dragging a bunch of nonproducing motherfuckers along in no wagon. Oh no. I'll always say hello to my old running buddies and wish them well. But friendships can't be based on me giving free rides to people. I didn't get to where I am by giving my money away. I invest my money in ideas and in people that I think will make my pile of money grow.

These people from the old neighborhood, they talk shit. If they had been producers, they would be here with me instead of in some bar or street corner in Liberty City talking about how they made me what I am. If you listen to people in the neighborhood, you would think I was carried from one event in my life to another on the shoulders of people in the neighborhood. Well, none of those people made me and I certainly didn't make them what they are now. I play to win and I don't waste my time with losers. They don't want to be down with me. They want to be down with the money they imagine I have. Some of them did work for me but they were either lazy or wanted a bigger piece than they deserved. A few were just plain jealous of what I had. They say I paid short money but I paid them more than they were worth in most cases and a hell of a lot more than they are making now.

Q   Back to the movie thing. You are interested in doing movies. In fact I remember once when David Chackler got some heavy people interested in casting you.

A   Yeah. When we were in Los Angeles and we went with David Chackler to visit Tom Holland, the director of *Child's Play* with that Chuckie Doll and *Fright Night* about the kid who has a vampire move in next door. Great director. No Spike Lee, but great for a white director. We went up there to discuss my role as the villain in a pilot called *The Owl*. We met this other guy who was the ex-head of CBS Entertainment. LeMasters. Kim LeMasters or something like that. They wanted me for the part. Hell, they gave me the part. They gave me all this here talk about you will be great. A natural villain. We'll work with you and here's the script.Learn the lines. Hell, write your own. You are the black guy, you know what you would say. I was on cloud nine. We were sitting in this big house in the canyon overlooking

Steven Spielberg's place. I had the script and a date to be out there. You were there. I was hired!

Q   Yes, you were hired.

A   On the plane, I read the script over, and when I got home, I told some of my friends and my family about it. Well, the date for shooting drew close and I had blocked out time. I was excited. I dreamed of being in films since I was a shorty. Well, the people never called. Finally word came that they had cast someone else for the role. They finally called Chackler and said that they had been too embarrassed to call and tell me that the network had freaked out when they mentioned my name. Not a real villain! A vulgar villain! They made some weak promise about bringing me in on a later episode, said that the star was afraid that I would upstage him with the press or whatever. It was a humiliating experience for me. See, I have never equated myself with Luke and the 2 Live Crew's character. None of us see ouselves as bad people and it hurts us when people think we are evil or whatever. Luke is my job. He pays my bills. But I am not Luke. I am Luther Campbell. The man is one of Hollywood's biggest directors and the other guy is one of the heavyweights and they couldn't tell me that I was out, to my face. Jesus. I may be a lot of things but I am a man. I tell people good news or bad news to their face. Especially if I have inconvenienced them or made them look like a fool. That's just common decency. And they say I'm the nigger.

Q   You have some strong opinions on the way blacks are depicted and how the movies are controlled to make specific impressions.

A   Anytime there is a black film the press starts predicting gang violence at the openings. When there is in fact any sign of violence, the film gets pulled from a large number of film houses. The AMC chain owns something like four thousand theaters but independent films have only a set number of houses that will show them. It's like eight hundred. Why is this the way it is?

I say that the white-controlled film industry does not want to see the black film community gain any real strength. They see the successful present black film thing as a short-term deal. When the momentum starts to build they will kill it off slowly or maintain control through distribution, advertising and that. The fact that *Boyz 'n the Hood* outgrossed *Terminator II* in some markets freaked people out. There is some trouble at the openings because there are some trigger-happy people who come to the movies. If they didn't have the idea planted that there would be violence by the media, who knows? The trailer for *Boyz 'n The Hood* made it look like a gang movie and it wasn't. Who produced the trailer that was shown on the TV?

Is that to discourage whites from taking a chance of being a target of black gang violence or black-on-white assaults? Would you go to the Omni where the audience might be ninety-five percent black to see *Boyz 'n the Hood*? You might join a mainly white audience to see that but what mainly white theater is going to show it? Even though it is still grossing at the box office. In fact, in those measly theaters it is still in the top four films in gross receipts behind *Terminator II*. But *Boyz 'n the Hood* has been out months and it is still selling tickets.

The plain fact is that the black man has to understand that they have to push things through. We have to solidify behind our own agendas. The white man does not want to see us driving his cars, living in his neighborhoods, playing golf at his country clubs, or dating his daughters, or directing his movies. Can you see a black director directing a white film? No. But white directors can do black films. We have to fight for everything we get. That's a struggle that we have to get into. They are not going to give us shit. We have to go get it and hold it ourselves and we have to help each other hold on or we will be the Plains Indians who have disappeared into the back pages of history books.

Q   I have seen how the music industry treats you. Like . . .

A   Like shit. You can say shit.

Q   Almost like the retarded son who is kept in the attic.

A   Well, it's their problem. I go to the Soul Train Awards. A black function, but yet and still my people have to go through hell to get me a ticket, period. Then they seat me up by the tourists back behind a pole. Sorry-assed old Don Cornelius who is so old he can't hardly walk is still thinking that music is Nat King Cole or something. He's dictating what is a hit and what should be listened to. People like him would rather that rap had stayed in the projects, in the alleys and parks. And my music might as well be from outer space.

When I went to the Grammys I expected to sit in the woods. But they dedicated the ceremony to censorship of music. I sit there and they talk about censorship and y'all know what is going on with Madonna! They didn't even mention 2 Live Crew. And I spend hundreds of thousands of dollars on lawyers and faced jail. They made it a white thing. I like Madonna. She's great. But she can fuck herself on stage with a dildo and people will say, Oh isn't that cute or Ohhh she's so wicked. But I'm the naughty nigger. She's white. But the Grammy people showed their true colors.

I don't judge anyone until they open their mouth. Then they will show what they are. I was threatened with jail. I stood trial. I am happy for her success but most of those people resent mine. If Madonna had been arrested for masturbating on stage or saying lick my asshole, the whole world would have been standing behind her. The support I got from this industry would have fit into an eyedropper. Sinead O'Connor and Bruce Springsteen and a couple of others.

Q   Were you shocked at the blacks who slammed you along with the right-wingers? Rev. Benjamin Hooks and the others.

A   Oh, all right-wingers are not white. Oh no indeed. Most blacks will say yeah, city street niggers talk that nasty shit there in Luke's songs, but we don't even know what shit is. And the whiter a black thinks he or she is, the harder they protest being thought of as part of "those" niggers that talk like that. Well, I got news for you. Benjamin Hooks and Carl Rowan and Jesse Jackson and everybody else you can name talk just like I talk when they are getting down with their friends. When all the white people are away and they are far from tape recorders, they loosen their ties and talk about poppin' that pussy! Ben

Hooks and the fellows just don't realize that everybody knows they are black. The difference is that I can be honest 'cause I don't have to convince anyone that I am not as black as "them street people" are. I talk like I talk, like my friends talk, like we talk all over these here United States. It upsets Hooks that I ain't talking white enough and I have drawn attention to the fact that we are not all looking to be accepted in polite white society. Most white people accept me for being honest and because I got a fat bank account. If I was poor I could talk like those other "house" niggers and I couldn't get a white person, other than a cop, to speak to me. Who they think they are fooling.

MTV was running PSAs [public service announcements] on getting out the vote. They had a naked Madonna wrapped in a flag in one of them. We called the producers up and asked if we could do a PSA. They said hell no! Wouldn't even talk to us. The white people don't want to see us do anything and neither do the blacks.

Q You sold almost three million copies of *Nasty*. That's mainstream, but I keep hearing you say that you hate being mainstreamed. Can you explain that?

A The best thing for me is to stay underground. I play to them. They are my people. I don't think I'll have another double platinum because half of the copies of *Nasty* were sold because of the controversy to people who just wanted to see what the fuck was going on. Those people won't buy any more of the music. I will always get some college kids and a few people who like the music but my audience is the people that live what I talk about. My audience buys records and tapes. The CDs are ninety percent white. *Nasty* sold twenty-five percent in CDs. *Move Somethin'* was five percent CD. See the trend there?

I would be losing money trying to stay mainstream. The truth is most black radio stations are owned by whites. The only time the DJs get black is when they lose their jobs. They make hits because whatever they play will be accepted and the whites like safe "Negro" music.

My music is pure anarchy. They hate Too Short and Public Enemy for the same reason. We are troublemakers because we believe that things are fucked up and have to change. I may own radio stations someday when the F.C.C. stops its racist policies. It should be so that if a black man wants to buy a station and has the money, they should make room for a station on the dial. You can't do that shit. They know that you are going to take the talent and play the black music. The right music. And tell the truth.

Q   You had a pirate radio station playing your music and interviews with you like twenty-four hours a day for a while.

A   Yeah, I heard that. But I never owned that station or had anything to do with it.

Q   Even though some people say it was in your building.

A   The answer for the record is that I don't know shit about that shit. And besides you can't prove shit! Jack Thompson might have done that station to get me in trouble. Who knows?

Q   None of your people were running the station?

A   What station?

Q   When I was writing a piece on you for the *Miami Herald,* you said I should call Jesse Jackson because you supported his Rainbow Coalition, so I called Reverend Jackson for a quote and his personal assistant said, "Oh, Mr. Jackson could never be quoted on that!"

A   Well, let me just say this about that. That hurt me because I had been a big fan of his and I had given them money. I expected something back when I was against the bars. I mean they were always calling me saying Reverend needs this and that and I had always written checks without asking for anything. When I was in court and he was going to be in the area I asked if he might come by the courthouse and sit in the audience for a few minutes to show his support for what was a racially based attack on me and my music by a bunch of fundamentalist pee brains. Well, no, he couldn't work it into his schedule or whatever. The Rainbow Coalition still calls me to help but as far as I can see the Reverend is just a politician with his own personal agenda. While I respect him for what he did in the old King days, he doesn't mean any more to me than say a local black councilman. Now I may help him or not but I don't feel the need to go out of my way for him. Maybe next time I am tried, he can drop by the trial to pick up a check. He didn't have to do an Al Sharpton number in the courtroom, just seem interested that justice might be served and let the world know that we were friends, which I thought we were.

The world is filled with people who didn't show up to support me. A few said something like, "Oh Luke is a nice guy and this censorship thing is scary but his music is really too rough." But nobody showed except Al Goldstein, the publisher of *Screw* magazine. If it had been someone else locked up and they had asked me, I would have come if I thought I was wanted or needed. I was really disappointed in a lot of people.

Q   One of your people told me that when you first started being attacked you went to Jesse Jackson for some help in mending your image in the black community and that he agreed to help but then hit you up for cash in exchange for doing you the favor?

A   I have no comment on that. [Shrugs]

Q   Do you admire Louis Farrakhan?

A   To a point, yes. I follow him until he gets to the point where he says that his religion is the one true religion. I'm Catholic and that's my true religion. But religion aside I admire his inspirational rhetoric. When he says that blacks must create their own jobs instead of leaving school to find work in the white-owned businesses, I agree with that. Why would the white man make room for us when he has the wealth. He doesn't have our best interests at heart. If the positions were reversed we'd probably be the same way. Black men and women need to create their own economic base. Without economic power there is no political power.

The Reverend loses me after that has been said. But the Black Muslims do a lot of good. They do a lot to build healthy self-images for black kids. They believe in being healthy and strong and proud. So you can say he's a maniac or whatever but he does a lot of good and a lot of what he says makes sense.

Jesse Jackson has a lot to say that is positive. But Jesse Jackson isn't the savior blacks are looking for. He's a politician. He also gives black kids a positive self-image. We need more black leaders at a local and regional level. Things have to be changed one kid at a time. If Jesse Jackson was elected President, you really believe he'd be any different from Jimmy Carter or George Bush or anybody else? No man, all the cats at that level only care about their own glorification, building monuments to themselves, and talking in generalities. He wouldn't do any more than a white, conservative Congress would let him do. He's just playing at politics and running for President for God knows what reason. If he wants to help he can roll up his sleeves, come down off his mountaintop, and do what Jimmy Carter is doing. Get into the streets and help people with your hands.

It's like he went to Africa to be photographed with Nelson Mandela when he was let out of prison. Mandela didn't want to be seen with Jesse. So what? He wanted it to look like he had exerted pressure on the government to release Nelson. Those blacks didn't know Jesse Jackson from Buckwheat. And he goes off trying to get hostages released and all that.

Q   Are there any black leaders you genuinely admire?

A   Are there any black leaders, period? They say that Martin Luther King was dedicated to nonviolence. King was probably killed because he went public against America's using the ghetto's black kids as targets in Vietnam. I think the non-violence gig was about up with old Martin. They have wiped out all of our best leaders. Keep on cutting the head off the snake. Malcolm X, King, Fred Hampton. And we got what in their places? Jessie Jackson? Louis Farrakhan? Benjamin Hooks? Andrew Young? How many leaders do we have? How many white leaders can you name? Hundreds. How many black leaders? See? We got a black supreme court nominee that don't even like blacks.

Q   We were talking about Benjamin Hooks and how he is whiter than . . .

A   Yeah. See, I talk slang. Black street slang. But I can sound white if I want to. "Like let's get laid, man! Ya know dude." In school, people were always telling me that my vernacular and stuff was common. You can talk to my brothers on the telephone and you wouldn't know they were black. They have mastered English. I never wanted to lose my ghetto language because it is my heritage and my culture. I am most comfortable talking the way I talk. I say motherfucker this and that shit and all that there and I talk like that there. Yet and still, I can drop the motherfucker and shit and all that stuff when it is inappropriate. I am dismissed as ignorant by those blacks who have worked to speak like white people and who were brought up in Miami Beach or wherever. The way I talk pegs me for the ghetto. That's what I am and even though I live on a golf course I am still the same bitch I was ten years ago. I ain't learning how to talk white, you can learn to talk black.

If people want to judge me for the way I talk, fine. If people want to think I'm ignorant because I don't speak like they do, fine. That actually gives me the edge in business deals. The fact is the people I employ speak that way and between me and my perfect-language attorneys I do okay. It is honest.

Q   You have had a lot of trouble on the road over the years. The thing that was most interesting to me was that the worst of all times was handed to you by a black mayor. Detroit's Coleman Young.

A   Oh, that motherfucker! Well, it's like this here. I still get pissed thinking about that self-sucking asshole.

Well, we went to Detroit and this black reverend contacted us and said that unless we donated to his whatever "church" fund, he would make sure that we didn't play in Detroit. He did. He said he could fix us one way or the other through the mayor's office. Well, I said something like, when hell freezes over preacher, and he suddenly had this big loud-assed organization, this typical Christians for Decency ding-dong deal. And he did what he said he'd do. Through the mayor's office.

The city people changed the venue three times. Each time we set up a sound check, here came the inspectors and it was, oh you can't play here because the bathrooms aren't up to code. The next place, same thing and so forth. Three times on the day of the concert. How was anyone going to follow that shit.

Mayor Asshole and the preacher put out the word. We had an interview and when we got there the radio station people locked the door and were looking at us through the glass window like we had leprosy and they were talking but we couldn't hear a word 'cause the glass was thick. It was crazy!

So we were scheduled to be on a TV show. A noon deal. When we got there the station security told us that the man we were supposed to see was out. He wasn't there? No, he was there. On the air. We were thrown out of the TV studio. Word was out. I still said FUCK THE PREACHER! That was Detroit! Where a black man was mayor. A lot of blacks like Mr. Coleman Young think they aren't really black like the rest of the niggers. They think they are better than the rest of us. I don't ever want anyone to think that I am ashamed of my neighborhood because I know how black I am. I'm as black as black gets. Jet black.

Q   We have talked about the talk shows that you have done. What was the worst?

A   That's easy. The worst talk show host in America is Geraldo Rivera. He doesn't have shows, he has opinions and he stacks his shows to get his opinion burned into America's brain. He seems like this intelligent, caring crusader but he is an egomaniacal, pompous, strutting, tiny man in platform shoes with greasy hair and the worst breath in history. No shit, you could smell his breath all the way across the stage. But it isn't his hygiene that makes him an asshole. In his book he talks about all the pussy he got in the "Green" room. I bet those poor bitches remember his breath.

See, his people stack his shows and he ambushes people. When we did the show I knew that Navarro and Geraldo were friends from when Geraldo and Navarro made asses of themselves when Geraldo followed Broward County deputies into a house and arrested an innocent man on live TV. It came out later that there are crack houses that the citizens have filed hundreds of complaints on over months and the sheriff hasn't done shit. Well, that's because he isn't a cop. He sees himself as a National Law Enforcement Celebrity.

So, anyway, in the audience Geraldo brought in Navarro's attorney and a whole section of deputies and Cuban supporters of his. These supporters are always getting involved in scandals and they are boosters and contributors. Then he put in a group of maniac religious blacks. A whole congregation of white-eyed Bible-thumpers. These people are the kind of fanatics that actually go to church during the week. They might have let ten people in off the street, maybe.

I have no respect for Geraldo. He's beneath contempt. He says he's against censorship. He's a fawning puppy dog who has a thing for cops. I think he's a pretty boy who has had his dick sucked so hard by so many people over the years that his brain has become dislodged.

Q So, most people with any sense hate Geraldo. Who do you like?

A That's easy. Arsenio Hall and Phil Donahue. Well, it isn't just because they are anticensorhip and ask intelligent questions and let people talk. They are, well . . . take Arsenio. He's a gentleman and a nice guy too. He doesn't come on with the star attitude. He works his butt off and he went out on a limb to help us. He has the strength of his convictions and he has integrity. He also has one motherfucker of a sense of humor. His people still stay in touch with my people. They send cards to my employees and call. He is surrounded by nice people who are real professionals. I would do anything for the cat.

Q And Donahue?

A Listen, Donahue is whiter than you are. He sparkles, he's so clean. But the man has soul. He really tries to understand people. He goes out of his way. Like the man sent his kids to a black school so they would get to know blacks and what we go through. He is a really nice person. He sent my mother an autographed picture because one of my people said something to one of his people about what a fan of his my mother was. He's thoughtful. And when we were in the dressing room the first time, he came in and spent time talking to us and preparing us for his show. He said, look, don't be impressed with me. I'm just here to try and mediate the show. I am not the star, my guests are the stars of this show. And he talks to you and you can tell that he is sincere and that he gives a shit about people. I have been his guest three times and each time I like him better. If someone like him was President and if the congressmen and senators in this country thought and felt like he did, this country would light up the universe. He is a truly peaceful man.

When Jack Thompson was on the show he started off by kissing up to Donahue sayin' something like, Oh Phil, please tell Marlo that she looks twice as beautiful as she did back when she was on *That Girl*. Phil Donahue looked at him like he was crazy. Thompson just sat there with this goofy look on his face and he didn't even realize that nobody likes an ass-sucker.

And during that same show, Bob DeMoss from Focus on the Family yelled out lyrics from *Nasty:* "SUCK MY DICK AND LICK MY ASSHOLE TILL YOUR TONGUE TURNS DOO DOO BROWN" and that stuff before anyone could stop him. The camera crew almost fainted. I guess that DeMoss thought the censors would bleep it, but it was going out live to, like, ten million people. You should have seen Donahue's face. After that I am sure he really disliked those guys but he stayed cool about that.

Q   Have you considered doing a TV show, cable or whatever?

A   The truth is they are scared of me. If I show what Downtown Julie Brown shows, a white ass dancing, people would lynch my ass. I'd love doing a show. I have a tape that runs several hours of interviews with hardcore rappers like Too Short and Chuck D from Public Enemy and Ice T. And we'll see if it runs anywhere. It's radical. I just MC it.

The truth is that damned near everybody wants to see me crushed. Well I ain't gonna get crushed. Man, I have just started. *Sports Weekend, Nasty Too* is the best record 2 Live Crew has done to date. I have a solo album coming out and this book and a TV movie deal with a major studio and I am putting together a movie using my own money and talented people and I have a great story to tell that is different and exciting. But I am far from being finished! Just wait till they hear "Pop the Pussy!"

Listen, when Jack Thompson's crazy old ass stirred up the shit, *Nasty* had bottomed out. Flat-lined. We had sold over a million units and we said, that was neat! We were getting ready to start accepting the returns that weren't sold. But old Jack opened his blowhole and the shit flew and we sold another one and a half million units. So thanks to old Punk Jack and those other shitsucks there are another million and a half units of *Nasty* available out there and it is still selling quite well.

Q   You guys have been around a long time. Five years or whatever it is. I have witnessed some friction in the group of late.

A   Is the group healthy? Is that what you asking me?

Q   Yeah.

A   Every marriage has its ups and downs. Ours ain't in divorce yet but there are some, what did you call it? Frictions. Yeah, there is some serious friction.

Q   Is it going to resolve itself or are 2 Live Crew dead?

A   Good question.

Q   And.

A   Well, I am not free to answer that. Ask them. Maybe they don't think they need me. Maybe I don't think I need them. Who knows. We don't really talk about it.

Q   But it's no secret that you are doing a solo album.

A   That has nothing to do with anything. I am doing that because I have some non-2 Live statements to make. They may have some to make without me. That's okay. The studio door is open wide. Let's just say that some things have come down and I have had to harden my thinking on the thing. But I don't need a megahit solo career to boost my ego. I am content with doing what I do. Would I have a career without 2 Live? Yeah. I am a businessman and I don't have all of my eggs in one basket. Do they? Ask them. If 2 Live stopped tomorrow I'd live the same as I do right now. Would I miss it? Yes and no. What else. You startin' to depress me.

Q   Oh, drugs. What about what drugs are doing to your community?

A   You want to talk about drugs?

Q   Yeah, I can take it.

A   You watch the news and you think the blacks have a corner on the drug dealings. No. Listen, have you ever seen a black man caught with pounds and pounds of drugs? Ever? Or a boatload of grass or a bale, even? No. You see white guys, Colombians, Italians, Panamanians or whatever. Blacks have a few ounces. We are the targets of the big pushers, the big drug dealers. The black pushers with their little ounces are the ones that get busted, get killed by the cops. It's a conspiracy. A white and near-white conspiracy. They use us for ready cash. We are the end users. We are the victims!

Q   Who controls drugs?

A   Well, the drug dealers couldn't stay in business unless the cops let them. When the drug pushers get outta line or cop a high profile they get busted or killed by the cops. Like Mercado. You think anyone knows that story? A couple of those cops have been beating up niggers for years. When the Mercado thing happened, there were a lot of people that had the names of the officers before anything was announced. They knew who they were because people been seeing them kick people for years. It was only a matter of time before they beat someone over the line. I think those cops beat that man to death. You know it and I know it. Are they involved in drug trafficking? Gee, I don't know. They might be. You white. You might be.

We blacks are selling drugs on a street level while the real pushers are sitting at the white country clubs and in the rows of the churches. If you sell some marijuana to your college friends, that's just helping out some buddies. But if I sell the same amount of grass to my friends, I am a drug dealer. If you get caught with a bag of weed, you might get your hand slapped. I would go to jail. You have friends that deal drugs. They might be doctors or lawyers or other professional people who invest in drug deals. The people in my culture that sell drugs are wild animals according to your culture when in fact a lot of them are good people who are making a living the only way available to them. It's a survival thing. The dealers, the real dealers who dump the shit in our neighborhoods in mega-kilo loads, rarely go to jail because their hands stay clean and their money buys them out.

Q But there is an awful lot of violence in the drug culture.

A Yes. And a lot of innocent people get hurt. The survival instinct is strong and guns are cheap. Plus a lot of these people use drugs as well. They have their territory like IBM or whatever. They stake out their territory and hold it the best way they can. They shoot because they think the other guy is gonna shoot. People are generally killed by a man who is afraid. Fear is the quickest motivator on earth. That's why the death penalty doesn't enter into anything. I got to survive today, this minute, and down the road a day, a week or ten years don't matter. If I am not afraid of dying on the street, of falling shot to shit, why will I be afraid of some electrician ten years away. Fuck that. Prison itself is no deterrent because jail is as gentle as the streets or at least in jail I can survive and my odds are better than on the streets sometimes. Jail is just another place to be for a lot of people. And the money in the drug deals is good enough that these kids without hope choose it as an exit even though it isn't at all. We have to give these inner-city kids alternatives that they can see will work. They need hope. They need to know that they are worth something. They need some self-esteem. If you have self-esteem, you can be anything and go anywhere. If you don't, you are dead meat. These kids are the white nightmare. The kid who will rob you and then shoot you just to see your brains splash. To change that, you have to get kids early and give them a clear alternative to being bad. Man is basically good but that good can be wiped out easily by leaving these kids to the streets. So pay now, or pay later.

Q   You did drugs?

A   You know I did. I did marijuana when I was a shorty. I got it from Jamaicans. I used to say that it was just grass but I had pals that were selling cocaine and I was around it. I hate drugs now because I see them for what they have done to my people. Drugs are bad news.

I am not that person now. Maybe I'm worse but I don't abide drugs. I tell kids that it's the shits. You can get an education and get out straight and never have to look back at part of your life, if you live that long, and be ashamed of anything. Black kids are just as good as white or Cuban kids and they will show the world that in a few years. We have to concentrate on getting the next two generations up to snuff and then they will take it from there. You'll see. I'm putting my energy in the little kids.

Q   You were involved in the Liberty City riots in 1980?

A   Yeah. This cop killed this black ex-Marine. Blew his brains out in an arcade or some shit. He got off. The black people went crazy as fuck. We was all running the streets and shopping in the stores that had been opened up for the evening. People always say we burn up our own neighborhoods during a riot, but we burn up the non-black-owned stores and the crowd knows which are which. I was there, right there, when the white guy was pulled from his car and they killed him and chopped off his head with a machete. The put a rose in his neck. It was scary.

Q   You don't hate cops.

A   No. Most cops are good guys trying to do their jobs as best they can. But no matter what, you get some jerks. Like the Cuban cop who got freaked by this bike flying at him with a cop car in pursuit and he puts a warning shot through this guy's head driving the bike. Well, the bike crashes and kills the passenger. Well, he probably didn't really know the biker was black because the guy had a helmet on but in that neighborhood you better be. The Cubans will get him released.

Q   The Cubans. You don't like Cubans?

A   No, It's not that. I don't necessarily dislike the Cubans. But they don't like us. But it was you white shits that let them all come in here and take over! Don't write that! But seriously, the Cubans and the Caribbean blacks gave this city its personality. The Latin style blended with the black, Caribbean rhythm and colors and that is what Miami is. It ain't the tired old people that come down here to shop and die. This place was dead until the Cubans started bringing Latin money here. This place was a jerkwater berg. Cubans and the other Latins gave this town a rhythm and the blacks gave it soul. Y'all put them crazy-ass Latins in police uniforms.

Q   Do you think that Cuban politicians are more corrupt than anglos or blacks?

A   I guess historically Latins are almost as corrupt as white people, surely more corrupt than blacks. [Laughs] But they are portrayed as so in the movies and the media. I see the movies like *Cuba* and all. I can tell you that of all the politicians that came to me for payoffs, the majority were Latins. A lot of them get indicted and go to jail or just get thrown out of office. The replacements do the same thing. Maybe it's in their hot blood and mixing that with politics makes them worse. Like political killer bees. Or maybe whites don't get caught as often because they're warned or protected. You tell me. My experience is that all politicians are corrupt. Black, white, Cuban and green.

But corruption is wide-ranging. Like Navarro who has used this obscenity business to collect money from all over the country by looking like he is the only thing between "filth" and the kids of America. He has gotten something like half of his donations from outside Broward County, and the state. And half of the contributions made up one-third of the total. Forty-eight grand, last count. He claimed that the "forces of evil" like the record industry were financing a candidate, which is complete bullshit and he knows it. Nobody is running that could beat him.

Hell, you would think that some old retired fart from Miami Beach could beat him with his record. Maybe he'll buy a better wig and a Belly Burner with the money.

Q   So talk about the old people on Miami Beach.

A   Yeah, you are gonna get me shot. I said that I think that these old people that I see sitting there are making those hotel porches look like storage shelves for cadavers. I thought when I was a kid and I'd see them there that they were being punished by God for having slaves and he wouldn't let them die because they had been so bad. But I was a shorty and they were mostly Jewish and Jews have never had slaves. Jews are a trip, but Jews have been nice to me, mostly. But somebody told me that they owned the slave ships and leased them to the slavers, but I don't know that that is true and I wouldn't say it if it took the heat off your people. Speaking of slaves. When are you going to give us our money for building this country as slaves. I know a few million people that could sure use some of it. It's racist not to give it to them. And me. [Laughs]

Q   Did you think that the attacks on you were racially based?

A   You don't! Please. The black community's businesses in South Florida are mostly controlled by Cubans these days and there is a lot of resentment there. I am a strong African-American personality and businessman who is out to grab back a piece of my world from them. So they don't like me and I accept that. And I will tell you that I believe with all my heart that my persecution was directed by those forces and that Martinez and Navarro were directed to knock me flat and that Gonzalez was their personal hammer.

See, I'm about money. I knew that in order to get rich I would have to have people working for me twenty-four hours a day, and I do. Even when I sleep I am making money in one business or another somewhere in the world. They hate to see that shit. Oh, it's racially motivated. I think Navarro is a racist, I think Martinez is a racist and I think Jack Thompson is a racist. It's lucky for Thompson that I have changed. Five years ago, I would have gone to that motherfucker's house and called him out in the yard and fucked him up. Even as nice as I am, I have come close to doing that.

Q   I have always maintained that you were arrested for talking dirty to white girls.

A   Yeah, ain't that some shit. See, the truth is that every form of American music owes itself to black music. Most white composers derived their music from black music because of the strength of that form. Only black music like the Motown stuff held up against the Beatles. The white music fell into a canyon because it wasn't strong enough to stand alone to the English music invasion of the sixties. That is all a fact and it is not taught in any school. But ask any good music critic. Now rock and roll was the first black music where white kids accepted blacks and followed them around. This was the first time young white people had dared defy their parents and follow and openly enjoy black people. This was race mixing and the white men in power freaked out and the white fundamentalists did what they are still doing. I believe in my heart that Jack Thompson, Reverend Don Wildmon and these others are just racists. Pure old racists just like the Klan, or the old Southern sheriffs, except the Klan and the Southern sheriffs are honest about it. And we are doing worse than any nigger in history has dared to do. We are telling white females that we have big black dicks and we know how to use them. The white old fathers are freaking out because they are afraid of the fact that once a white girl has slept with a real man, white or black, she won't settle for the stuck-up, pencil-dick motherfuckers that her daddy likes.

Jack might not think, and he will never admit, that he is a racist but he is. He says that his life was threatened when he stood up in some cracker city and said that they would have to integrate because it was the law. Thanks for nothing. Were the townspeople so stupid they didn't hear about the laws or think it didn't apply because their city was totally white? Where did they get the blacks to use to integrate? Hell, knowing him there probably weren't any blacks within a thousand miles of there.

What I have to say to Mr. Jack and his buddies is this. Is he in our neighborhoods teaching us how to better ourselves? Is he working with black kids to teach them that white people care? Is he doing anything positive or is he just another nigger-hating cracker faking concern for children, white and black? I think we can close our eyes and imagine the answer to that. Give me a Klansman in a sheet any time to a slime ball that is but can't deal with it.

Q   What about the way the Haitians are being treated?

A   Oh, it's pathetic. United Snakes of America. It's a racist deal. The federal government is so full of shit! There's no way you can justify taking in every Cuban they can find. They might stop at the Krome Detention Center for a few hours to appease the blacks. But they beat the shit out of the Haitians and chain them in cages on ships. They have forgotten "Give us your tired, your poor, your huddled masses yearning to be free." Just make sure the huddled masses aren't poor and black. They are all dried up like prunes and trying to survive. Castro filled this country up with his scumbags on those boats. From prisons and mental hospitals. Most Haitians are good, honest, hardworking people. They work and they help their people. American blacks should learn from them. The US is a motherfucker.

As long as the TV is controlled by the government it's gonna be fucked up. Like *1984*. It's all about the spin that they put on stories. The first part of any newscast is about how many blacks fucked up somebody, white people or each other, today. That keeps us down by destroying black kids' self-esteem. And it makes white kids scared of black people. And it scares white kids and makes them think all we do is steal and murder and sell crack. The media perpetrates and maintains the old racial myths. They can say that Luke jumped out of his car and beat up some bitch. Or if they like me, this week, I was responding to provocation. They got a thing against black people.

The jails are full-up and half the brothers in jail are innocent of the crime they put in for. They got white gangs and Cuban gangs but there ain't no organized black gangs in Miami. The media keeps the races apart. The only thing you see blacks doing is killing and shit. Then they end the newscast with white people doing something nice, like a park or a bed race. Start with negative blacks doin' shit and end with Cubans or white people throwin' frisbees. That's the same in every city I go in. They'll find some atrocity and put it on the local news but they won't cover an event we put on for inner-city black kids.

The other day there was a thing on the news where these Haitians were beaten by the INS and shipped back to God knows what hell or death in Haiti. Then there were these Cubans that had brought their dog on a raft with them. The Cubans were probably being smart 'cause you can eat a dog if the raft goes east instead of north. These one hundred and fifty Haitians were on this boat that was about to sink but they picked up these Cubans that they found floating in the ocean, way off course. And the American Coast Guard plucked the Cubans off the boat and turned the Haitians back out to sea. They say, oh well, the Cubans are welcome because they live in a country where a despot has destroyed their economy. Let them all come. But, yet and still, this country dealt with the Duvaliers that stole their country blind and had their own people killed and tortured by the thousands and starved them down to prunes. But it isn't the same thing? Well, this country is racist. That is a racist policy. Starving Cubans and starving Haitians and Dominicans is the same thing. I have no respect for a government that behaves like that.

It's no wonder that black kids have such a negative self-image because everything they see on television, with a very few exceptions, shows the American black as bad. The news reports concentrate on the killings within the black community. Black-on-white or black-on-black crime.

I helped found the Liberty City Optimist Club to help give kids a place to play where they will be safe from the corners. A place where there are afterschool sports programs for them to participate in. We have done a lot of fund-raising and have had several events to raise the quarter of a million dollars in seed money. We have sent out numerous press releases to the print and electronic media. Have they responded by promoting this activity? No.

Recently there was an unfortunate shooting and a fourteen-year-old was killed in a drive-by shooting across the street from the Luke Records Entertainment Center. Since I own the building the kid was leaving when he was shot, the press was looking for me all the next day. I was at a scheduled event for small children at Hadley Park when the TV crews caught up with me. I gave them hell for looking for a negative story and trying to show my involvement in that killing, I guess. And there I was in front of two hundred children and the news crew was asking me about a killing that I had no knowledge of.

Is it any wonder that our children suffer from inferiority complexes? Is it any wonder they lash out at society? Would they if they felt anyone cared about them and their futures? A few black men in Miami are trying to make a positive change in our own community and we are not only not getting any help, the media is trying to discredit us. The media tries to discredit any black who finds himself in a leadership position. They want blood on the airwaves and unfortunately there are always blacks committing crimes for them to report on.

I hate to admit defeat but it seems to me that the kids above the age of twelve are goners. These little jitterbugs are always shooting each other and sticking each other and have no respect for their parents or anyone else. If we are going to make a change it has to be a long-range change, working with the little kids. And when they grow up, they may have a shot at a good life. I know that is a defeatist attitude but I watch the kids and I tried to have a safe place where they can go and hang out so they'll be off the street corners, and they end up shooting each other or some innocent bystander. They have no respect for anyone or anything. It doesn't do them any good to say that it's your fault or his fault. There may not be anything anybody can do to change it.

I just found out by accident that Wilt Chamberlain has a restaurant called Wilt's in Boca Raton, Florida. I have never seen anything about that fact on TV or in the newspapers. See, the kids in Liberty City and Overtown would love to see a black man who is making it after a brilliant sports career has ended, but what they get is some crack house shoot-out or something. The stories on black athletes that the media loves are the ones where one of them gets into drugs and loses everything. A black athlete's best route to making headlines, even in the sports pages, is to get caught doing something wrong.

The black kids need a barrage of positive role models. They need blacks who have made something out of themselves without turning to drugs or crime for the money in their pockets.

Q   What does censorship buy? You have said that you have fought censorship since you were a child.

A   Censorship isn't new to me. I have been censored all my life. My school textbooks were censored. Official black history is slanted. What chance we got until we learn our history? Black history is always an elective but white history is mandatory. And it is slanted against us.

There are only a few black leaders in this country. Every leader that has come forward to unite blacks has been neutralized. Do the textbooks say that J. Edgar Hoover's FBI was a racist organization? Not that the FBI is particularly racist but there were racists running it. There are no racist corporations but there are racists running many of them. What they do to us is racist.

It's no secret that blacks are exploited. The black community has been exploited by the powers that be from the government to the major corporations for decades. Look at the liquor companies and the products they target to our community. The malt liquor is a drink designed for black people. It's basically a sodium cocktail. I say, watch what the white people eat and drink and follow suit. Malt liquors come from the bottom of the barrel. White people drink off the top of the barrel. It's like the difference between gasoline and tar. They are both by-products from the same oil. Blacks get the short end of the stick. Blacks have to band together if we are ever going to get anywhere. WATCH THE WHITE PEOPLE.

How much money goes back into our communities from the corporations we support?

Q   You said that you felt censorship was generally subtle. It only becomes overt when strong examples need to be set to maintain . . .

A   Hey, it ain't no secret that the world wants me to go away quietly. They want to sweep me under the carpet but it ain't going to happen. Okay, it's like this book. The white publishers didn't want this book to be published, for several reasons, so they said the only people who would be interested in the story was blacks from the ghetto and they don't buy books or read. Well, what they are saying is that they don't want to take the chance that the book could draw a big white audience, which it surely will. What they don't say is that women don't want the "sexism" aspect of my culture to be explained or discussed. They don't want my culture explained, period. They want everybody to keep thinking that we're dangerous and our neighborhoods are ambush points.

Rich people are always smarter to stick to their own neighborhoods. When poor people have nothing, black, white, red or yellow, they might take what you got. That's not a black thing. It's a survival thing. It's a universal thing.

In short, the publishers will put out a million-dollar advance for the story of Marion Barry being a drug addict in the mayor's office because that paints a picture of a corrupt "nigger" and reinforces their idea of how blacks behave when they have power or money. If this book had promised a totally negative picture of me and slammed me, it would have been published. But my story is positive in the end and they don't like that. It's not a clean story and I don't get mine in the end. So they'll publish a thousand books on subjects that nobody gives a fuck about. But I sell a million or two records and my fans will buy the book. White people will buy the book to try and understand what happened in the trials, to see the lyrics for themselves. People who are interested in my culture will buy the book. Plus the controversial subject matter will get up their curiosity.

But the idea of my having a forum for my ideas and lifestyle and to show what you can do with your life and how a black kid doesn't have to sell crack, or go to school like my brothers did to escape the ghetto or conform to white America's ideals, codes and ethics to be a success, is just too much. So fuck Simon and Schuster and Random House and the others. The Jamaican press isn't afraid of telling it like it is.

That is censorship. How many books are out today on black anything? Scandals, yes. That is scandalous!

The truth is that I don't talk like you, I don't have sex like you do, or you would admit to. I don't have the same values, the same attitudes on women or whatever. So I must be crushed as a role model. Right? Well, I'm no worse than anyone else and no better. I am out for me and mine. Everybody has freak in them. I just don't try to hide mine. I show it because it's there and nobody else was showing that side of life. Of human nature. That part of natural life. More people are freaky sexually than will admit it. Any variation of the missionary position is freaky. But I guarantee you that everybody from the judge in Lauderdale to the bailiffs have done it doggie style, or in the buck, or against a sink in a washroom. And they have had someone suck their dicks and a lot of them have eaten pussy, had anal sex, or popped the pussy, made a pussy go splack, and some have had two women at the same time or watched two women. The difference is that I say all of that is normal. That freaks them out. I said this is how it is and that freaks them out because it is!

If I hired enough detectives to research the lives of Judge Gonzalez and Jack Thompson and the prosecutor Jolly and Dijols and that lady Robson, sooner or later I'd turn up someone that they tricked with or done something unnatural with. They don't think I should talk about it. Well, fuck them! Their hang-ups don't have to be yours or mine. That's what America is all about. If they want to draw lines all the time, they should move to South Africa or Latin America or somewhere else. This country is about freedom. Not just their idea of freedom.

Sure, some lines have to be drawn for the actual protection of citizens. I never agreed that my music hurt anyone and there is no evidence that it has. Like people who make child pornography or physically injure others need to be stopped. But cross-cultural ideas are different. You have all these immigrants whose cultures are not the same as ours. And they have to conform or lose their freedom. Haitians and Jamaicans are not going to bring the same experiences to bear as someone who was raised in Palm Beach and they are treated by the law as though they were.

White religious groups condemn me and rush to save my people from the language we use. Let them come save us from starvation, let them bring us jobs. Let them either help or mind their own fucking business. Or better yet, get the fuck out of our way while we go for our own slice of the American Pie!

Q   Was that racist? I have never thought of you as a racist?

A   God knows I try not to be racist but it is hard sometimes, John. See, I won't like you just because you are black or dislike you because you are white. Skin tone is an accident of birth. I have preferences for things of my culture. My Jamaican blood likes spicy food and reggae music. I am comfortable with myself and like my skin dark. I am happy to take money from anyone of any color and I am comfortable in Carroll City or Miami Beach or Miami Lakes, where I live. I was taught to like myself and I do. If you have self-respect all things are possible. Without self-respect very little is likely. The most important thing we can teach our children is to love themselves and all others. Hate between the races is counterproductive and it is learned behavior. We teach our kids to hate by letting the media show negative images of a race out of all proportion to reality. We teach it in subtle ways everyday. It's like the book *Little Black Sambo*. And all that kind of garbage. Can that part which seems to be human nature and historically deeply rooted be changed? I hope so. I really do. It's like your kids and my kids don't see the color like kids a few years older do. I don't know. I tell you what. I won't make my kids hate your kids if you won't make yours hate mine. Ten million deals like that between blacks and whites and we'd have a start.

Q   What do cultural differences have to do with persecution of 2 Live Crew's music? You seem genuinely perplexed that your lyrics generate so much anger.

A   Yeah, you grow up using this word to mean this and to mean that. Like if I say cock to you, you might think I mean a dick. But on the street I say I want to get some cock and I would mean pussy. If I say that during sex I want to bust the walls or break your backbone about a girl, I just mean I want to bend her so there is more tightness around my dick, and bust the walls is just a way of bragging about how big my dick is. It's just street humor, you know, laughing at ourselves. When white people and those libber bull-dykes and girls with balls hear the lyrics, they think we are dissecting women with hatchets. See, that's a cultural thing that doesn't cross over. We are laughing and y'all are crying. But you can ignore the lyrics and dance. People who don't speak English are in bliss at our concerts because the music is solid.

But, you tell me. You been doing this here book for all this time. Tell me what you learned about the cultural differences?

Q   Cultural differences account for a lot of misunderstanding of the lyrics of 2 Live Crew's music, according to your expert witnesses. They have been taken out of the context of the black urban experience. Among those lyrics that caused the biggest furor was describing a father whose daughter was deflowered in "Me So Horny." "You know he'll be disgusted when he sees her pussy busted." This refers to her loss of virginity and not to physical mutilation of her vagina beyond the natural loss of her hymen due to the initial penetration.

For instance in "Put Her In the Buck," when you say "Put her in the buck" that is referring to a position that is a variation of the "missionary" position in which the female is flat on her back with the backs of her legs on the man's chest and her knees broken at his shoulders. Her backbone is "broken" in that the base of the spinal column is bent at the small of her back. This position tightens the vaginal muscles and enhances the pressure or sensation against the shaft of the penis. It also serves to push the top of the penis shaft against the clitoris, giving the woman more pleasure and hopefully an orgasm.

2 Live's music is vulgar, lewd, and very, very dirty even in the context of the culture. But it is, when taken in context of your culture, merely "locker room" talk.

We guys, white, black, rich or poor, get together and let our hair down and tell off-color jokes to establish that we are all cut of the same cloth. At a party we will subject our girlfriends or wives to the same humor. Sexist humor isn't a racial thing but something that you find in most cultures.

Words are powerful but they are just that. Words. And who decides that "fuck" is inappropriate and "intercourse" is cool. It's exactly the same thing. Words are words are words.

How was that, Mr. Campbell?

A   It'll do. Let's go play some golf.

13 Epilogue
by John R. Miller

Today, at thirty, Luther Rodrick Campbell lives like a potentate in a first-class fairy tale world that "naughty" words built. He has made millions of dollars. He has managed to invest enough of those dollars so that he will be able to retire whenever he likes. There are people who think he has semiretired already since he spends several hours a week on the golf course. When he wants to play he drives his custom cart out onto the course through his back yard.

He lives in a beautifully appointed eight-thousand-square-foot pink palace built on a golf course in Miami Lakes, just north of Miami. He has a closet the size of a normal bedroom, filled with expensive clothes and fifty pairs of shoes. For transportation he chooses between his Jaguar, the black BMW convertible with the custom Bavarian power plant, a four-wheel drive Ford muscle wagon with a rack of lights on top, and a two-tone Acura NSX. He also has a private, eleven-seat Jet Commander.

Luther enjoys sports. He has a sky-box at Joe Robbie stadium and a block of choice seats at the Miami Heat games, and he flies first class around the country to prize fights. He travels across the country at will, stays at the best hotels, plays the best golf courses, and eats wherever he chooses. He hangs out with sports, recording, and film celebrities. In short, Luther is enjoying his wealth and fame. The religious right which advanced his record sales by half again stares at him all pouty-faced.

Money. It takes millions of dollars to run Luther's empire the way Luther runs his empire. His monthly overhead compares to the retail cost of a matched pair of Rolls Royce convertibles. As Luther will tell you, a million dollars just ain't what it used to be.

Luther is so comfortable that one would never guess that he was born to the streets of Liberty City. On the golf course in Arizona, Luther and I paired with two middle-aged men who were three-star generals in the corporate army. They had no idea who Luther was until we had finished the round and were having a drink in the bar. If the waitress had not asked him for his autograph the men would never have put Luther with Luke and the 2 Live Crew or the obscenity trial. In the year and a half that I was with Luther, I have yet to see anyone confront him about his music. Without exception, people have said that they either are fans of his music or at least support his fight against censorship. I understand that he has been engaged in debates in unusual places but I have yet to witness one. Little old ladies love him, kids love him, and women love him. It becomes obvious that while most Americans do not particularly enjoy his music, the majority agree with his right to record whatever he wants. These Americans see him as a hero of sorts. To his fans he is the black urban equivalent to Lenny Bruce.

Luther's language usually fits the circumstances. Bruce Rogow's wife was initially upset that Bruce would defend the music of 2 Live Crew because she thought, as do many, that the music is violent, misogynistic and vulgar. While she was aware and accepted that it was his job, she was verbal in her denunciation of Luther and the rest of the group. When she was introduced to Luther, Chris and Mark she was disarmed at once. The young men she met in her living room were well-mannered, courteous, considerate, and genuinely interesting. Mrs. Rogow has never heard any of the three utter one word of low language. But when he is stirred, Luther makes low language an art form.

Offstage, Luke, Mark and Chris are all soft-spoken. Mark is extremely shy, moody, constantly withdrawn and seemingly depressed, in direct opposition to his stage persona where he laughs, struts and says things best described as overt and suggestive. He is the group's clown, its heart. Chris Wongwon has a crisp sense of humor and seems to genuinely like what he does. As the main writer he is a bit of a "blue" poet. His left arm is paralyzed (from a car crash where he was tossed through the opened sun roof) and hangs from his shoulder like twenty pounds of wet ribbon. David Hobbs was not arrested in the Broward "Club Futura" case because as the DJ his contribution was not considered significant. If the group was compared to the solar system, David Hobbs would be Pluto. He is on the far side of the group and appears to move in only long enough to play and then he seems distant to the enterprise. He has the least amount of stage personality of the group members; but it is truly amazing to watch him at his turntables.

If David is the furthest planet in the 2 Live solar system, Luther is the sun. It is Luther's strong personality that has held the group together so long, although it is that same personality that is probably responsible for the emotional schism that separates it. Because Luther has the majority personality he controls what can be controlled of 2 Live Crew. He owns the group's name, is its leader, spokesman, producer, and regulates its finances. As the sole proprietor of Luke Records he controls every aspect of 2 Live Crew's product including promotion, covers, studio sessions, concert dates and so on. While the members helped elevate him to his position, it is natural that they would rebel as though he were their father. Luther seems genuinely disappointed and even perplexed by the problems that the group is having. While he has always tried to hold them together at all costs, he seems resigned to let the cards fall where they may—like the father who has tried everything, but the kids still get drunk and wreck the car.

The truth is that 2 Live Crew has lasted a long time by industry standards. Until the members expressed dissatisfaction recently, Luke had never considered making a career change. Luther is putting the finishing touches on his first non-2 Live album. Like any band leader, he is open to keeping the group together though he is mentally prepared to accept the breakup if it happens, and to replace departing members.

Luther is learning the painful realities of the music business and his responsibilities in heading a major independent label. The multimillion-dollar distribution deal that Luke Records entered into with Atlantic Records, on July 4, 1990, is indicative of the complexities that Luther has faced in operating in the national arena and becoming mainstreamed.

According to David Chackler, record industry veteran and, until recently, the chief operating officer of Luke Records, Luther Campbell got one of the three biggest deals in the history of that record giant. The Stones got considerably less. The eight-digit advance was the largest dollar advance commitment that any artist had ever received from Atlantic. Period. Scarcely a year later Luther seems to be displeased with the record-breaking deal. The reason is both as simple and as complex as Luther himself.

He thinks that in those mahogany-walled executive offices he was told things that turned out to be untrue. He feels that Atlantic said that they would stand up against the censorship forces and make the record chains take the product. They told him of the powerful PR and promotions machine that would insure him and his artists great success beyond their wildest dreams. However, not only have they not gotten his product added to the racks in record chains, but he has been tossed out of several chains since signing.

Luther was, in fact, not pleased with the wording on the short-form contract. When what he had been told verbally failed to be written into this initial contract (basically a letter of agreement), he was told that the long-form would iron out the problems.

Reading the long-form contract, he found that it had remained the same, and he simply refused to sign it. (He has never signed it and still operates under the short-form.) Luther feels he received nothing and paid for it through the nose.

Basically Atlantic is pressing Luke's records, tapes and CDs, for a percentage of sales, and making a healthy profit on that enterprise. Even if a record fails to sell, and is returned to the company, Atlantic makes their profit.

But the first major problem, as Luke saw it, came with the initial album made under the new Atlantic deal, *Banned in the USA*, which was rushed out to take advantage of the controversy and suffered in quality when compared to the other 2-Live records. Atlantic had slapped Luther on the back and vowed to be his ally against the morality police. Then they balked when they discovered that Luther had attacked Tipper Gore in a song. They urged Luther to remove it. He bristled, then thought it over, and took it out because he still wanted to please the company. This felt like censorship to Luther but, after all, the law suits had given him major dollars and promised him a rosy future complete with a picket fence around a vault filled with money.

From then on Atlantic became less the pal and more the father figure. Luther's refusal to sign the long-form contract did little to build the relationship. He felt that Atlantic all but refused to promote 2 Live or the other Luke Record acts and made more and more demands on him. When Luke recorded *Sports Weekend*, Atlantic balked at the photograph he selected for the cover. In the shot the members of 2 Live Crew are sitting shoulder-to-shoulder in one queen-sized brass bed. They are reading the sports pages. Four women's posteriors are stuck up into the immediate foreground, knees on the mattress—asses in the air. Their faces are under the covers at the crotches of the group members. The Crew, not wishing to be confused with singing nuns, thought it was a funny shot that their fans would certainly appreciate. Besides, Luther reasoned, "Atlantic can't get the fucking record on a rack because of the language, so what difference is what's on the cover going to make?" He planned to print stickers over the female asses on the "clean" version of the LP but Atlantic demanded stickered cheeks on both versions. Luke stood firm. This brought two powerhouses eye to eye waiting to see who blinked first. Atlantic did.

The company insisted that Luther remove three cuts from the album. One, "Pop the Pussy," includes a good-natured poke at a comedian from the popular ethnic TV show, *In Living Color*, who had made fun of Luke more than once. He also couples Michael Jackson and his chimp Bubbles in this musical sexual innuendo and some other popular celebrities are targeted. Luke refused.

Atlantic responded by having one of their legal flunkies inform Frank Tabino, Luke's chief of production, that the company was demanding that neither their name nor logo appear on the labeling of *Sports Weekend*. Luke, who has never settled for landing the second punch, fired off a few dozen faxes to members of the press saying that he seemed to have traded one set of censors for another.

Luther had discovered what anyone who has been long in the industry knows all too well: that record companies have no real loyalty beyond a dollar bill. They are just another corporate entity with merchandise to sell and no soul beyond a bottom line.

The next day reporters are responding to the faxes. By noon Luke's people are fed up with the numbers of calls. They can't get their work done. That evening the music reporter from *The Miami Herald* calls to say that the story has been effectively killed. He had just spent all day tracking the correct people at Atlantic and had been stone-walled at every turn. Then by late afternoon, as if by magic, the reporter could suddenly talk to any of the people who were involved. In fact, the senior partner at the law firm that represents Atlantic told him that there had been an unfortunate communications problem. "Why, we have straightened it all out. It was an honest mistake. We love Luke and the 2 Live Crew's latest record. We support them one thousand percent and wouldn't dream of suggesting that any of this wonderful material be altered. We're expecting really big things from this record!" The reporter then spoke to the woman who had "supposedly" told Frank that the Atlantic people were pulling the logo and label ties. She didn't even recall the incident. The bottom line? A unified company line.

The reason for the majority of problems between Luther and Atlantic is an incompatibility of styles and methods. Luke is a successful guerrilla entrepreneur whose formal training in business was at the ass-end of a heavy stick or from jumping headlong into uncharted territory and carefully watching what happened. He never makes the same strategic errors twice. Being a product of the streets Luther has never felt quite at ease with slick corporate types who sometimes make the mistake of thinking that they know his business better because they were trained in fancy schools. Once when Atlantic was telling Luke how to promote an artist, Luther's former entertainment attorney Allen Jacobi reportedly shot back "Leave him alone! You guys have never put together a string of successful records the way that he has! Don't fuck him up and get him thinking like you think."

When it comes to dealing with institutions, Luther Campbell is his own worst enemy. Because he does not understand their way of seeing the world, he insists that they try to see it as he does. For the corporate soldiers at Atlantic, seeing the world through Luther's eyes is about as easy as spotting the rings of Saturn through a Coke bottle in broad daylight.

David Chackler summed it all up when he said, "Nobody but Luther Campbell could have gotten that deal out of Atlantic Records. Unfortunately, it's the story of a street fighter and a gloved fighter trying to blend their styles into one. They are trying to do their best and so is he and they are both disappointed with the net result. But the problems can be worked out. I think everybody wants to continue the relationship. They have simply never dealt with anyone like our dear Mr. Campbell." But who has?

Luther is working hard these days. He is developing a movie loosely based on his Ghetto Style experiences. (Recently, a major production company optioned the story of the Broward County Trials for a made-for-TV movie.) He is presently planning a 2 Live tour for the winter of 1991–92. And with twenty active groups, he continues to produce records and music videos for his label. Luke also keeps close watch on his club operations. Add to this a stacked social schedule and what you have is a man who works hard.

Luke likes to keep things stirred up. He hates complacency. The only person whose job is one hundred percent safe is Luther. It is under a super-competitive atmosphere that the employees work. Some thrive; some fall by the wayside. Turn-over in the outer perimeter positions is common. The inner core jobs, closer to the throne, are a little more secure. Very little.

The Luke Records complex is a spreading, two-story, con-crete, almost windowless (Luke's office has two) bunker that occupies the best part of a Liberty City block at 8400 N.E. 2nd Avenue.

The reception area is more of a holding tank where people often wait for hours to see Mr. Campbell, as he is called by all of his employees. Some wait forever and still never see him.

There is the warehouse with twenty-foot ceilings and boxes of records, tapes, CDs and tee-shirts. It also holds the shipping and receiving department. Then there is the forty-eight track studio. Through the warehouse doors there is a seven thousand square foot entertainment center, designed to be utilized as an alternative rental space for the native black and Haitian com-munity as a banquet hall on weekends. It may qualify as the largest nightclub in Miami when it is functioning as the PacJam Teen Club.

Luther often strolls the halls of Luke Records carrying a golf club. He has been known to stand at one end of the hallway and slam a golf ball the fifty yards to the far stairwell door while people are inside their offices. The ball will ricochet about in the hall and occasionally go through the ceiling panels. The object is to hit the door. He has been known to slap the club down on the desk of a worker while making some point.

Luther usually arrives at work around noon. He parks under the green awning nearest the front door, under the watchful eyes of the warehouse staff. Pals for many years, they are the only people at the company that Luke really trusts to watch his back. The prevailing attitude of the warehouse guys is "We see 'em come and we see 'em go. We'll be here long after you are gone." They may be the only people in Luke's life that are constant.

Luke knows the record business, specifically the rap music business, as well as anyone. He pioneered most of the sales techniques that are employed by other labels, including the majors.

What he knows about the rap industry is that nasty lyrics sell.

He knows his market, and knows what his market wants to hear. Luther makes his music for his peer group. If the rest of us want to eavesdrop, fine. In so doing, he is talking dirty on a grander scale than most other people get to do, or want to do, for that matter. But it is doubtful that Luther really cares what other people get to do, as long as *he* gets to do what he wants to do. Make money. Once I asked Brannard Campbell when Luther would stop making dirty records. He thought for a second, smiled, and said, "When it quits selling."

Luther doesn't see what the excitement is about in the first place. As Luke says, fellatio is polite speak for blow job; having sexual relations is the same act whether you call it having pum-pum or fucking. The whole debate is a cultural thing as to which words are correct and which are obscene or nasty or merely dirty or off-color. A word cannot be but what it is, letters in a string.

I think pop music critic Dave Marsh summed it up better than anyone else when he wrote:

> Luther Campbell and the 2 Live Crew member, Christopher Wongwon, spent only one night in jail and they were acquitted. We are meant to understand this as a great victory for the system. But in reality it is an indictment of it. One night in jail for men who have done nothing worse than sing a song, no matter what the lyrics, is one too many for any nation that dares call itself a democracy. The fact that there was a trial at all, for rhymes whose kin have been recited in junior high school locker rooms as long as there have been children, gives the lie to the idea that we live in a system of equal justice for all. I refuse to ask why Andrew Dice Clay was not prosecuted for reciting many of the same dirty nursery rhymes. Instead I ask why anyone was prosecuted at all.
>
> Until that question receives a satisfactory answer, we do not live in a democracy and the First Amendment is merely a bunch of words, a mouthful of much obliged without a handful of gimme. Until Luther Campbell has the right to say what's on his "dirty" mind, none of us do. And if you aren't willing to defend the principle involved, don't just sit there. Write a letter, draw a picture, make a speech, sing a song, tell a story, grab your video camera, or call a friend. And follow the best advice I have to give you: Move Something—or lose everything.

On March 25, 1991, Luther flew to Atlanta to hear Bruce Rogow plead the *Nasty* case before the stone-faced judges of the Eleventh Circuit Court of Appeals. Rogow explained to the venerable justices how Judge Gonzalez had twisted the law, and ignored the experts, to rule *Nasty* obscene. It did not fail the three prongs of Miller vs. California, he said, and he led them through the case in the slim amount of time allotted to him. "Bunch of tired-assed old motherfuckers," Luther commented later. "Bruce had to talk to them like children and they were asking dumb-shit questions."

Although Rogow remains confident that his argument should win, the Eleventh has upheld some conservative lower court rulings. "Seems to be the trend," an attorney told me. Should they not reverse the Gonzalez obscenity ruling, the final appeal will be to the Supreme Court. Of late, that body has been extremely conservative. The Supreme Court may even elect not to review the case. So the odds are that if Luther loses with the Eleventh, the ball game may indeed be over.

What does that mean to Luke? It means that he spent well in excess of one hundred thousand dollars on a game he didn't understand and never wanted to play. What does it mean to record sales? It means that *Nasty* will sell another few hundred thousand copies to people who want to know what the big deal is. It means that Luther will have succeeded where thousands of others have failed. He will have created the first "obscene" record in history. It will mean that the music of 2 Live Crew is completely without any redeeming value. It will mean that the United States Constitution has lost a great deal of its ability to protect any and all of us.